Y0-ABC-416

OPHB 42

30—
——
6s

The
Manuscript
of
HUGO
POTTS

*An
Inquiry into
Meaning*

By
CREEL FROMAN

Southern Illinois University Press
Carbondale and Edwardsville

Feffer & Simons, Inc.
London and Amsterdam

BD
450
.F776
West

Library of Congress Cataloging in Publication Data

Froman, Lewis Acrelius, 1935–
    The manuscript of Hugo Potts.

    (Southern Illinois University centennial publications)
    1. Man   2. Meaning   (Philosophy)   3. Truth.
4. Reality.   5. Human behavior.   I. Title.
II. Series.
BD450.F776   110   73–5915
ISBN 0–8093–0608–5

Copyright © 1973 by Southern Illinois University Press
All rights reserved
Printed in the United States of America
Designed by Gary Gore

Southern Illinois University Centennial Publications

EDITORIAL BOARD

Basil C. Hedrick
Harold M. Kaplan
Carroll L. Riley

For Katie, Lizzie, and Katrina;
in memory and with thanks
to Crete Sewell, from
wherever he appeared; and
to Tellurians everywhere.

Contents

Acknowledgments   xi

BOOK 1   *The Search, by Hugo Potts*

1 Tellurian's Study   3
2 Tellurian's Study (continued)   23
3 Letters From Lewis   35
4 Seeker's Apartment   107
5 Peter Pope's Poems   113
6 Tellurian's Study   145
7 Margaret Fleece's Play   155
8 Seeker's Apartment   171
9 Seeker's Philosophical Notes   177
10 Seeker's Philosophical Notes (continued)   241

BOOK 2   *About Hugo Potts*

1 The Office   289
2 A Meeting   295
3 Teaching   305
4 Writing   320
5 Marion   331
6 Voices   352

Acknowledgments

I would like to thank the Ford Foundation and the National Science Foundation for their support while parts of this manuscript were being written, and the University of California at Irvine, the British Museum and the Kensington-Chelsea Library for providing the settings in which the writing took place.

For permission to reprint the William Butler Yeats poem "To a Friend Whose Work Has Come to Nothing," from *The Collected Poems of W. B. Yeats,* Copyright 1916 by The Macmillan Company, renewed 1944 by Bertha Georgie Yeats, I wish to thank The Macmillan Company (New York), Mr. M. B. Yeats, Macmillan & Co. Ltd., and the Macmillan Company of Canada Ltd.

Several people helped at various stages of manuscript preparation, and I would like to thank them: Gayle Hill, Elaine Ficociello, Patricia Montgomery, and Sharon Maier.

My wife, Katie, was most helpful in many ways throughout the entire period in which this manuscript was being written.

Finally, I would like to thank the members of the Southern Illinois University Centennial Editorial Board and the Director of the Southern Illinois University Press, Vernon Sternberg, for their willingness to take on what is probably a somewhat unusual manuscript, and to the Chief Editor of the Southern Illinois University Press, Beatrice Moore, for her kind assistance.

Creel Froman

Newport Beach, California
October 1972

The Search,
by Hugo Potts

1
Tellurian's Study

We are in a large study in the home of Lewis A. Tellurian, Jr. The room is quite stunningly furnished, with paintings, sculptures, and other *objets d'art* generously placed about. Tellurian, a formidable-looking man of about sixty, is speaking with a younger man of about thirty-five (Peter Pope) and a woman of about forty (Margaret Fleece). Tellurian and Fleece each have a drink. Pope has just entered.

POPE:

This is really a lovely room. I'm quite impressed.

TELLURIAN:

By what?

POPE:

By the obvious taste with which someone put this room together. There is an idea here, a theme, a feeling. I wouldn't be able to get a thing accomplished in this room. The atmosphere is overpowering. It reminds me of the feeling I have in almost any Frank Lloyd Wright building. Anything *in* the building is diminished, and especially the people.

FLEECE:

Now that's an interesting way to put it. I've always been uncomfortable with Wright's work, but I could never put my finger on just why. Take the Guggenheim Museum, for example. It really is an inhuman building. If you start from the top, as some people suggest, and walk down the ramps, you get the sensation of being pulled, or being unable to stop or linger. Starting at the bottom is a little easier, but the feeling of having to exert oneself is constantly with you, that it is, in some way, an obstacle course. And the pictures are so difficult to look at. There's an angle problem since you stand on an incline and, if not actually uncomfortable, one is aware of himself. As you say the building itself dominates the contents, including the people. I find it most appalling.

POPE:

You think so? It depends, I guess, on what you think of someone or something that can dominate you. Can you imagine being capable of designing a building that will not let one concentrate on all those magnificent paintings? Anyone, it seems to me, could design a building which could show art. But to design one, *and get it accepted,* that so dominates that one finds it difficult to enjoy the pictures—that's sheer genius. One is constantly coping with the building, thereby coming under the influence of Frank Lloyd Wright, not the paintings. For example, have you ever had to visit the lavatories? Each is so small, and so inhumanly designed, that you're frustrated for the rest of the tour. One will remember the Guggenheim not as a place where art hangs, but as the place where it took fifteen minutes to go to the bathroom. Absolutely fantastic.

FLEECE:

But don't you think there's something wrong with that? It's a terribly designed building. After all, the paintings hanging there are worth seeing, and if one is so struck by the building . . .

POPE:

(Interrupting.) Yes, but that's the point, don't you see? I've been in art galleries in which the paintings were difficult to see, or poorly placed, or whatnot. Perhaps the building was designed for some other purpose, or is overcrowded, or has poor light, or is even badly designed. But the Guggenheim is none of those. The difference with the Guggenheim is that it is designed with the *express purpose* of discombobulating the patrons. And it succeeds admirably in doing so. But at the same time it is not badly designed. Quite the contrary. There is an idea in the building, an idea so overwhelming that one is constantly thrown off his guard. When you enter the Guggenheim, you contend with Wright. And *that* is no small accomplishment, especially in the distinguished company that it houses. Wright has upstaged other geniuses, and has been given permission to do so by holders of large wealth. All while developing the reputation as one of America's leading architects. His fame lies in his ability to dominate—the quality of all great genius. (There is a pause as Pope strolls around.)

This room gives me the same effect, but on a smaller scale, of course. Which is why I said I couldn't work in it. It's too overpowering.

TELLURIAN:

Thank you.

POPE:

Did you design this, Lewis?

TELLURIAN:

Yes, I did.

POPE:

It's quite remarkable, you know.

TELLURIAN:

Your kind compliments remind me of a passage I once read in something by Kierkegaard. He suggests how beholden we are to those who praise us. If someone is critical, we can safely ignore him, get angry, or act in any manner we please. We are justified in choosing among a number of offenses or defenses. But if someone flatters us it places us in a debt which most of us find difficult to repay. Most people know how to take an insult—but a compliment presents problems of an entirely different kind.

POPE:

But I didn't mean anything by . . .

TELLURIAN:

(Interrupting.) Of course you didn't. I simply find Kierkegaard's comment extremely interesting. And if you look carefully, you may find that I have just illustrated his point.

In any case, as to this room, I'm struck by the notion that if one does not live in his own world he is, *ipso facto,* forced to live in the world of others. If you don't like certain parts of the world, as all of us don't, and if one can't change them, and most of the time they can't be changed, then one either adjusts, withdraws, or is constantly frustrated—or he does something about it for himself which, as much as possible, allows him to live in a world of his own construction. There are obvious limits to this—limits of time, energy, and money as well as taste and imagination—but one does the best he can.

POPE:

(Looking away, and noticing a picture hanging on the wall.) That's a deKooning, isn't it? Quite nice.

FLEECE:

I'm inclined to agree. But I feel at a loss for words to try to describe what it is that the picture is saying.

TELLURIAN:

I'm afraid that if one attempted to summarize what a deKooning picture expresses, or a Giacometti sculpture, one would be left with a trivial statement, like "Man is in great trouble" or "Life is hell." The function of art, it seems to me, is to add an aesthetic dimension to a universality which, if expressed alone, would sound trite.

POPE:

(Eagerly attempting to recoup the losses suffered in the last exchange with Tellurian.) I wonder whether we can even speak very well about what paintings or other art forms say. I can remember seeing the first deKooning retrospective in London and being impressed with two points: one, that I wanted to paint, and two that I wanted to paint two pictures having a conversation with one another. So struck was I with my inability to say anything to the paintings or even about the paintings.

TELLURIAN:

There are lots of jazz musicians who would agree with you that art products speak a language of their own and that to

6

talk *in* jazz on an instrument and to talk *about* jazz in ordinary language are two quite different things. Many saxophone players would rather talk to a piano in the language of music than to talk about music to a piano player.

FLEECE:

But don't you find that people like deKooning or Giacometti are saying something essentially degrading of the human condition, that pessimism, or cynicism, or whatever you wish to call it is the central theme of their work?

TELLURIAN:

Most of us wish to elevate man, and there are many artists who attempt to do so in their work, some of them very famous, such as Michelangelo or Renoir. We are led to see man not as he is but as he might be or as he should be, without any consideration as to whether he could be so elevated, whether he is able to reach such heights. It is not so much that deKooning or Giacometti are degrading as that they are making a statement about what they believe man to be. This is something which Michelangelo never attempted. His theme was man as he should be. What I am saying is that I prefer artists to tell me how they see things as they are—not how they see things as they should be. I don't even have to agree with the artist in his interpretation—just that he concern himself with his idea of the human condition as it is.

FLEECE:

But surely you wouldn't deny that man must have his hopes and his dreams, that we must all live in an illusion? Isn't that part of what we mean when we describe man?

TELLURIAN:

Yes, I think so, but illusions need not necessarily be synonymous with hopes and dreams. We all have visions, but some are of what the world should be like and some of what the world is like. (Pause—Pope continues to admire the room and its furnishings.) I'm sorry, here we've been talking and I haven't offered you a drink. Please, what would you like?

POPE:

> A beer, please. Thank you. (Pause.)
> (Tellurian goes over to his desk and pushes a button. A butler enters quietly and goes over to Tellurian, receives the order for a beer, and withdraws. In a few minutes he returns with the beer for Pope, brings it to him, Pope acknowledges him, and the butler then withdraws. This action takes place as the dialogue continues, interrupting when necessary.)

POPE:

> (Continuing.) But if we all live in an illusion, then the person who says "We all live in an illusion" is also living in an illusion, namely, the illusion that we all live in an illusion. (All three chuckle over this.) And if that's true then what's real?

TELLURIAN:

> But don't you find that the situation you describe so eloquently (all three again exchange a smile of recognition) is true of all interesting philosophical positions? It is just that many sentences are of such a type that what they say are also true of themselves. For example, if what Freud says is true, that intellectualizing is a form of rationalization, a defense which is meant to cope with a threatening situation, then isn't Freud's intellectualizing also a rationalization? (Pause.) Or, if a person says "There are no true statements," is that statement itself true? Or false?
>
> Most of us think that paradox is something to avoid. Many academic philosophers feel it their duty to *solve* paradoxes. But perhaps all we can do with language of this sort is simply to discover them and to recognize that they are inherent in all that we do. The world is so complex that any attempts by us to make distinctions are bound to run into difficulties. Just the fact that we use language itself presents us with simplifications, distortions, boundary problems, *and* paradoxes. These are the natural products of language and should be seen as part of our difficulty in ultimately coming to understand our world.

POPE:

> But that should be disturbing. If the person who says we live in an illusion also lives in an illusion, then is there any reality?

8

FLEECE:

Perhaps reality is simply the illusion we decide to live in.

POPE:

Well, but aren't there *really* trees and rocks, and won't I bump myself if I walk into a tree?

TELLURIAN:

There may be trees, yes, but because there are trees doesn't mean there is intelligence or beauty or virtue. We must distinguish, I think, between what we discover and what we create. We do not create trees or rocks, but we do create intelligence, beauty, and virtue. It is no argument to say that because material objects exist it is therefore possible for anything, including nonmaterial things like people's motives, to exist as well. Reality may mean one thing with respect to physical objects and quite another with respect to social distinctions. We may live in a world of multiple realities, in which what we say of and how we come to know one kind of reality may have little to do with another kind.

POPE:

But by your own admission, language distinctions are likely to create boundary problems and other difficulties. If you distinguish between material and nonmaterial, then presumably this distinction itself will lead to difficulties.

TELLURIAN:

Yes, of course, but that is simply to agree with something else I said: that all interesting philosophical positions assert things which are also true of themselves. Besides, you know, I'm a great fan of Oscar Wilde who once said, "If it's worth doing, it's worth doing badly." (They all laugh at this.)

But with respect to the problem of reality I am reminded of Pirandello, who premised his plays on the distinction between reality and illusion. His major argument, it seems to me, is that one can never know when he is in one or the other. One can't know the difference. My argument differs from this. We live in different kinds of realities and hence there are different kinds of illusions. Physical objects do not belong to

the same reality as people's emotions, for example, or interpretations of their behavior.

POPE:

But is there really this difference? Can't a tree be an illusion?
Can't we fabricate physical properties? For instance, when two
people see the "same" accident? Is there really a physical
reality?

TELLURIAN:

I'm afraid that these matters will take us some time to un-
ravel. Like most conversations our thoughts and questions are
proceeding at a more rapid pace than our answers. In a simplified sense some discussions may be likened to speedboats—
they leave big waves, but after a time the sea goes back to
normal. People often leave a large number of unsolved problems in their wake as they speed on.

Intellectual discourse, after all, is only a game. No better
or worse than any other game, but a game which some people
like to play. I'm afraid I'm going to have to say that we would
have to shift the level of discourse a good deal to pursue some
of these questions further.

POPE:

In other words, you don't want to play this game any more,
at least at this level?

FLEECE:

I think what Lewis is saying is that to play the game we are
playing would involve a commitment inconsistent with this
setting. Is that correct?

TELLURIAN:

Perhaps something like that. We are expecting our "guest"
soon, anyway.

POPE:

Speaking of that, I'm not really sure what I am supposed to do.
Any instructions?

FLEECE:

You really won't need to be told. Just do what comes naturally.

POPE:

(Chuckles.) That sounds too much like the advice my mother used to give me: "Just be yourself, Peter; just be yourself and act naturally." I never did know what that meant.

FLEECE:

Yes, but you're a big boy now. Presumably you're here because you now do know.
(The butler enters, whispers something to Tellurian, listens while Tellurian says something in return, and withdraws.)

TELLURIAN:

Our guest has arrived, and I'm having him shown in.
(The butler opens the door and shows in Duran Seeker, a very well-dressed man of about forty-eight. Tellurian goes over and introduces himself, shaking Seeker's hand and warmly welcoming him.)

TELLURIAN:

(Continuing.) How do you do Mr. Seeker. Please come in. I'm Lewis Tellurian. And these are colleagues of mine— Margaret Fleece (they shake hands and exchange greetings) and Peter Pope (they in turn shake hands and greet one another).
    We are certainly delighted you could come. Why don't we all sit down. (Pause as they find places to sit, all except Tellurian who remains standing near Seeker.) May I get you a drink?

SEEKER:

(Looks around sheepishly—he is obviously uncomfortable and unsure of himself.) Well, yes, what are you having?

TELLURIAN:

Whiskey. But we have most anything.

SEEKER:

I think I'd like a Scotch and water then, please, if I may.

TELLURIAN:

(To the butler who has remained near the door.) A Scotch and water, please.

(The butler comes in shortly after and serves Seeker.)

SEEKER:

You certainly have a nice place here. (Meant to be said kindly but comes out awkwardly.) This is a very nice room. (Pause.) There's something about it which interests me, but I can't quite put my finger on it.

TELLURIAN:

Thank you.

SEEKER:

Do you work here?

TELLURIAN:

(Exchanging quick glances with Fleece and Pope.) In a way, I suppose I do. Although I really don't like to call what I do work.

SEEKER:

I hope you don't mind my asking, but what do you do? Does it have anything to do with why you invited me here?

TELLURIAN:

It's really hard to say just what I do. Certain kinds of activities tend to resist labeling, at least in the sense that people would agree on any one label. I have a feeling that what I do, or rather we do, would be described quite differently by different people. In a way I suppose I'm a kind of professional pest.

SEEKER:

(Laughs nervously.) Well, at least you're honest about it. I know a lot of pests who would never own up to it. (Pause.) But what do you really do?

TELLURIAN:

I am a pest, you'll see. We're all pests, actually (again indicating his colleagues). You might even want to become a pest some day. (They all chuckle.)

12

SEEKER:

(Beginning to get a testy edge in his voice.) Yes, but I'd really like to know what's going on here. What do you people want?

TELLURIAN:

Let me see if I can help you to understand. We are simply people. Like all people we want to know, no, that's not quite strong enough, we *need* to know something about those around us. We are, to put it one way, curious. And we are very overt about our curiosity.

You are also a person. You too would like to know something about us. The more we know, the less like strangers we are to each other, the safer we feel. At least that's the hope. So, let's begin. But let us also take our time. If forced to say too much too quickly, we will all simply become nervous. We will be inclined to resort to names and labels which may be quite inappropriate, being the product of fear rather than of safety. We will all have a better idea of who we are and what we are doing when we have finished. Until then I can assure you that you are in no physical danger.

SEEKER:

(Obviously not calmed by this statement.) Not in any physical danger? What in the world is that supposed to mean? I don't understand. Why am I here? Who are you and what do you want from me?

TELLURIAN:

You are here, I take it, because you are mildly stimulated and excited. Your curiosity has been ignited. If you wish to leave now, you may. I would guess that you will not. (Pause.)

We would like to discuss some things with you, ask you some questions, and later you may do the same to us, if you still think you need to. But by then you will not actually wish to do so as you will know what is happening.

Please, then, let us begin. Who are you?

SEEKER:

But that's preposterous. I'm Duran Seeker.

FLEECE:

> Mr. Seeker, we are all given names. These labels help us to distinguish ourselves from others, for all sorts of purposes. *Your* "name," you say, is Duran Seeker. But that doesn't tell me who you are, it merely tells me which human being I would send a particular check to if I employed you, or which person owns a particular house, automobile, or what-have-you. It has been estimated that something like a hundred billion people have lived. Names help to keep this conglomeration straight.
>
> But as a label it is very peculiar indeed. Why, even if I go to the store to purchase boysenberry jam I know approximately what I am getting. But what does the label Duran Seeker tell me? Nothing, I'm afraid. For example, if I buy the boysenberry jam I can ask if it is a good jam or a bad jam. But can I ask if it is a good Duran Seeker or a bad one? If Duran Seeker is unique, how can I say whether he is a good or bad example?

SEEKER:

> (Becoming somewhat agitated.) You people are crazy! (Pause, as though expecting an answer.) You're really crazy.

FLEECE:

> Please, Mr. Seeker, we really find that unnecessary. You imagine that by calling us crazy you're actually describing us, don't you? But words like "crazy" are not really descriptive words— they're names, "bad" names. We don't want to engage in name-calling. Just the opposite, in fact. Mr. Tellurian asked you who you are and you gave him a name and we told you we didn't want a name. We don't want to play that game.

SEEKER:

> Look, you people asked me who I am and I've told you. What do you want if you don't want my name?

FLEECE:

> We want to know who you are.

14

SEEKER:

Like what, for example?

FLEECE:

How would we know? Do we know who you are? (Pause.)

SEEKER:

I'm a sales manager for a paper company. (Said softly.)

FLEECE:

I'm sorry, you're a what?

SEEKER:

I'm a sales manager for a paper company.

FLEECE:

What do you mean you're a sales manager?

SEEKER:

I supervise the sales staff of the regional office.

FLEECE:

No, no. I know what the word "manager" means. I mean, what do you mean you are one?

SEEKER:

I don't understand you.

POPE:

Let me see if I can help. If I told you I was a sculptor, you would know that I sculpted, but would you know who I was?

SEEKER:

I'd know part of what you did.

POPE:

Yes, but again we haven't asked you for part of what you do, we asked you *who you are.* (Long pause.)

SEEKER:

I'm a husband, father, golfer, friend, shopper, etc., etc.

FLEECE:

You are proceeding under the assumption that who you are is a sum of the roles that you play?

SEEKER:

Well, aren't I?

POPE:

Could you ever exhaust labels for what you do?

SEEKER:

What do you mean?

FLEECE:

Well, does that "etc., etc." include thinker of lecherous thoughts, loafer, churchgoer, hypocrite, drinker, defeatist . . .

SEEKER:

(Interrupting.) Now who's calling names?

FLEECE:

Exactly. Are you telling us who you are, or just calling yourself names, and an incomplete set at that? Are we allowed to add our names for you to your list? Or are you only what *you* call yourself? Are you also what you can't call yourself because it's too painful for you, or because you haven't sufficient insight? What do we know, exactly, when you've told us these things that you claim for yourself?

SEEKER:

Well, if you're not satisfied with my name, or the things I do, just what the hell do you want to know? (Pause.)

TELLURIAN:

Can you tell us, please, who you are? (Said patiently.)

SEEKER:

Now look. Apparently you think you're making some point, and it looks like the point is me. (Getting progressively more agitated.) Are you trying to break me down, is that what you're trying to do? I've heard of people like you—who seem to take great pleasure in getting at others. But I just want you to know you can't do it to me.

TELLURIAN:

You may not believe this now, but you will later. We are simply human beings, and we are interested in who you are. We want to know *who you are.* (Said with increasing fervor.) Who are you? Why are you here? What's your purpose? What's your meaning? Why do you do the things you do?

SEEKER:

(Jumps out of chair, and speaks with great emotion.) I'm a human being too, goddam it, that's who I am, and you have no business treating me like this. Who the hell do you think you are, anyway? You sons of bitches. (Long pause.)

FLEECE:

As you've already heard, you're free to leave any time you want to. (Pause—no response from Seeker.) You don't have to stay. (Another pause.)

You want to know who we are, don't you? And you're also curious about what we're up to. You're beginning to want to know yourself who you are.

TELLURIAN:

Tell me, what do you mean you're a human being? What does that mean? (Pause.) Mr. Seeker?

SEEKER:

Damn little, I'll tell you that.

POPE:

You mean you haven't thought about it?

SEEKER:

Apparently not.

POPE:

But why not?

SEEKER:

Well, what's to think? You just do what you do. If you start thinking about those things you can get awfully depressed.

POPE:

What do you mean, "those things"?

SEEKER:

About life, and what it means.

POPE:

Do you know about life, and what it means?

SEEKER:

No.

POPE:

Do you want to know?

SEEKER:

Maybe, if it doesn't cost me too much.

POPE:

What do you mean, "if it doesn't cost you too much"?

SEEKER:

Look, I've got a lot of things to do and a lot of things to worry about. I've a wife and family, although the kids are grown up now, a job, financial responsibilities. How much time do you think I can spend worrying about who I am?

POPE:

But what's more important, living your life the way you describe it, or realizing that life is being lived? What will you do when you're seventy? Will you look back and say, "My God, what did I do with my life? What happened to it—where did it go?" It's never too late to start, but it will mean more to you if you begin early. The less you have to regret the greater the chance you'll survive the disaster that will hit you, if it hits you, of course.

SEEKER:

Who the hell are you to preach to me? Just who the hell are you? You make it sound like I haven't given this any thought. Well, I have. And I can't handle it. I feel depressed—I feel . . .

FLEECE:

(Interrupts.) Have you ever thought that it might be just the other way around? That you think about it when you're depressed, rather than becoming depressed when you think about it?

SEEKER:

You're going too fast for me.

TELLURIAN:

I doubt that. We may be opening up a wound, and it may be increasingly painful, but I don't think we are going too fast.

FLEECE:

Look, we all need time to come to grips with ourselves. But if we stop when it begins to hurt we'll never get beyond scratching the surface, so to speak. (Says it as someone who knows she has just made a pun.) If it doesn't hurt then you aren't doing anything. If there's no pain you won't remember —there'll be no trace—it won't have made any difference to you. (Long pause.)

TELLURIAN:

A moment ago you told us you are a human being and that we have no right to treat you like this. Exactly what did you mean by that? Did you mean that people have no right to ask questions of others? Or that we should not encourage you to think along certain lines? Or that we shouldn't badger you? Or what?

SEEKER:

I meant that you are asking me a question I don't think I have a very good answer for. Maybe if I had an opportunity to think about it for a while, I could come up with something— maybe. But I don't think I have anything for you right now.

TELLURIAN:

But do people not have the right to ask others questions they might not have good answers for?

SEEKER:

I suppose they do. As long as they don't expect a good answer.

TELLURIAN:

You've said that you are a human being. What do you mean by that?

SEEKER:

Are you serious? Do you really want me to answer that?

TELLURIAN:

If you would, please. We're trying to find out who you are. You've told us you're a human being. That's a beginning. But we would like an elaboration.

SEEKER:

(Somewhat embarrassed.) Well, I suppose the major thing about a human being is that he thinks. He has the ability to figure things out, to answer important questions.

POPE:

Tell me, what's the most important question you can think of?

SEEKER:

I don't know what you mean.

POPE:

I mean, if you had an opportunity to learn *one* answer, what would the question be?

SEEKER:

I don't think I can answer that . . . But I'm beginning to think I'd like to know the answer to the question: Who am I?

FLEECE:

If a human being is someone who can answer important questions, that might also mean he can *ask* important questions. You say you're a human being, but I get the feeling you're not sure you know an important question . . .

SEEKER:

I know *an* important question. I just don't know what I would say is *the most* important question. It seems to me one would have to give that a lot of thought. But I can think of some important questions, like: How did the world begin? Or, is there a God? Or, is peace possible?

POPE:

Why are they important questions?

SEEKER:

Because if we knew the answers it would make a difference. If we knew how the world started, then we'd know something about the universe and what we're here for. If we knew there was a God, then more people would believe in Him and it might be a better world. If peace could happen, then maybe we'd work harder for it.

FLEECE:

But what would you say if we *knew* we couldn't know the answers to those questions? Would that answer make a difference too? (Long pause.)

TELLURIAN:

I have the feeling we are now very well launched. I wonder, Mr. Seeker, whether it might be possible for you to visit us again tomorrow? It seems to me that doing what we are doing and thinking are not activities which can go on at the same time.

SEEKER:

I am a bit done in. You people certainly know how to make life exhausting. (Pause.) Yes, I could come back tomorrow.

TELLURIAN:

Good—we're delighted. We'll look forward to seeing you then. (They all begin to stand up and move toward the door. Each shakes hands with Seeker, and says his good-byes.)

Oh, by the way, I wonder if you would do me a favor. Mr. Pope, here, has recently completed a book of poems. There aren't many, but you might find them interesting. You might look them over before tomorrow if you get the chance. That's all right with you, isn't it, Peter?

POPE:

(To Tellurian.) Of course, I'd be delighted.

POPE:

(To Seeker.) Maybe we'll get a chance to discuss them tomorrow.

SEEKER:

You've given me quite a lot to think about already. But I will try. Thank you. (To all again.) Good-bye.

ALL IN CHORUS:

Good-bye.

2
Tellurian's Study (continued)

Tellurian, Pope, and Fleece move back from the door and to their seats, or to stand and admire the art available in the room.

FLEECE:

My gracious me, I wish they wouldn't get so exicted.

POPE:

But what do you expect?

FLEECE:

Oh, I expect them to get excited, but I just wish they wouldn't. I much prefer talking in a normal voice and in an unemotional atmosphere. When people get like that you have to be so careful.

POPE:

He is a man of many problems.

TELLURIAN:

We are all men of many problems.

POPE:

Maybe we should open up those problems, and get him to talk about them. He certainly does seem to be catching on, and I would guess he could be cooperative.

TELLURIAN:

There are people he could go to for that, people who are perfectly content to listen to the problems of others, in fact people who gain their own sense of importance in diagnosing and prescribing for people's ills. Most people seem to need weakness in others—it gives them strength. (Pause.) No, I don't think we need proceed that way. Intellectual discourse is only a game, but it's the one I happen to enjoy playing. We all talk about our problems in different ways. People can be bitchy and complain constantly—but I'm not interested in hearing their gripes and complaints. Or they can want to tell you about their insides—their pains and sufferings. I'm not interested in that either. But personal problems can also lead to a kind of intellectualizing which is *not* the problem but the *product* of the problem. It is this way of talking that I'm most interested in. Their complaints and their own descriptions of how they feel I will leave to others.

POPE:

But you aren't interested in just any kind of intellectualizing, are you? My God, even if you ruled out the gripes and pains you'd still be left with a lot to sort out.

TELLURIAN:

Yes, I think you're right. I'm interested in what I would call "interesting" discussion. Most of us, even by this very subjective criterion, spend most of our time listening to ourselves and others saying quite uninteresting things.

And I'm interested, in a way, in hearing people who have given the matter some independent thought talk about or intellectualize about what life is about, why we are here, and various subjects related to the very broad category of "the human condition." People are very reluctant to talk about such things, partially because it's obviously so threatening to even think about them privately, especially in terms of oneself. Most of us, to the extent that we have anything to say about such matters, simply repeat some simple platitudes we've learned in church, or out, which are meant to *close off* further discussion.

Of course there are many people who do have something to say whom we don't let talk. We tend to assume that because what people do is routine and uninteresting that what goes on in their heads reflects this as well. This is true more often than we would like—but we tend to equate public performance with private experience, not realizing that we ourselves harbor interesting thoughts which we are frightened to share with others.

FLEECE:

Yes, and we also err on the other side as well. If people live an "unconventional" life we tend to think they must also have something interesting to say.

POPE:

But don't you find, really, that most people have nothing interesting to say? And don't you suspect that even if you opened them up there would be nothing much there? Many people confuse intimate talk about themselves as "interesting" talk. And that's what you often get when you "open people up."

TELLURIAN:

Yes, you may be right. On the other hand I would not want to prejudge the matter. Perhaps by our very nature we are uninteresting to most people. Perhaps people must find, to preserve their own importance, that others are dull and of little worth. Those who escape this, the "stars" of any field of endeavor, escape it because people don't know them, not because they do. They are revered because they are thought to be different from other people. But to the people who know them they are just like everyone else. We tend to put a good deal of faith in the process of evaluating people by their *reputations,* without ever realizing, I believe, what this commits us to. Among other things, of course, it commits us to allowing others to define for us what is of worth.

POPE:

But you're not saying, are you, that there aren't *really* differences among people, that some people may have special talents and geniuses which allow them to do things better than others, or, better yet, which allow them to do things most people simply couldn't do? I'm amazed, for example, at the number of people who can't write a novel, or a poem, or even paint a picture if you put a brush in their hand. It's not even that they would do these things badly. It's that they can't do them at all.

TELLURIAN:

What I'm suggesting amounts to something like the following. We all make judgments of people. And we label some as interesting, some as bores, some as kind, some as crude, some as intelligent, some as evil. But not everyone concludes the same thing about any given individual. We seem to agree that the labels themselves make sense—we disagree about to whom they apply. And what is true of our observations of others is also true of their observations of us. Some might see us as exciting, imaginative, bright, etc. Others might see us as crass, arrogant, uninspiring, or whatnot. And we don't have any control over these evaluations. In most cases, of course, we don't even really know what they are. We have relations with people all the time who think things about us which we would be quite surprised to know they thought *if we knew* what they thought. But we don't. They have, somewhere, from someone, or something, labeled us by reputation, or by what we do, or by who we appear to be occupationally, etc.

POPE:

You are suggesting, then, that it's in the nature of human beings to find fault with others, to judge their fellowman?

TELLURIAN:

Something like that, yes.

POPE:

You're not really interested, then, in Seeker's problems? Only in his abilities, if he has any, to intellectualize?

TELLURIAN:

That's partly true, yes.

FLEECE:

Of course, as an intellectual matter some people's problems are interesting. It *would* be interesting, for example, to know something about Einstein's problems, or Picasso's, or anyone else who has already demonstrated a capacity to intellectualize in extraordinary ways. But, as I understand what Lewis is saying, to listen to *anyone's* problems is a disaster. We all have sob stories—Einstein's aren't any more interesting than anyone else's. We would pay more attention to his, that's all, because of what it might tell us about Einstein's product. To listen to problems *before* one has any reason to believe that the person has something interesting to say, is to act the role of therapist—something to do if you like that sort of thing.

POPE:

You're saying then, I take it, that you would rather see how people give meaning to life than to listen to anything else. That's kind of interesting.

FLEECE:

Not only that. We always assume that people have "problems" of some psychic sort. Maybe people's problems are philosophical. Maybe they simply haven't been able to think some things out. (Pause.)

POPE:

Do you think Seeker will be back? (Addressing this question to both Fleece and Tellurian.)

TELLURIAN:

Yes, he'll be back. Our experience has been that people's curiosity becomes strongly aroused—not to mention the fact that they are genuinely interested in finding a solution to the questions raised. Mr. Seeker appears especially perplexed. I think we were correct in assuming he has already done a considerable amount of thinking about these things on his own.

FLEECE:

You remember Maris Oates. (Looking at Tellurian while saying this, but actually speaking for Pope's benefit.) He became so enthusiastic after the final session that he himself *asked* if he could come back the next day. After the second session he quit his job and took his family to Montana. He's been writing short stories. (Turning to Tellurian.) I put a new batch on your desk, by the way. He certainly has an interesting turn of mind.

POPE:

You mean you actually keep tabs on the people you bring here? You follow their lives afterward?

FLEECE:

Of course, it's up to the people themselves. We encourage them to let us know what they are doing, and to send us anything they've done that they would like us to see or comment on. In lots of cases we keep up a continuing dialogue.

TELLURIAN:

It's also a question, in a way, of actually seeing one's impact on people. Very few of us are able to see tangible proof that what we do actually makes a difference. Most of us, in fact, have the sneaking suspicion that what we do has no significance for anyone. Oh, we talk ourselves into half believing many things, but if we ever begin to question seriously what we do, we can open up quite a gaping hole. Perhaps we soothe ourselves with the thought that someone has to write insurance policies or loan people money. But we seem to work for reasons which, if we ever did know, are now long forgotten. How much we make becomes a criterion for success in this kind of void.

POPE:

Do you really believe that's true? I have been offered positions for more money and have turned them down.

TELLURIAN:

We must come to an understanding. Anything I say which you find "negative" or unflattering of humans in general is not meant to apply to you. You can simply pretend you are not a human being and exempt yourself from the remark. Although this is obviously a pretense, I find it less annoying than having you attempt to defend yourself by showing how you are an exception to the rule and therefore a "good" person. When you do that you insert yourself in between me and my argument, and in order to continue my argument I must run over you. Now, while I am perfectly willing to do that if necessary, I would prefer not to.

POPE:

I don't understand. (And obviously uncomfortable.)

FLEECE:

I think what Lewis is trying to say is that he doesn't want to have to talk about you in order to talk about what he wants to talk about. When you make a comment about yourself then it's necessary, or seems to be necessary, to talk about you. But since you are the only one who has "evidence" about yourself, we are left with nothing to do but to come to some conclusion about you personally. Lewis is saying he really doesn't want to do that. He wants to talk about people in general, but not in such a way that evidence about yourself can "defeat" or "confirm" the argument.

I think, for example, that Lewis is not really saying what you attribute to him. But even if he were, the world is so complex that he has to be wrong. But he knows that. To point to yourself as an exception must mean, then, that you are trying to say something favorable about yourself rather than to comment seriously on the argument he is making.

TELLURIAN:

Please excuse me a moment. (Tellurian rather abruptly gets up and leaves the room.)

POPE:

(After Tellurian has left.) What an extraordinarily interesting man. What did he do before this?

FLEECE:

Lewis was a college professor. And a very successful one at that.

POPE:

But why did he give it up?

FLEECE:

Why do you think?

POPE:

(Chuckles.) I guess that was a silly question. (Pause.) But

what I can't understand is why he doesn't write, or paint, or something. Why has he decided to do this?

FLEECE:

Creativity is a personal matter. There's no law that says creative people have to be artists, or writers, or whatever. One can be creative and be a lawyer, a businessman, or anything else. Apparently Lewis wants to see if he can get others started on the same road he thinks one must travel in order to do what he thinks people should be doing.

POPE:

But his significance gets wrapped up in other people that way, and his influence, if he has any, becomes anonymous. He'll have nothing to show for his efforts except the effect he's had on people.

FLEECE:

Yes, that's right. But don't you find it a bit peculiar that you find that a bit peculiar? Creativity need not always require a tangible product. One can be creative and do nothing but talk. And besides, what's wrong with measuring one's significance by the impact one has had on the lives of others?

POPE:

But you know as well as I do that one earns intellectual recognition through one's products and *not* one's influence on others. Lewis will never be respected for the obvious contribution he is making, especially in history, unless he does something of his own, unless he produces something tangible.

FLEECE:

I have a feeling Lewis doesn't want other people's respect. In fact, I think he might even say he has failed if he earned anyone's respect. He doesn't want to be admired—he wants to be an irritant.

POPE:

But wouldn't you say that he will lose his ability to do what he wants to do if he goes around irritating people?

FLEECE:

> To the contrary, not if one believes, as he very well may, that the consequences of irritation with oneself, especially with one's worth, is the only valuable thing we have.

POPE:

> Wouldn't you say, though, that . . .
> (Tellurian reenters. Pope stops. Tellurian knows that they have been talking about him. But he expected they would.)

TELLURIAN:

> Excuse me, I didn't mean to interrupt.

FLEECE:

> Not at all. I must leave for a moment myself. (Fleece exits.)

POPE:

> (Still somewhat embarrassed.) I certainly have found this interesting. (Pause. No reply from Tellurian.) Margaret is certainly a dedicated person, isn't she?

TELLURIAN:

> That's coercive.

POPE:

> What's coercive?

TELLURIAN:

> Ending a sentence with a question which asks for agreement. The English do it all the time. I find it irritating, don't you?

POPE:

> Yes, I guess . . . (Tellurian begins to smile and Pope finally catches on. He starts to laugh and Tellurian joins in.)

TELLURIAN:

> I assume, by the way, that when I came in just now you and Margaret were discussing me.

POPE:

(A little frightened about the prospects of where this might lead.) Yes, we were. I was asking Margaret what you did before you began doing this.

TELLURIAN:

I thought you might. Would you be interested in learning more about it?

POPE:

(Eagerly.) I certainly would.

TELLURIAN:

(Goes over to his desk, opens a drawer, and pulls out a typed manuscript.) Why don't you have a look at this when you get the chance? You may find it interesting. (Hands Pope "Letters From Lewis.")

POPE:

What is it?

TELLURIAN:

That will become clear, I believe, when you read it. I'd appreciate it, by the way, if you'd return it. It is the only copy I have. In fact, it may be the only copy anyone has. I am no longer in touch with the person who sent it to me, and that represents our complete correspondence. When you read it, you will know as much about him as I do.

POPE:

I shall take very good care of it. (Begins to leaf through the manuscript.)

TELLURIAN:

You did very well in your first session. We are going to enjoy having you on our staff. Assuming, of course, that you wish to be.

POPE:

Thank you. (He smiles and looks down—embarrassed. He is obviously pleased with the compliment.)

TELLURIAN:

When did it happen to you?

POPE:

Just last year. It had been building for about a year before that. In retrospect, of course, it looks like I had been preparing myself for even longer. I would do things that didn't conform to what others were doing. I would make it impossible for myself to achieve all that I thought I wanted. I now see, from hindsight, that it was all part of the process, only at the very early stages.

As I became more and more frustrated I began to strike out more freely. I began to have strange ideas, ideas that led me to question my whole being. Well, as you might guess, despair followed, but accompanied, occasionally, by glimpses of real creativity. Then, at the end of last year, I finally realized what it was all about. I began to go my own way, and all on my own. It was a giddy experience at first, but now it's very comforting—although I still have my moments of doubt. But I don't seem to mind as much. I'm not sure I even want to be. Despair is the edge that will keep me nimble. Or so I hope, anyway.

TELLURIAN:

There does appear to be a pattern in these things. Very much like yours, actually. What is so interesting is that there seems to be no particular age that is immune. It's true that many are between thirty and forty-five; few before thirty and few after fifty. But we have recruits from all ages. You're extremely fortunate, my friend, that it happened to you so early. One of the most pathetic things I can imagine is to have it toward the end of one's life. To look back over such a vast stretch and have to call it a waste. (Shudders.) That's what frightens me a bit in the case before us now. Mr. Seeker is forty-eight. I'm afraid it will go very hard on him. (Fleece comes back into the room.) But I do think it's better than nothing, how about you? (Both laugh, and Fleece joins them, sensing immediately the joke.)

Shall we go to dinner?

POPE:

> If you don't mind, I think I'll stay behind and take a peek at this manuscript. I'll join you later.

TELLURIAN:

> Suit yourself. (He and Fleece leave. Pope settles down in a chair and begins to read.)

3
Letters From Lewis

Dear Lewis,

I have taken the liberty of putting our correspondence together in the form of a manuscript. I hope you will not be offended. I have added a short introduction, which you may enjoy.

Good-bye and good luck.

Crete

Introduction

When I was a younger man and just beginning to see the possibility of having thoughts of my own, I decided it would be interesting to try to engage someone in a possibly protracted discourse concerning human behavior. I am not sure what "motives" I would be willing or able to assign myself for wanting this. Why I did what I did obviously depends upon how you wish to look at it. My own explanation to myself is that I wanted to see whether I had anything interesting to say, and one way to do this was to talk with someone. But others, I am sure, will assign different reasons for my behavior. If one approves of what subsequently occurred, then perhaps I will be given worthy motives—but if one disapproves, as well he might, then perhaps judgment will be more harsh.

It was, of course, in many ways an outrageous thing for me to do. Why should I want others to consider the positions which I hold? Why should I argue with someone with a different point of view? What are the obligations and responsibilities which I or he might assume once the encounter was begun? I am afraid I gave none of these questions any thought whatever. To me it was a question of my own desire to find out what I thought, and whether what I thought could have any grounding among others. And, as I said, I was young and new to the intellectual world. I cared not for practicalities—nor, I am ashamed to say, for the feelings of others. At least not when ideas were at stake.

To carry out my plan I needed a correspondent, someone who looked at things differently than I did, and someone who did what he did successfully. Someone who would not only feel himself that he was successful but who had the markings of a successful person—the rewards and honors from his peers. I needed, in short, a somewhat older man, someone who had had the opportunity to be successful and who had taken advantage of it. To this end I chose Lewis A. Tellurian, Jr., a very well-known, successful researcher in human behavior. There were, undoubtedly, some special or "contextual" reasons for choosing him—I had heard of him, for example—but at the time he seemed to me typical of the direction in which human analysis was then going and was himself a heavy contributor.

Tellurian was a professor at a large, high-status university in the United States at the time I decided to contact him. Because of his abilities in his chosen field he had managed to publish a large number of works and to rise quickly to his position as professor. He was, from all appearances, devoted to his work and committed to his ideas. He seemed to have all of the necessary qualifications which I desired. The difficulty would obviously be in encouraging him to engage in such a project with me.

The fruits of my labors are presented in this manuscript. This consists of the unedited correspondence between Tellurian and myself over a two-year period. I have taken the liberty, in presenting these letters, to distinguish three sections. These are meant to have significance only for the reader, marking convenient stopping places, as chapters do in normal books. Otherwise, the correspondence is presented as it occurred.

1   The Fall

Dear Lewis,

I hope you will not mind my writing to you and, incidentally, addressing you by your first name. Although you are somewhat older than I, it strikes me as indulging in unnecessary formality to call you by your surname. I, of course, have heard of you, and you will recognize me only as someone of no reputation, so perhaps you will think I take advantage by bypassing hierarchy. But I trust that such matters are not of much concern to you. At least I feel that must be the case.

I have a proposal to make to you which I earnestly hope you will accept. On the surface it may seem that the advantage will all redound to me, and I will not try to persuade you otherwise. You may find, however, once we have made a start, that my proposal has something to offer you as well. I would like to suggest that we engage in a regular exchange of letters in which the subject matter would be entirely at our discretion. It is not even necessary that we should conduct a "dialogue" and discuss the same topics. This more random procedure will give each of us the opportunity to put our thoughts to paper, no matter how tentatively we might hold them or how embarrassed we might be if they were given in a more public context. That we are personally unknown to each other will be an advantage as feelings of friendship or dislike will not be at issue. People's friends usually agree on most matters—if not at first, then certainly very quickly —and enemies are too busy polarizing themselves to say anything very interesting. We will have neither of these encumbrances.

There is one major difficulty, of course, and that is that either of us might find the other uninteresting. This would end the correspondence, as it should. The purpose of an exchange of letters for me is to seek stimulation under circumstances in which neither of us will arrive at the point of dismissing the other's arguments because we have dismissed the other's competence to argue. So often we protect ourselves from examining the perspectives of others because to do so would mean, at the minimum, a willingness to grant the possibility that what *we* believe is also *a* perspective. We then dismiss the threat by dismissing the person, and the world becomes safe for our thoughts once again.

If you agree that such an enterprise, as I propose, might be of some value to you (at least to the extent of giving it a try), I would be happy to hear from you.

Cordially,
Crete Sewell

Dear Mr. Sewell,

Thank you very much for your letter in which you propose an exchange of letters on various "topics." I appreciate the fact that this might be an interesting experience, but at the moment it would be difficult for me to find the time it would undoubtedly require. I am currently engaged in several projects and hope you will understand.

Sincerely yours,
Lewis A. Tellurian, Jr.

Dear Lewis,

It has taken me a good long time to realize that there is a difference between resistance and dissent. To resist is to respond with one's usual social cover—to take flight from threat in conventional activity. To dissent is to proclaim that the self will no longer tolerate a state of affairs. I take your response to be resistance—it would have been fruitless for us to continue had I not encountered it. Of course you are busy, and of course you feel you must get on with it. This is one price we pay in collecting society's respect (which we then proceed to confuse with our own). I think you will find however, at least at first, that it will take very little of your time.

In some ways I envy those who are caught up in life's work. Commitment gives life zest and meaning. From commitment we derive the benefits of feeling that what we do has significance. But what happens if we become aware of this function of commitment? What happens to the commitment? Self-awareness of the function in life of one's participation can be likened to a sleeping giant—there may be little which can survive its awakening. Once up and about it may lurch heavily, smashing objects which are in its way. Most of us manage to prevent this from occurring. We *do* feel that what we do is important, and self-consciousness, rather than being a tool which destroys commitment, serves, rather, to reinforce it. We use our awareness of our commitment as a moral club, justifying ourselves and denigrating others. Self-consciousness of this sort facilitates the construction and maintenance of an individual life and serves as a shield to ward off threats to one's sense of significance. If one begins to think that commitment may be a struggle in which one attempts to gain control of one's meaning through subjugation of awareness, to put to work against the alleged enemy the justification for tyranny from within, then one has a new and dangerous struggle with which to contend. Awareness of the function of commitment and the commitment itself are natural enemies, for the human enterprise is an historical record of man's construction and destruction based on commitment, and awareness of this can bring the process to a halt. Which raises an even more difficult question: whether man's creativity must be paired with his viciousness. But clearly we cannot move ahead rapidly—reflection is a brake which burns up time. I have heard it said, however, that we must count by geological clocks.

Cordially,
Crete

Dear Mr. Sewell,

What is all this chatter supposed to mean? I get the feeling (uneasy I will admit) that you may have an interesting thought or two, but the muddle surrounding them is so great that ideas are lost. Can you possibly say what you wish to say in a more precise summary statement? Perhaps, then, we can see more clearly just what your points are.

Sincerely yours,
Lewis A. Tellurian, Jr.

Dear Lewis,

There develops a fashion, in most *academic* subjects, to say things with what the practitioners insist is precision. What this amounts to, in almost every case, is a demand to conform to a particular writing style which is derived, even more perniciously, from an ideology about how intellectual activities should be conducted within any particular discipline. The demand for precision is, then, a demand for conformity masquerading as precision since what is precise and what isn't is more a product of familiarity than it is with independent standards of what precision "really" is. Precision, then, is one of the labels by which we attempt to judge what comes before us without having to contend with the content itself. It is, as any labeling system, an economizing device which frees us from considering that which is strange, and which even justifies, morally, such rejection.

The argument in favor of precision is usually that with a new and common vocabulary, free from the connotations words collect as they roll through generations, clear thought and understanding will be abetted. Words are thought of as arbitrary symbols, to mean only what one says they mean, as though thought must be free from feeling. The argument often heard against, usually mounted by those who have the most to lose, is that such a new and pure language will be sterile and trivial. Again the mistake is in assuming that words and not sentences are the purveyors of meaning.

Rather than pretend that we make things interesting by our choice of words, we could assume that we use words and we may or may not say something interesting, but that the two are independent of each other. Whether what we say is obscure or precise, long-winded or condensed, fashioned from cold, scientific jargon, or flowery, poetic imagery the criterion we must use to judge another's thoughts is whether the *content,* the *meaning* of what is being said, stimulates us to think further on the subject. By this criterion, of course, we would reject most thought regardless of style. We do, in fact, develop a preference for certain styles over others—it is all part of what is meant by being comfortable. But such preferences will always break down in the presence of brilliance no matter in what style it comes. Our prejudices will grant exceptions when the alternative is to alter our prejudices. But the cost we pay for the safety of familiarity is the company of mediocrity. This is not to argue that because something is confusing or different it is therefore brilliant. Many strategists who are incapable of making it in the established way justify their failure by flying off into a land where they think there are no standards by which they can be judged. We are all familiar enough with this phenomenon not to be overawed by those whose styles are designed to shock. On the other hand, one does not want to reject all those things which are confusing or unfamiliar, primarily because creative ideas may possibly be lodged there. Each new form deserves a fair hearing.

Cordially,
Crete

Dear Mr. Sewell,

We proceed in our knowledge of things step by step. Such progress requires dedication, patience, and hard work. It is also essential that the results of often very complicated (and tediously collected) material be put in a form which does not confuse or mislead the reader. It is unfortunate enough that we have arguments over real differences of opinion. To compound these with potentially explosive misunderstandings which could have been averted by clearer presentation is anathema to anyone who prizes intellectual clarity. I agree with you that what is said is of utmost importance, but how it is said can affect people's understanding of it. We have too much in written form which is badly written. We also have too much which is longer than it needs to be. The points of many books may be summarized in several pages. The ideas contained in many articles may often be condensed into a single sentence or two. And especially when we attempt to inform we must say what we have to say with a minimum of our own judgment thrown in. We must try to say what is, without confusing it with what should be. Otherwise we come perilously close to crossing the dividing line separating education from propaganda, knowledge from opinion, fact from value judgment. Because we know that the general public is susceptible to rhetoric does not mean that we should give it to them, nor practice it amongst ourselves. Our job is to discover what is true, and to pass it on to others in as clear and precise a manner as possible. All else leads to hopeless argument and misunderstanding.

Sincerely,
Lewis

Dear Lewis,

There is a very serious problem that arises out of people getting together in groups, and that is what happens to "the middle people." The few high-status ones take care of themselves, and if they do not we would consider their troubles their own fault. How can those so fortunate to begin with expect help from anyone? And those whom society defines as stupid or demented are taken care of in ways which are a lie to our own nature. In the effort to create a dignity for ourselves we hide them, deny them, and think them deviations from what *Homo sapiens* are and ought to be. But the so-called "middle people" who make up the overwhelming majority of any group, these are the ones who must work for their significance. Neither brilliant nor dull, grotesque nor bizarre, justification does not come easy.

Most of us would like to think that we are making a contribution. And if our part is small there are a number of ways we can make it appear larger. Indeed, this is one of the major products of any society—the definition of distinction. One form this may take, especially in intellectual societies, is to suppose that something called "progress" is the result of the cumulative efforts of large numbers of people. Such an idea, of course, is quite seductive since it not only gives most of us a feeling of significance, it also enables us to judge others by the extent to which they are a part of this social enterprise. But in creating a society, of course, we inhibit the efforts which individuals might make if they were not a part of a group in which success is defined in terms of conformity to certain standards and ideals as established within the group.

Few of us are capable or willing to admit that it might be otherwise and that significance might not be the consequence of cumulative effort. This is not to deny functions to daily routines. It is only to question why we must make more out of it, or glorify its obvious demerits by pretending that tedium added together ever sums to more than a pile of tedium. Quality is not a function of weight, although some qualities may be heavy. Brilliance is not a function of size, although brillance may, on occasion, be produced in quantity. The "middle people" plod along, keeping ahead of the stupid and demented in a struggle to become human by invidious comparison, carping at each other in the everlasting effort to turn individual differences into matters of first principles, and generally begrudging the efforts of those outside the group, feeling it safe to acknowledge brilliance only when their own egos are not at issue. Indeed, they are even likely to explain a brilliant performance by giving to the performer extraordinary intelligence, thereby neutralizing the damage to themselves. The "middle people" have their heroes, but certainly it is rare that a producer of brilliance will be among them. The "middling" keep busy and do the things that middle people do. Let us not pretend it is any more than that. At a later time we might consider whether what is has to be.

Cordially,
Crete

Dear Crete,

Are you, then, a cynic, a man who despairs of the human efforts he witnesses, thinking men should be angels rather than men but knowing full well they cannot be? You credit too highly answerless questions, and as a consequence, disparage the efforts of those who try. Do we really know all that much about man? Have we, then, so much insight into man's behavior that judgments such as yours are anything but self-destructive? To preoccupy oneself with pessimism is only to belie an inability to cope. There are things to be done, and all we can do is do them. Your moral indignation is hollow against a good, solid achievement. There is suffering in the world, there is poverty, injustice, bigotry, war, famine, and hundreds of other evils. Given these, how can one spend his time talking to himself? Does man not have a responsibility to leave the world a better place than he finds it? Are we not to attempt to preserve and extend man's dignity? Have we not goals like freedom, brotherhood, and virtue to pursue? Faced with these challenges, it strikes me that negativism is quite out of place.

Sincerely,
Lewis

Dear Lewis,

In the presence of strangers, especially those with "peculiar" manners, it is natural for humans to feel frightened. Self-preservation is a powerful instinct, often demanding behavior which, upon reflection, cannot be explained but only justified, and which others criticize as peculiar and selfish. And, speaking historically as well as biologically, fear among strangers is often justified. As a consequence, we usually avoid strangeness and seek the familiar. But when frightened we have at our disposal many stratagems which are employed contextually. When a person senses danger he searches for a possibility of escape (assuming time to do so). If he finds one, he may or may not take it, depending upon his assessment of whether he can win and how important what is being challenged is to him. If he is in doubt about the possibility of escape, he may panic, especially if the danger comes upon him suddenly. If he feels he has to escape, and no chance of winning, he may simply give in to his terror. Among these more general categories of response are, of course, the names of many others: fighting, anger, resentment, hatred, fawning, withdrawal, etc. But they all stem from a common source: a sense of being threatened, produced by the introduction of an incongruity. Whether one refers to the experience in terms of moving away as in flight or fear, or as attempting to move toward safety or self-preservation, it is still the same experience. (We have words that do mean different things, but those "differences" are not always meaningful.) Incongruities in turn have as their source expectations of how things ought to be (both normatively in terms of how things should be and empirically in terms of one's expectations of what things will be like). Events (internal or external) give rise to incongruities which in turn produce fear. If the incongruity is shown to be silly or harmless (perhaps not until considerably later) tension release may take the form of laughter.

One may, of course, recognize these things and still be subject to their occurrence. If one attempts to state something about the human condition, one should not assume that he himself is exempt. Nor must one assume that because one understands, one can control. We usually know things only *after* they happen.

Crete

Dear Crete,

I am afraid I do not share your way of doing things. You speak speculatively and never make an effort to adduce evidence for what you say. You contend that people do this and people do that. But people are different and "they" don't do this or that—some do one thing and some another. One must then try to discover the causes of these differences, the conditions which underlie this diversity. When one speaks of man in a general way, as you do, one says very little about people in particular situations. And, after all, people do behave in particular circumstances. In addition, of course, the level at which you seem to want to discourse produces such vague concepts as "the human condition," "human nature," and other similarly abstract notions which have not taken us very far in our understanding of man. In the face of the obvious diversity which we see before us, attempting to collapse that diversity under a single heading is simply asking for empty generalities and statements without meaning. We must be more cautious about stating such generalities, and we must spend more time *verifying* the statements we do make so that, for example, I do not simply have to take your word for the truth of something, I can look at the evidence and draw my own conclusion. We must have some agreed upon way of deciding that a statement is true or false, or we will never get anywhere. And we need to spend more time collecting data and less in armchair speculation.

Lewis

Lewis,

One of the reasons why we believe some things to be true and some to be false is because we are taught to believe in truth itself. In a manner of speaking, we come to believe that the statement "some things are true" is true. If one accepts the concept of truth, then one will naturally separate things out in terms of the concept. And if we do not believe in truth, we run into a fundamental paradox: is the statement "there is no truth" true? How does one judge an assertion if not by the criterion of truth? There is, I think, an answer to this question. We judge things by how we feel about them. Do they strike us as being what we are willing to believe in? And we are willing to believe in something for lots of different reasons. But primarily it is because we understand things that way. Our understanding may change— we may even change our minds, but we all have ways of handling incoming material which essentially rejects those things which "make no sense" to us because we do not believe that "sense" looks like that.

One of the ways in which we are taught to come to a conclusion about what is true is to suggest that "the evidence" supports us. The question, then, is not so much evidence versus no evidence, but the kind of evidence which will satisfy us. It is fashionable in some fields of inquiry to require technologically produced evidence to demonstrate the validity of an assertion. This is true in many areas of the humanities and social sciences as well as in physical and natural science. But what one is really requiring is that one argue in a particular form and within certain prescribed boundaries. And, of course, the importance of evidence becomes less and less as the assertion becomes more and more general. An indication of the fact that things may be "true" or "false" independent of the evidence and that evidence is used as a matter of persuasion. Clearly, for example, evidence may be "wrong," irrelevant, or in other ways removed from the validity of one's argument.

Put somewhat differently, you and I could agree to the procedures necessary to verify that there are twelve books on that shelf. But how would we agree to the procedure necessary to verify the statement: "A primary factor in the human condition is fear"? In the former we share a perspective, a way of looking at things, that allows us to check the accuracy of the statement. In the latter we are *suggesting* a perspective. Perspectives are neither true nor false, only statements within perspectives are. So that unless one shares the perspective in which the question of truth is at issue, one can reach no agreement.

A good deal of argument, of course, is over this very problem. We assume that there is such a thing as "truth," and a *single* truth, and so we cast our disagreements in terms of what is really true and what is false. But rarely are our arguments about validity as defined here. Those who share a common perspective can easily distinguish between truth and falsehood. Indeed, most falsehoods will simply be errors which, when pointed out to us, we will readily rectify. Most arguments, however, are only *cast in terms of truth;* they are actually disagreements over perspectives or how things are looked at. No amount of "evidence" will persuade someone of the truth of a statement if he does not share the perspective which makes legitimate the evidence in the first place. And often, of course, no evidence at all is required to be convinced of the truth of something if one shares the perspective in which the "truth" is lodged.

Crete

Crete,

I think one either believes there is an ordered world out there to be described accurately, or there isn't. In the former case our task is to discover the order and to avoid error, in the latter we must construct the most useful fictions possible in the face of chaos, prepared to be eclectic in our beliefs as we shift from one construction to another. Your position, however, seems to be both.

You suggest that ways of looking at things or perspectives are neither true nor false. Presumably, then, they are constructions, creations of the mind, and we live in a world which requires that we construct plausible interpretations. But then you suggest that within these perspectives a statement may be true or false, which suggests a world that is ordered, which we can discover, and about which we can be correct or in error. But if this is your belief, then the world is both ordered and discoverable, and constructed, and our task twofold: to approximate what the world is "really" like and to build convenient fictions. It seems to me difficult, however, to hold both positions at the same time. I choose the former, and I have heard that some people prefer the latter, but you seem to want both.

Lewis

Lewis,

There are a few who attempt to construct orderly systems of thought and, of course, there are many more who make some effort to see things within a perspective already provided. Within these systems certain statements are logically true and others are contradictions. Whether a fallacy is committed, then, depends upon the system with which one starts. But of course, it is perfectly possible to hold a position which is a contradiction in the context of one perspective but not within another. The basis of a disagreement between people may therefore be quite complicated and may require the explication of the differing perspectives.

My concern here, however, is in any case somewhat different. We may come back at a later time to the point you make. People do certain things and think in certain ways. It is fair to ask what those things and ways are and, just as important, what the behavior and thinking imply. For example, one could insist that the way one looks at things is true, and many people do. But to do so would be to insist, equally, that other perspectives are false. There are certainly enough people who do this. But the word *truth* here is not the same "truth" as in the case of the number of books on the bookshelf or any other assertion of "fact" for which we agree upon procedures necessary to test its validity. In the latter case we share a perspective about books, bookshelves, counting, and the like. And this raises an additional difficulty. Very often when discussing these matters we use examples which are within a perspective which we share to explain a position which is outside the shared area. For example, to "show" that the world is ordered and that truth is to be discovered we might refer to "facts" such as books on a bookshelf or other "observations" which are likely to occur within a common perspective. Normally within a society there is some agreement, some sharing, with respect to common objects and matters of everyday living. Socialization procedures within societies help to insure some common ways of looking at things. Often the smaller the society and the more frequent the interaction among members compared with those outside, the stronger the shared perspective. But from this position one cannot argue that the perspective itself is also "true."

Of course most people have no single system of thought but rather a series of more or less connected but disjointed opinions, beliefs, and feelings. It would be too much to expect logical consistency from those who make no pretense to it except possibly when pushed to do so after the fact by taunts that contradictions and inconsistencies are somehow "bad." Most of us share this bias in favor of logic and consistency and are therefore vulnerable to charges of violation. The tortured arguments designed at the spur of the moment to "bridge" the inconsistency are often ingenious.

Perspectives, however, unlike matters of fact (and what is a matter of fact will not be known until one finds that others accept what one asserts), are a mixture of assumptions, hypotheses, judgments, definitions, values, beliefs, etc. (the "etc." referring to whatever vocabulary one finds most suitable to discuss these things). In some cases, for example, one might want to say that a part (or whole) of a perspective was immoral, dangerous, or beautiful, more than one would be tempted to say it was true or false. Indeed we might be disappointed if denied the opportunity to assert that something was wrong or monstrous rather than merely false. Perspectives, then, provide one with a whole context in which to see, judge, and interpret. And sharing a perspective means sharing some relatively standard ways of deciding not only what is true and false, but what is right and wrong as well. There will, of course, be disagreements even within a perspective. In some cases these disagreements may simply be our errors, mistakes in using the accepted procedures. In other cases disputes will arise because one or more of the disputants are unwilling to follow precedent or feel that the precedents are ambiguous. And, indeed, in some instances of this the major reason is lack of agreement about the perspective. That is, there are margins to almost all perspectives which will not be clear. Methods of adjudication are designed to meet just such contingencies. In any case, it is useful to know when one is dealing with a difference of opinion which might be settled by collectable evidence the parties would be willing to accept as legitimate and as sufficient to establish "truth," and those in which no such procedures are possible. Most of us too readily assume that evidence of agreement about "truth" in one area (within a shared perspective) is evidence that there is "truth" in a more absolute sense. And, of course, it is one's own perspective which is viewed as being true. But disagreements which entail differences in perspectives are not at all parallel with within-perspective disagreements.

Crete

Crete,

I must confess that I am somewhat intrigued by this notion of truth which you are developing. But before making any extended comment I need answers to two questions:

First, is not what you are saying itself a perspective, and hence neither true nor false but (as you put it) a "way of looking at things"?

Second, how does one choose between and among perspectives?

Lewis

Lewis,

The answer to the first question is "yes." But this raises an even larger (and more interesting) matter. All interesting perspectives contain within themselves built-in paradoxes. That is, in our effort to understand human behavior we are forced to simplify. And these simplifications lead to nonsense, absurdities, and other "illogical" phenomena when pushed too hard, especially near the boundaries. One of the most interesting products of a simplification is the "paradox of self-reflection" (as I will call it). If, for example, one makes the assertion that nothing is true or false, then the question "Is that assertion true?" becomes a "self-reflective paradox." If, as Freud suggests, intellectualizing is a form of rationalization which hides a deeper conflict, then is that also true of Freud's intellectualizing? Is what is asserted as a negative universal also true of the assertion itself? Is what a perspective says of other things not in the perspective also true of the perspective itself? And herein lies the answer to your first question. My discussion of perspectives is also a perspective and hence the things I say about perspectives also apply to my perspective as well. Hence the seeming paradox.

Most academic philosophers, especially logicians, spend a good deal of time and effort attempting to do away with paradoxes, treating them as doctors do curable diseases. We have many fine edifices of philosophical discussion built on this effort. But it might just as well be a function of philosophy to point out to us where paradoxes exist and to suggest why, without also going through contortions of attempting to do away with a "naturally" occurring phenomenon. It is as though a landscape architect attempted to do away with a mountain by building a fence higher than the mountain so it could not be seen. The mountain is still there. But one must now climb up the fence, or go around it, or poke a hole in it, or build a stand behind it, or go further back from it, or do something else in order to see the mountain. So it is with those who build fences in front of paradoxes.

The second question cannot be so easily answered. The nub of the difficulty rests with the concepts of "choice." Do we ever have an opportunity to *choose* in the way that most people mean to use that term? Some of the things we do preclude doing alternatives, but some of these turn out to be logical puzzles (e.g., if we choose to marry, we cannot also choose to be a bachelor), and others may not be dilemmas at all (e.g., if we are offered a choice between an apple and a banana, we may often have both). It may sound frivolous to say that we do what we do, but it is no less so than to say that we choose to do what we do. Given "alternatives" some are more attractive (for sometimes very complex and even strange reasons) and we do them. Given alternatives of equal weight (including indifference) we are likely to "choose" willy-nilly. Choice is not a helpful concept, primarily because it presupposes a "rational" individual (at least when actual "choices" are being made) "free" to select among "alternatives" with more or less "knowledge" of the consequences and implications of his selection, and hence a "responsibility" for his actions. This rationality model of man has never proved very satisfactory, either as an explanation of how we do in fact behave, or as an ethic. It is clearly a "way of looking at things," complete with assumptions, values, judgments, beliefs, definitions, and the like. And it is a perspective which many people share (at least when discussing the responsibilities of others). Actually, the key to the theory is "responsibility," for those whose morality presupposes that man is in some way responsible for what he does will be very likely to share the beliefs and other components of the perspective.

Let me answer your question, then, more along the lines you undoubtedly intended it, i.e., "what criteria might you offer which would constitute grounds for holding any particular perspective?" (This is somewhat akin to asking what perspective I might offer on perspectives.) To this I answer that I believe things to be the way I see them when I "feel" that my perspective reveals secrets to me and when the world outside (or some part of it) makes "sense" to me. Some of these feelings will be stronger than others and I can therefore be convinced that some parts of my perspective are less sound than others. I may also find it necessary to "make up" (create, construct) some notions of my own if, for some reason, I find those around me inadequate. In some cases I might be persuaded by "evidence" (if I share a perspective or a part of one). In other cases I might come across an insight so compelling that large areas of understanding are opened to me that were not so previously. Insights are usually accompanied by a good deal of "rethinking" of my previous perspective and some new thoughts along related dimensions. Often I am simply reinforced in my perspective and made to feel correct, right, just, etc., when the statements of others (perhaps put differently, or in a different form such as in poetry or literature) coincide with thoughts or partial thoughts consistent with my own perspective. But the common dimension of all of these is the feeling I have that I am seeing things properly. Since I may prefer not to be disturbed, I may expose myself to those things which I feel will reinforce me, I will "see" things in terms of my perspective, and I will justify my behavior in ways consistent with my view

If I am disturbed, if I feel uncomfortable with an event, or a thought, I will engage in behavior which attempts to reconcile the disturbance. The number of stratagems available are large indeed, from denial, answer, and resentment to acceptance and change. Although we do find some stability in our perspectives, we must also rather constantly attend to disturbances of one kind or another.

Crete

Crete,

But if you hold a perspective or believe something to be true simply because you "feel" things are that way, it seems to me you have pushed the problem in the wrong direction. You wish truth to be a matter of someone's inner state rather than some correspondence with the world outside. Are such feelings a valid reason for distinguishing between truth and falsehood?

More importantly, you indicated earlier that things were true or false within a perspective but that truth was not an adequate concept by which to judge a perspective. But certainly statements about what is true are part of a perspective, or are at least deductions from the axioms or premises of a perspective. But if this is the case then there is no objective standard of truth at all but simply, ultimately, different statements which claim to be true, each of which is part of a perspective which can be neither true nor false. But then we face the ontological problem quite squarely. Is there an ordered reality out there to be discovered or isn't there? Are our theories merely the creations whose claim to validity depends upon how we feel about them? I do not think we can beg this question any longer. It seems to me that your distinction between perspectives and truth does not make your idea of truth any less relative, in which case we then have no standard to judge whether we have arrived at the truth or not other than our own feelings. But how, then, do we come to any conclusions about what is *really* true?

Lewis

Lewis,

Truth is an attribution which we give to assertions, and in just the same fashion as we attribute beauty to some object, or virtue to some action. Truth is what we call those assertions which, by whatever criteria we may have, we have decided correspond to what "is." The questions of whether "that is true" would continue to be true if people weren't there to say it is the same order of paradox as, do sounds exist if people are not there to hear them? There is something—but when we call something true we are not simply acknowledging that thing—we are giving it a meaning lodged in truth. Just as when we call something beautiful we are not simply acknowledging something but giving it meaning lodged in aesthetics. So I can believe in a "world out there" without being committed to the concept of truth. To deny truth is not to deny the ontological question of an ordered universe. It is simply to acknowledge that truth as an absolute being in itself is as paradoxical as hearing as an absolute being in itself. Human beings call things true or false. This does not make those things real or unreal. When one questions the "existence" of truth, then, one is simply saying that truth should be treated like other man-made concepts. Truth is not a part of "reality" but *is* a part of our talk about reality. We can be a part of reality, and we can talk about it, but we must never confuse our talk about reality for reality. "Truth" is the way we try to make talk about reality and reality the same thing. Its force is obviously a moral one—binding on those who believe in the morality of truth. And by "morality of truth" I mean that people would generally say that it is good to say things which are true and bad to say things which are false. So saying something is true is injecting a moral dimension into the discussion. It is making a claim for goodness as well as for validity. This claim for goodness is independent of the content of the statement. That is, one could claim that the assertion "Hitler killed six million Jews" is true (and therefore good in the sense that truth is good) even though the content, most people would agree, is bad. But the major point is not only that truth is a judgment which we make about assertions which adds to the discussion a moral dimension—but that most people would not even agree that this is the case (that is, would not agree with this interpretation of things).

What is true, then, is what we feel or believe to be true (we may, of course, have doubts). To say that something is true is equivalent to saying that I accept it to be true. A person may change his mind about what he believes to be true. But, one might ask, won't that show that he was wrong to begin with, and that there is therefore a difference between what is true and what is believed to be true? My answer is that a person may indeed have believed something to be true which he may now no longer believe to be true, but that does not mean that he was "wrong" or "mistaken." One may speak of error only in the context of a recognized violation of something agreed upon and in which one would agree he made a mistake if it were pointed out to him. A change from one "truth" to another "truth" does not guarantee "real" "truth." Normally when we say we have changed our minds we mean that we do not see things now the way we saw things then because something else has changed. For example, if I believe it to be true that someone is an honest man, and then I believe that he cheated me, was my first belief in error and is he now a dishonest man? I think not, or at least only in the sense that men are honest or dishonest if we call them one or the other. In the first case we call a person honest, something happens which we call cheating, and we change our mind and now believe the man to be dishonest. The first statement was not untrue—it was simply arrived at before the occurrence of a particular event which led us to change our minds. But we will agree that he did "in fact" cheat only if we share the same perspective, only if we look at his behavior in the same way. What he did from his perspective (or from a third party's perspective) may be quite different. Which is *really* true? What do you mean, which is really true?

Within a perspective there are usually rules, either implicit or explicit, and more or less detailed, about how one arrives at true statements. We, therefore, often accept as true those statements which we feel have been arrived at correctly. For example, there are some people who will accept statements as "true" only if there is statistical or "hard" evidence of some sort in their favor. What is true then becomes more a matter of how one arrived at them than where he arrived.

Or we sometimes grant the ability to say the truth to certain individuals, books, or what-have-you. Whatever X says is given the status of truth because of our faith in X, because we believe X to be smart, because we believe X to be close to special sources, etc.

Most of us have "shorthand" ways of granting the status of

truth to certain kinds of statements and of denying (or questioning) the truth of other statements. In most of these cases truth
is granted to those who we believe share our perspective or who
have a perspective in which we wish to share. Truth, in this
general sense, is then *socially* determined. A group of people of
some sort who share a community, a region, a religion, a profession,
an organization, etc., comes to share a perspective and to grant
certain truth-saying ability to those who are members of the
group. How people achieve differential truth-saying power within
a community or group is related to the claims which they make
for themselves and the willingness of others to know those claims.
Disputes which occur may often be looked upon as struggles
over who will be granted truth-saying power. In all groups some
procedures have been devised which specify how legitimacy is
gained. And, of course, there may be revolutionaries, heretics, and
crackpots. The struggle for truth, then, is a struggle for the right
to claim legitimacy for one's own perspective, and hence the
right to claim the statements within the perspective as being
"the truth."

Crete

Dear Crete,
   I am going to complain a bit in this letter, if you don't mind.
I was always one to divorce my scholarly life from my personal
one, or at least to try to do so. But now I see (as I guess I always
suspected) that to try to separate them is impossible. I used
to think, for example, that criticism of my work was not to be
taken as criticism of me, and that one's intellectual activity was to
stand on its own, apart from personal feelings. Similarly, I felt
that my criticism of the work of others (and I will confess to my
share) should not be taken by them as in any way personal
criticism but merely intellectual comment on their work. As I look
back on it I must have been very cruel indeed, and my belief in
the separation was quite necessary if I was to criticize so severely.
Your comments, however, have found a home, not only
"intellectually" but "personally." It is no use trying to hide
behind a mask of intellectual activity. What I did was an expression of myself, and I am not very proud of it.
   I feel, now, as though I have lost something, something which
I really didn't want, but because it was part of me something

which I could not let go nor easily replace. I will discuss the loss as "intellectually" as I can, full well realizing the "personal" aspects of it.

Most people need a sense of certainty, a feeling that they are engaged in something solid and maybe even important. This was provided for me in the feeling that I was working to establish *the* truth, that I was engaged in the important task of teaching and writing about the world as it really is, and not just the elaboration of some perspective. There was comfort in this for me. It gave my life an orientation, a sense of purpose.

I now see some of the ways in which I was using this perspective for my own purposes. For example, there is an enormous amount of reading to be done. One simply must develop economizing devices, and mine were probably very common ones. For example, I would dismiss certain kinds of writing as not worth reading without knowing what was in them. I would ignore certain authors on the grounds of their not being capable of making a contribution without even reading them. I would take other people's word for things, and I would find certain arguments unsuitable simply because they were not consistent with my particular perspective. I would read only those whom I expected to find intellectually congenial, and I would grant truth to statements on the basis of the methods employed and the people employing them. I was a member in good standing of a rather select group of scholars, and I did not realize what that meant. I was caught up in the sociology of my profession and not the pursuit of . . . of what? What do I put in its place?

I feel that I have had a career, and that I am now at the end of it. I don't know which thought disturbs me most. I do not have the sense of an intellectual experience or, perhaps better, of a feeling experience. I have been successful, but I now see how easy that was. I had a reason, but I see it was a mask. I had a purpose, I now see it was someone else's. I am not sure what I shall do now. I will just have to wait and see.

Lewis

Dear Lewis,

It is too early to say now what I am going to tell you. It will not make as much sense as it might at a later time. But I will say it anyway, in the hopes that further discussion will take place.

Our greatest fault is to stay with one perspective, to look at things in only one way, and to think that life consists of filling in that perspective. Such a life is limited by one's own sense of comfort. It is also a mistake to accept the perspective of someone else. Obviously most of us do so—most of us "have" to. But the excitement lies elsewhere. The stakes are high, and one's chances of "winning" are slim, but one may commit his life to creativity. Most of us find comfort in society, it is easier, safer, and the rewards more predictable. Few choose a different path. But one has a mind and he can try to do what no one else but humans can do, and what even few of them attempt. Do you want to write creatively? Chances are you don't know how and, worse yet, have nothing much to say. But once you try, who knows? When you discover you are empty perhaps you will want to construct something of your own. But does your career depend upon your doing something else? Then at least you will recognize that you do what you do for your career and not because you are seeking truth. And if you come to this conclusion, as apparently you have, you will probably give up your career.

There are many people, most in fact, who prefer not to be creative. The hazards of such a life are very great, and other values are tempting. But if you want to be, be prepared for a life different from that of most intellectuals. For one may be intellectual without being creative. To be creative is to attempt to construct one's own perspective while most intellectuals adopt the perspectives of others.

And let me add one further thought. To aim for success as a creator is to substitute one career for another. You already know what that means, and one can see the effects in other people quite easily. Do what you do—work things out for yourself. Creativity is a personal matter.

Crete

2   The Struggle

Dear Crete,

A prolonged melancholy, which I am not yet over, has forced me to think about a question I haven't given thought to in a very long time: What is life all about anyway? It is a question with very great significance to me at the moment. I suppose it might be a first step in a rebuilding process (it would certainly be difficult to think of a *prior* step). I would like to think it is anyway.

It is peculiar that one feels a bit childish in telling others he is thinking about the meaning of life. Even now I am holding back a chuckle. I know perfectly well that others are uncomfortable and don't wish to discuss it. It is such a disruptive question which if one is going to answer he must put aside almost everything else (except diversion if he can manage it). And those around you must be prepared to put up with a period of sombreness the end to which is never in sight. I suppose the reason the question is so embarrassing is because everyone senses how discombobulating it really is and how dreadful the consequences could be in, as it were, voluntarily putting oneself through the process of trying to answer it. Obviously we should all have an answer. And some people do. But not everyone, and not everyone with an answer is satisfied.

In addition, there is also a sinking feeling that the question may have no answer at all, that it is, therefore, a foolish question to be asking. But the enormity of trying to realize what it would mean if there were no answer drives me even more to find one. But yet I am torn between believing that those who think there is no answer think so merely to avoid facing the question and believing that those who think there is an answer are escaping from themselves.

But once one gets involved with the question, it is difficult to let it go. It seems to envelop one in its comprehensiveness, leaving one stunned. It is the final standard by which all can be judged, and a devastating standard at that. For there seems little that man does that can survive its scrutiny. And that is why it brings on such a melancholy. One must confront himself with the personal question of the meaning of his own life and the things he does and thinks in it. The criteria become intensely subjective, as though some great angry parent has one by the scruff of the neck and is shaking one to pieces while at the same time yelling, "What the hell are you around here for?" and one isn't sure how to answer. It is a frightening experience, but at the same time one finds relief in coming to grips with such a humbling question.

And one also feels the excitement of doing something

important. So often we find ourselves doing things in order to enjoy the consequences rather than the activity itself. But not when wrestling with this question. What one is thinking about is its own justification, and stimulation is inherent in the activity. It is, or at least it appears to be, a kind of euphoric obsession, art for its own sake, a thing to do because it is worth doing.

I must apologize for not writing these past months. I have been doing a good deal of reading and thinking. It was important that I did this alone. My major product during this period was a poem, or what I will call a poem because it felt like one when I wrote it. I am sending it to you as a gesture, I suppose, and as a way of sharing with someone the experiences of a place I would not want to see again but found I had to visit. Some never return.

Lewis

Thoughts From a Half-Way House

The people are in the yard,
    demanding blood.
Shall it be given them, so they may go
    home?
The hearth too
    is fragilely placed in man's hope chest:
Blanketed in violence. Little children witness
    death at sunrise—unlike their sowers,
Substance without form. Appearances are
    real: beneath embarrassments lie additional masks.

Why search, and why pretend? Why teach
    to expect too much?
The wounds of events are quick—self-made
    as though for a purpose. Are they
Gaping? But why? Where did space
    come from that man so unfulfills it?
Sisyphus can do more than be defiant—in
    the name of drama he can act
The play a different way—which thought gives
    rise to his stone.

Passion is an answer. But so is its
   denial.
To grow unwetted by nature's apogee
   conscious
Of one's consciousness, blocking
   commitment
A particular answer—but what of the
   people in the yard,
Demanding blood?

Synthetic anxiety lies between
   a thing and its antithesis.
We confuse middle courses for
   wisdom, the begging of questions for
Transcendence. Is time a gentle slope or a ragged edge?
   a constant line or striving steps? The tension of
Fellowship numbs the soul,
   the game a bouncing ball—
When left suspended, ambivalence makes way
   for contemplation.

The hour of crisis is an
   embellishment, anticlimatic when
Viewed from a distance. Who,
   then, will say whether
One has arrived, when the Host is
   busy feeding off his guests
And the servants are running
   errands?
Is it even time for a party, or are
   we important enough without such struts?

The end is never in sight; how can
   it when we obscure one purpose with
A hundred others? If the grasp could
   branch the hands that reach—
But then, few want to know what lies
   hidden.
The consequence of not evolving out of
   fear is
That moralizers are in the yard,
   and I must think of something.

Is it our language, then, which
    leaves us so impoverished?
Are there yet unknown symbols which
    may dehumanize?
To get together is to gossip, in never-ending
    enrichment of the I—the temptations
Of Francis stretch before us—
    but only if
The ark will not sink with the
    weight of controversy.

The past contains no precedent for salving
    generalities
The early fruits of intercourse must
    be retained by each.
But in hounding one another
    what is further
Gained, save to decimate the
    tranquil with a wreath of
Suffering? Attachments need
    sharp edges, dulling the senses.

Awareness with its passion, is
    it worn without despair?
Disappointments must be shouldered, loose
    ends must find their own
Ties. Enough that one should
    escape, who by example may serve
as contrast. It would be well that those
    howlers in the yard learn
The quiet of
    singularity.

But does one escape or merely flee, when
    surrounded by knots of an
Earlier time? In what sense is the
    hunter ever free?
Serial efforts preclude close harmony,
    simultaneity a dream—
But why should it not be so,
    if heaven is so very far
Away? The same is true for all
    but a few—let them alone.

The struggle is pleasing, if the
  efforts are staged, for should
Not the actors really act? Performance
  is not extemporaneity, and there
Lies the good. To scribble may
  be our due, but
On the backs of giants. The
  ladder has no direction, to
Distinguish the many
  sideways.

Yet one knows that
  alleys end—
That is why we make so
  many of them.
The thought disrupts only
  when process is underrated
For who is to say what the castle
  shall look like when Kings are democrats.
We yearn too much for blossoms, and think
  manure putrid.

Detachment feels with neuter probes
  the underside of tragedy,
We are free to stretch the hours
  and analyze our analysis.
That could almost be enough
  if it weren't for the yardbirds
Who must by mental prowess be
  transported over the fence—
Such a task requires a gaggle of dedicated
  teachers.

Abandonment is chaos: one does not
  leave the world to nurses
And priests to fall into the hands of
  the sick and godless.
Nor are the lies of civility to be
  cast aside—it is only
Withholding knowledge that does the
  damage. It is hard enough
To walk when maimed. Exposure for inspection
  gives man the edge.

Conflict is refuge in a world where
  congruity is sanctified.
We are driven to shadows
  our stature provides—
Reflections are creatures postures
  produce, light the source
Of chimeras. Enlargements are
  not whole pictures—but when
We focus what do
  we see?

Order requires maintenance, and who is to
  do the sweeping?
Prevention counts for misery and routine
  an excuse for idleness. Can we
Cast aside the cause? Who can achieve
  such tolerance? It is no wonder we
Scream and howl: the pains of despair
  are real where beauty
Discards its spores in order
  that we may know it.

Seasons do not change—our feelings
  come from how
We live them. Charity has not been
  kind to us—our minds are
Sponges and we must be merciless,
  wringing from what we have
To make room for what we make. No
  other world is satisfactory
For those who have an
  opportunity.

We wonder at the misery caused
  us by others' convenience, yet
How can we ever know of the hurt
  our wake inspires?
Is it such a hard thing to
  endure the awkward
Silence—in the name of conversation
  need we all be carpenters?
How can we ever reckon our
  outbursts?

The people are in the yard demanding
  blood—how I wish I were
Not among them. The work is hard
  and there are shortcuts
Tempting us all. Who would not
  scoff in the place of
Anguish? The swells of torment
  guide me and
I purge the soul of the
  devil.

Sanctimony: why do we embrace you
  and practice your liturgy?
The heathen is considered dead and
  the apostate a fool.
We are driven to be vile for the
  sake of maintaining
Cordiality. Commitments
  create opposites
Even when our choice is to be
  so directly.

What I say of others is self-
  revelation, for who will
Truly deny his birthright? Is
  it always left to us to
Gull the clouded countenance? Is
  not the choice available
To announce forthwith our
  pretense by conjured deed
And conscious
  drama?

The falsehood is to be thyself, for
  who could stand such an
Invidious comparison when the characters
  of the mind cry out for imitation?
With image and appearance, what of
  nature and her rapture? Who
Is to win the struggle, when the
  poisons are so plentiful
And the underbrush so filled with hollows?

God constructs our sites, but
   sight is less divine,
The competition is enviable only
   when we leave
Memory to cite the
   blocks from which design
Fashions eternity. A day is
   nothing and everything
Since we are given
   so few.

Is it possible that dialectics take
   us so far as to dictate
The depths of evil from the heights
   of virtue?
What of transcendence, then? Is
   it mere outcome, temporally
Following the violent night
   as a dawning?
Beware of those who have found
   the answer.

Without my consciousness
   I still sense, but in
A way that my fellow
   phyla do
There is still in and out
   dressed in its several
Manifestations—I have
   these as any would, as
Functions to be done
   with.

But mind allows me another
   range of senses not
Afforded bodies. To
   cast myself upon the barren
Desert and make the flowers
   bloom from cactus
Which I find there—what
   monster would tempt my
hand and so my mind
   dry?

There are some certainties, and these
   give us pain. It is only
Comedy which is ephemeral / so
   we value it all the more
For in a bounded leap with
   suffering is all the
Void of which being is
   composed. How else would
Meaning establish itself, if not
   by grasping at other things?

Self-conception is the essence—
   all else is merely truth
Which black, does not allow
   us to distinguish shadows
From figures, shifting forms.
   How much is given by the
Cries of composition? How much
   to lose when we play
It
   out.

                          Lewis A. Tellurian, Jr.

Dear Lewis,

    There was a man, sitting near a great rock, staring out into
the sea. His face was taut and he appeared to be thinking. The
man hardly moved the whole time I watched him. Occasionally
he would stand up and walk a few paces. But he would come
back, assume the same position, and continue gazing out to sea.

    The next day I returned to the same spot and found the man,
lying next to the rock, writhing in agony. I asked what was the
matter, and he replied simply that he had eaten a pickle. I asked
if I could help, and he said that only the sea could cure his pain.

    The following day I forced myself to that great rock, afraid of
what I would find. There was the man, as on the first day, quiet
but reflective, looking seaward.

    A month passed before I returned again. I don't know why
I expected to find him still there. Curious, I made inquiries about
him. It seems that two weeks after I had seen him, a child and its

mother had observed a man, near a large rock, shout a triumphant yell and run with obvious delight into the sea. The mother was frightened and started for her child. But the child had already gone.

Seven years later the body of an old man was discovered washed up on that beach. And engraved on a silver amulet hanging from his neck was a message which said: "Don't bother to look for the child."

Crete

Dear Crete,

It strikes me that I know very little about who you are. Would you want to tell me something of yourself? Like where you're from, what your family is like, whether you're married.

Lewis

Dear Lewis,

One can have many different kinds of friends, but there are three more or less ideal types which may stand out (ideal types meaning an intellectual distinction which may have no other basis). The first is the friend who is warm, open, ready to listen, and with whom one can talk about his troubles. It is often this kind of friend that one speaks of family and personal problems. There is, in this kind of friendship, a trust that secrets will not be abused, nor personal information used against one. One feels he can speak freely about himself as a person. Sometimes one's wife or husband is this kind of friend—a sharer of personal troubles and a sympathetic listener to complaints. But more frequently it will be someone else. And sometimes there will be no one except a stranger who temporarily fills in.

The second is the friend with whom one shares his successes, to whom one can brag, talk of future plans, fantasize, and build any manner of hope. This is the friend who doesn't mind if one exaggerates his own strengths, who allows one to compare himself favorably with almost anyone, and who shares one's opinions and attitudes. And, of course, one does the same for him (but not without feeling slightly uncomfortable). It is usually a mistake to bring one's troubles into this kind of friendship, for this is the friendship of optimism, of idealism, of joy, of laughter and good times. Smiles, not tears, are the cement which bind these friends together, and it is dangerous to think it will stand under other burdens.

And then, my friend, there is a third kind of friendship, a kind which few ever experience directly. It is a friendship which exists to share thoughts, mostly of a highly abstract nature, and therefore has a profound but, with this kind of friendship, unspeakable relationship with one's personal circumstances. What matters is that one tries to transcend his own life. *Ad hominems* turn into rancor. Among joyful and sad friends one uses his life as an illustration and as a standard. To the ears of the sombre one whispers his explanations—in the presence of the lighthearted one sings his song. But to searchers after meaning one enters a different world, a world in which all exists for itself rather than as a pillar for one's cracking veneer.

It is undoubtedly possible to exist without any of these friendships. There are substitutes for almost everything. But each, in its own way, serves a purpose. The first makes it possible for us to understand ourselves, to come to terms with the question of how we came to be as we are. The act of telling transforms the material from a thorn to a simple piece of clay which one may now work and shape. It is a search for the unique.

The second is at once man's hope and man's faith, a denial of existence. There is, in this relationship, a horror in disguise.

The third is an effort to create—to fashion a universal. It belongs to those who have peered over the edge.

Crete

Crete,

I sometimes feel you a bit elusive, but no matter. I feel I am changing somewhat and some things which once seemed important to me no longer are. I must confess that I do feel a bit uncomfortable in what I regard as a perpetual one-down position with you. It may be the case that some people can operate at the "intellectual" level alone, but I do not have a lot of evidence for that proposition. It seems to me, to the contrary, that all interactions are at two levels: the content of what is being exchanged or discussed, the actual substance of the interaction, and the state of the relationship itself, the social phenomenon of people interacting with each other and their relative positions in that relationship. I would argue, of course, that each of these levels (content and relationship) affects the other. The content of an interaction in a hierarchical relationship is likely to be quite different than a relationship among peers. Conversely, threatening content is likely to have a major affect on the relationship which people experience. Some of these processes can be very subtle indeed—one "feels" them but would have a difficult time explaining what has happened. One can be having a conversation, for example, and suddenly feel very uncomfortable. Prior to this point one might have felt buoyant and alive. Afterwards one can feel quite wounded, as though in some mysterious way someone has pulled the plug. One feels as though he is being emptied of himself. It may even be a bit frightening when it happens because one is never sure how much of oneself one might lose. Yet there may be no observable signs that anything has happened or that the person with whom one is interacting has in any way changed. But nevertheless something has happened, either in what was said or perhaps in how it was said which has had a profound affect on the relationship. Nor is it clear what is to be done once something like this occurs. One often needs to be aware of the relationship one is having as well as the content of the interaction. But even then one may not be able to pinpoint the difficulty or even to plug it up in time.

Because of this duality in social interaction we have some interesting variation in the way in which people have an interaction. For example, there are large numbers of people whose almost sole concern is with the social relationship and who shape their substantive contributions to fit what they think or wish the social bond to be. In most cases this concern for the relationship is quite unrecognized. But what is produced is an interaction in which people "say things" for the sake of the relationship, mostly in hopes that it will in no way deteriorate. There are, of course, many conversations of social interaction which bear witness to this. And it appears that the admired (and resented) wit is the person who knows how to play at the edges of these conversations, threatening the social relationship sufficiently to make the interaction exciting but not enough to destroy it. There is, in these people, a somewhat more explicit and recognized skill at manipulation of the relationship, often in such a fashion as to elicit the desired one-down posture in the other. There are also those who refuse to participate in certain kinds of gatherings (e.g., a "wallflower" at cocktail parties), or who have styles of interaction inappropriate to the occasion (bores and boors, for example). The amount of essentially "contentless" social chatter which we all engage in is, I think, a tribute which we pay to the importance of the relationship. When the content of the interaction does loom more important we often find quarrels, anger, resentment, hurt feelings, and other examples of human frailty dependent upon a supportive social environment. Indeed, interesting reputations are made by those who have little regard for the effects of the substance of their remarks and who, thereby, show some disdain for the relationship aspect of the interaction. And, of course, there are many examples of blunders or tactless remarks which can change the relationship entirely. In any case the burden of bearing the strain of the interaction is placed on those who are least able to tolerate uncomfortable social relationships, a partial explanation of why bigotry and stupidity are not punished more severely. Many people will become more sensitive to the relationship aspect of the interaction because of the concern of others for the content.

Indeed, to relate these matters to a discussion we had earlier, you yourself have suggested that the notion of what is "true" is often determined by support given certain individuals in a social group. Concern for the group itself sets limits on the kinds of challenges which are to be permitted and, indeed, restricts the kind of control which will be considered legitimate. Similarly concern for content makes improbable certain relationships, especially with those who are considered to be outside the group.

Both substance and relationship, then, contribute to the overall impression one receives and gives off in an interaction. Some individuals may be primarily concerned with content and might be defined as serious, quarrelsome, and/or ideological by most of those with whom they interact. Others may tend to center their attention on the relationship and may be described as sociable, pleasant, or fawning. And some will be essentially inarticulate, who cannot say anything for fear of damaging the relationship, but who cannot have a relationship for fear of having to say something.

We all, I think, are aware of these two influences when we

interact with others. Some may be more aware of them than others, and some may be able to exercise some degree of control over the direction of the interaction and of their own participation in it. But the two processes are at least implicit in the very act of having a social interaction.

Lewis

Lewis,

When you view a picture by Manet, for whom do you think he is painting? When you listen to a cantata by Bach, what is his intended audience? When you read a poem by Eliot, a book by Dostoevsky, or a play by Shakespeare, to whom are they writing?

It is, of course, somewhat unfair to cite only those who are well known. There are also large numbers of unknowns, of "failures" (by public standards), who were creating for themselves, who were communicating to themselves, who were attempting to say something about everyone but to no one in particular, who were trying because they wanted to, because it was their way of establishing the meaning of being. One can be substantive, *even in an interaction,* without having a relationship and even though others might be trying to relate to you. One can exist as a creator in which the communication is internal, to oneself and for oneself. Those who listen are like eavesdroppers, witnesses that something is occurring, audiences at an event. Those who desire a relationship must do so in terms of what is occurring, not in terms of who is doing it. It is the message, the content, the meaning that is significant, not the fact that the somebody who said it is a particular individual with a personal, unique background. If one wishes to relate, he must do so in terms of what is being said.

"Failures" are those works which do not, for possibly many different reasons, gain outside recognition and status. And in this context I mean those who attempt to be creative but who gain no particular attention in doing so. It is no easy matter to say something relevant about the human condition. Most of us are so engrossed in our own concern for uniqueness that we, paradoxically, produce nothing but commonplaces. To immerse oneself in Everyman, and try to tell oneself what the experience is like, is transcendence in which the universal and the unique merge. One cannot say something about everyone by observing the details of one's existence. How many layers one is able to cut through is not as important as being able to see the layers as layers in the first place.

But you are right, of course, about most people in most situations. We do have relationships with people as we interact with them. And the reasons, I think, are two: fear and self-importance. On the one hand we seek the excitement and stimulation of individuality, of differentiating ourselves from our fellowman, of rising above the level of others, of being singled out for special attention and praise. But at the same time such efforts at individualism expose one to danger. It is in the nature of excitement to be a little frightening (and in some cases very frightening). Threats to the self lurk everywhere for those who dare to leave the safety of similarity. Anxiety is the constant companion of those who find the unfamiliar. And so most of us are driven back into the community to find comfort in being like other people and to draw strength from submerging ourselves in their warmth and fellowship. Our yearning for self-importance and our boredom with routine send us out into the unchartered— our fear of what we find there and our desire for a haven force us back. And this becomes a part of the human experience: the endless dialectical spinning out of one's life from one end of this dilemma to the other. We find ourselves in a predicament—striving for uniqueness and becoming frightened, finding safety only in our return to be like others. We need stimulation, but it is tolerable only within a context of safety. We desire a home, but only if we may occasionally wander off.

And partly as a consequence of this, many of us take our thrills vicariously, through the lives and creations of others. We read, look at paintings, listen to music, attend plays and motion pictures, watch television, to experience a sense of being different in what we know to be safe surroundings. The function of art and entertainment is to stimulate by transporting one into a somewhat unfamiliar world, yet in the context of never having really left one's own, to provide an incongruity without "actual" danger. Most of us live from rather "simple" fare and escape the routine of our existence for the stimulation of someone else's. But for most of us the meaning of life is not yet a question—we are simply getting through it. Those with this latter interest will choose arts with wider vision, will expose themselves to the dangers of those who have asked themselves what life is about.

And those still left unsatisfied must create for themselves a world of their own devising.

There is, then, drama in life, tension created by the incongruities to which we expose ourselves. We develop ideas about how we expect the world to be, either how it should be ideally or how it should be as we have come to know it. But our expectations are incomplete and our idealism the product as well as the source of incongruity. Comedies occur when our sense of what should be conquers the cause for alarm and makes the world safe again, where things are like they ought to be. The threats are shown either not to be serious (and we are relieved), or if serious, they are removed (often without a struggle). There is, of course, much drama in all of this, and we are sustained in our dilemma.

The drama of tragedy lies in being unable to cope with an incongruity, to "lose" to the forces of reality. Tragedy is a time for tears, a prodding to introspection, an opportunity to see just how powerful the enemy is. It is also, of course, the acceptance of tragedy which gives such force to comedy, for it indicates that life is a struggle and that winning does not come easily. We like to know that our existence, which most of us value, is in some ways a product of our own efforts. It provides a meaning to life and a context for tragedy which might otherwise be overwhelming.

And this is why, of course, tragedy is conducive to continued thought. For none of us can really accept tragedy. We must somehow "handle" it, either by transferring it to the category of valuable experience, turning it into a "devil," or explaining away what happened in a fashion which satisfies man's need to preserve his dignity. For above all man must conquer—life must, in the end, be a tribute to man's capacity to overcome. Comedy is its own justification—the tragic requires an explanation.

Life, then, may be seen as a series of dramas. Indeed, for most people, it is drama which gives meaning to everyday existence. We attempt to impose order on a world full of surprises. We are delighted when our expectations are borne out, and forced to contend when they are not. Through our ideas of what life ought to be like we create the conditions for incongruities—and the latter fills the world with opportunities for significance.

But the great dramas belong to those who voluntarily risk themselves rather than simply expose themselves to events. Certainly there is sufficient drama for most of us in either the "natural" comedies and tragedies which come our way through the force of events, and the vicarious drama which we in some ways seek. But one can distinguish between these and the act of subjecting oneself to the possibility of actual (rather than pretended) danger. And this can be done in many ways. At one level one can subject himself to possible physical harm. A jungle exploration, joining the army during a time of war, exposure to an area or to people known to be potentially violent, some forms of sporting activities (e.g., mountain climbing). In some cases this might even be saying something or doing something which one suspects might bring on some physical assault. At another level one can subject one's mental prowess to possible attack. This can occur in conversation, a debate, or some form of writing in which one is concerned about the reaction of the audience. One generally learns these mental games in school in which rewards often go to those who "succeed" or who "win." But one may confront intellectual competition from many sources, not the least of which is simply in everyday social behavior. And at another level the risk may come not from exposure to outside forces at all but by subjecting one's self to a demand for justification in full view of the same self looking on (the self as both subject and object). Man's consciousness is fully capable of providing the ability to engage in this enterprise. One is conscious, one can be conscious of his consciousness, and one can be conscious of this consciousness. It is this ability to build layers of consciousness which allows man to question the meaning of what he is doing, and it is this risk which, in some ways, has proved the most troublesome for man. For, in the first place, most of us are too busy fending off the dangers to mind and body and dealing with drama on those levels. To get to the point of asking oneself what it all means is something which some never face (for some good reasons which we may have time to discuss at a later point). But those who do come to grips with this question, not just as *a* question but as *the* question, and not just as a small segment of one's life but as the entire of one's life, and not just for a short time but for a long enough period to break oneself down, these are the people who then face the possibilities of creation. The despair that is involved in this, the risk that one will never succeed, that one might in fact get "caught" as one looks into oneself and never surface, the fact that one must sever his relationship with society to such an extent that one can literally "talk to himself," the long, hard effort to try to construct something for oneself to replace what was so painfully torn down, and the likelihood that one will find he has little to say, all combine to make the risks unbearable for most people. The temptations to relapse are many—the chance to play before an audience perhaps the most seductive of all. One can think the old is uprooted only to find it growing back. And we even have some capacity to live with what we know to be self-deception.

And this process, lest there be some doubt, is not self-psychoanalysis. It is, however, a *self* analysis in conjunction with the appraisal of meaning. One does not, as in psychoanalysis, concern oneself with inner conflict within one's personality. Rather one attempts to see himself in relation to the question which confronts all men. It is an experience which induces one to think in universals and not, as in psychoanalysis, unique personal history. Nor does one take on someone else's perspective of the self. Rather one slowly finds he discards the perspectives of others and attempts to construct his own perspective to take the place of what others would prefer one to have. For it is only in developing one's own perspective that he is finally "at one" with himself.

And so we all have the possibility to be in the most exciting drama of all, the drama of life in which one literally writes his own script. No, this is not quite accurate. A script is something which actors follow purposefully and which is written beforehand. It would be more accurate to say that one becomes his own interpreter after the fact, providing the reasons why the actors have been following the script written by someone else who seemed to have nothing in particular in mind when he wrote it. One becomes his own commentator rather than relying upon the comments of others to understand what has happened, is happening, and will happen. But in this case the main drama, far from being enjoyed vicariously, and not even participated in directly, is in the creating of meaning. Activity, including one's own, becomes at the same time both subject and object. For what one does is create, and the creation itself becomes an activity.

Crete

Crete,

Why are you so insistent on denying your affinity with your fellowman? Why must you think yourself different, set apart, above what everyone else is? You are making a case for a very special sort of person, an artist, a creator, who speaks only to himself about the meaning of life. But are you not falling into the trap of countless dissatisfied visionaries before you? You seem to recognize what man is, but at the same time deny that man has to be that way. In place of the life man leads you attempt to provide an alternative. And you seem to think that not only could men do it but it would work if they did. I feel I must demur on some of these points.

In addition to this, however, you also seem to imply that creativity is not related to intelligence. You would certainly grant, wouldn't you, that there are some men of genius, men of extraordinary intelligence and gifts quite beyond the endowments of the average person? Can we not account for great feats of creativity by these factors?

There are some ways in which I wish this were not the case. It would give me hope. For I do not consider myself of much greater than average intelligence, nor possessed of any extraordinary gift. If you are right then perhaps I too may be capable of creativity.

Lewis

Lewis,

There comes a time when one begins to question what one knows or thinks he knows. In some cases the precipitating event may be some sudden tragedy, in other cases it may simply be a slow accumulation of incongruities which one has now realized can no longer be handled by how one currently looks at things. But in any case this "crisis" is likely to come to most of us. And some men meet the crisis, struggle with it, and find the only way they can "win" is to develop a perspective of their own. This does not mean that one ever achieves this "completely" or even "correctly" (in the sense of satisfactorily understanding those things which are included in one's vision). But one can develop a perspective that, quite literally, illuminates the world. And so one could stop. Why one does or doesn't is something we won't go into here, but it ultimately depends upon one's willingness to keep going, one's desire to push on. And it is in this act of dissatisfaction, this need to go over it again and again, where one begins to part company with one's fellowman. For it is only by voluntarily experiencing agony in order to come to an answer that one has any hope of even beginning.

You are quite right, I think, to be wary of the potential elitist tendencies inherent in any position which attempts to distinguish some men from man in general. Therefore let me emphasize that *anyone* may become creative in the sense in which I have been speaking of it. One does not have to be a "genius" or a man of special endowments. We each have it in us to try to become creative. This *process* is available to any willing and able to confront the challenge of meaning. That few may decide to engage in the struggle should not be surprising. Many of us have responsibilities which make such a deeply personal experience appear to be quite impossible. That we may in fact take on or use these responsibilities to avoid the confrontation does not lessen, for many people, the moral issues which they see involved. In addition, of course, the entire enterprise is itself quite frightening. It is challenging to look over the edge. It is even more risky to jump, ultimately, into the water.

But even after the process of self-analysis one is confronted with how one fills the deep and painful void. To fail at this stage is undoubtedly even easier than to give up at self-analysis. The temptations are many to grasp at the first interesting perspective which comes along and to take it for one's own. For the vacuum is difficult to maintain and the pressures to occupy it are great. Self-communication may be lonely, at least at the beginning, and someone else's views to take the place of yesterday's is no small comfort. Further, in discarding a shared perspective one has to forfeit his right (or expectation) to congenial and sympathetic company. These are not inexpensive prices to pay. It is only in hindsight that one sees that it was truly necessary. Indeed, the entire endeavor relies on hindsight for justification, as one can rarely see beyond the day one is living as he struggles to survive.

But the development of a perspective is not the same thing as intelligence. The important matter is not "native ability" (whatever that may be) but a way of looking at things. Inspiration comes more from wanting to see clearly than from intelligence. I have a piece of art, for example, a sculpture, that was created by a person who is mentally retarded. This person has made many pieces —the piece I own is not an accident. I originally purchased this sculpture because I found it an expression of someone's vision, an attempt by someone to try to say what he saw. I value this sculpture as a brilliant piece of work, as a tribute to creation as perspective, for it was not until some months after I had purchased the sculpture that I learned by whom it was made. The fact that it is a work of what others might call "genius" gives it additional value, for it holds out hope for the rest of us.

One additional point. A perspective is not synonymous with what philosophers of science would call "theory." The latter, as it is usually construed, is a set of assumptions, "empirical" in nature, from which other statements may be deduced. If the deductions are "true" (verified) then support is given to the original assumptions of the theory. If the deductions are "false" (shown not to correspond with "reality") then the assumptions are challenged. (Obviously this whole stream of thought takes place within a perspective which one may or may not share— hence the large number of quotation marks.) A perspective, on the other hand, freely admits what philosophers of science would call "values" into its system. (The scientific definition of theory, then, is a perspective in which values are denied, but still present.) It also admits of potentialities, possibilities, visions, and other quasi-mystical phenomena. For how else would one account for the attraction of one way of looking at things over another? Man lives in his constructions and calls them the world. If one pretends that these matters can be separated, the discourse takes on an entirely different "meaning." For in the end we all live in someone's perspective. My argument is simply, why not one's own?

Crete

Crete,

It seems to me that teaching at a university would offer an ideal setting for acts of creativity. But I take it that what most professors do, in the form of scholarly work, would not be so classified by you. But even more generally than this, you would probably not find most intellectuals—writers, composers, poets, painters, researchers—on or off the campus, to be creative. Yet I am interested in how you would classify those who spend their lives working with and producing intellectual materials. And I would be especially interested in your views of academic scholarship, since I have spent my life in academia and, like all professors,

78

have always had my doubts about the utility of what others do but never, until recently, of what I do. The university exists to further knowledge, and research is its major tool. But I would say that very few of my colleagues are creators in the sense in which you seem to mean it. The production of intellectual work and creativity are not synonymous, I know, but is there not some overlap?

Lewis

Lewis,

I wish to digress. I have already suggested that one of the ways in which people maintain a sense of their own importance is to compare themselves favorably with others. One method of doing this is to be critical of other people (or even events or objects), to make observations which, in placing something else in a bad light, by implication puts oneself in a good one. Indeed, one of the major functions of one category of "friend" which we discussed is to facilitate just this kind of experience.

And in a more general sense a very large amount of conversation follows this principle. One does not usually speak generally about things (that is, including oneself by implication in the sweep of the generality) but rather in terms of one's judgments about differences which one observes. Rather than make the assumption that all humans are alike and share in the human condition (and hence anything we say about someone else also implicates ourselves) we start, rather, with the premise that humans are quite different from each other, especially in the sense that some are to be considered "better" (superior). For this reason, conversations often involve one person telling another his personal feelings, his likes and dislikes in other people, events, or things. People "express themselves," they present to one another the conclusions of their own (usually invidious) comparisons. If these people are friends, they are likely to agree with and support one another's observations and to grant the status of "truth" to them. Those who are not friends often do not challenge these judgmental statements on the grounds that harmonious social experiences are preferable to disharmonious ones (in being less threatening). For disagreement may easily be interpreted as a form of challenge. Not only are the "ideas" being disagreed with, but one's "person," one's self-importance, is also at stake. The "truth" and one's own efforts to demonstrate superiority are wedded in one's comparative judgments. If one is willing to pay the social costs, he may find himself in a dispute in which each of the parties must fight for the "correctness" of his experience and insist upon its general validity because it is, from this point of view, a form of expression in which one is asserting his self-importance. One "loses" face if he is forced to back down or change his view.

When, then, one is having a conversation with someone at an abstract, general level in which the parties recognize differences of perspectives, there is often a very strong temptation to do one of two things, both of which have a very similar effect. One may identify the generalized argument with one's own personal experience which, in effect, says to the other person: "Look, I disagree with you, so if you persist in your opposition to me not only must you disagree with my ideas, but you will also have to take me on personally. I will intervene 'myself' between your argument and my argument." Or, with very similar effect, one can point out to the other person how his (the other person's) argument depends upon personal experience which thereby places the other person in the position of having to defend the logic which one thereby imputes to him of inducing a general statement from personal experience. In the first instance, if the argument is to continue one must argue personally—in the latter one in effect accuses the other of "really" carrying on a personal argument masked as a general one. In each case the "victory" usually goes to the one who initiates either of these variations.

One's response to all of this, predictably, is "But I didn't mean it that way." Of course one didn't. People "protect" themselves in conversation without knowing it. Especially if one is at all involved in the conversation, such commitment excludes simultaneous consciousness. In this sense one rarely "consciously" pursues strategies in the process of conversation (which helps explain one's fantasies *after* an unpleasant conversation at which time one *does* attempt to figure out, consciously, what he might have done) . But one is able to analyze the consequences of what one does regardless of "intentions." It is one of the most perplexing characteristics of the human condition that man is able to reflect upon his behavior and state "laws" or principles to which he himself is also subject. So irritating a position is this that most of us exclude ourselves from our own perspectives.

Crete

Crete,

Touché. I apparently did insert myself into the argument, thereby making the discussion personal. That is an interesting point. But on this matter I have one question: Is making explicit the consequences of someone else's behavior also a form of defense?

In addition, of course, you managed to avoid answering my original questions. I am now self-conscious, but I still wish to know even though I have inserted myself in between my position and what I know will be your criticisms. It is clear that I still strongly identify with the university community. It appears that I was attempting to communicate this to you in the hopes that you might not really say what I have a feeling you will say.

Lewis

Lewis,

The university is said to exist for the purpose of discovering, disseminating, and learning truth. And indeed I would suspect that almost all of its teachers, researchers, and students believe they are doing just that. If one could take them one at a time to a place above the university where they could see how passionately its scholars believe in a point of view, how committed each is to a perspective shared by a few others (and more widely by friends and colleagues at other universities), and how earnestly they go about attempting to convince, perhaps they might be able to see themselves in this apparent bubbling confusion, to suspect that they themselves might possibly be like everyone else down there. But, of course, from such a lofty position the temptation would be great to conclude how silly the *others* are and to draw strength by invidious comparison that one's own work is somehow different and better and not subject to the same standard of criticism. (The great disadvantage of a detached view is that one is not himself among the passing scene.) And so one simply reinforces one's own inherent belief that at least one's own work will make a contribution. And this thought will be so stimulating (and hence frightening) that one will want to rush back down to join the others without ever realizing that what one seeks is the opportunity to display one's erudition in a context made safe by rules.

Most scholars, of course, share a particular perspective with other adherents. This intellectual position may stretch back many

years or it may be somewhat new. But in any case there will exist
a community of scholars who will share the same perspective.
Research, although seemingly an individual effort, is always
conducted in terms of an intellectual context supplied by others
and consists primarily in elaborating upon or supplying details
for a point of view, a way of looking at things, which is shared by
some subset of those in the same discipline and which is anchored
in the writings of some particular group of people. Each scholar
draws intellectual sustenance from those whom he and others
consider to be "the giants" of his field who have opened and perhaps
still blaze the trail so that others may follow. In this context most
scholars would openly admit to being proselytizers, as long as one
understands by this that the truth is being served. The intellectual
life of a scholar, then, is highly social. A scholar thinks of himself
as one of a group, differentiated from other groups in the sense
that one's own group is "right" (correct) and the other or others
are "wrong" (or perhaps simply irrelevant). There is, I think, a
prevalent belief, even among scholars themselves, that their life is
one of independent pursuit of truth, wherever it may lead. A more
appropriate imagery would be of a person, alone in a room, surrounded by a limited number of voices, taking notes rapidly and
then transferring these notes into notebooks. (It is, indeed, an
interesting situation when distillation increases volume.)

In addition, of course, and quite related to this point of
scholarship as a community enterprise, is that scholars, as other
organized people, have careers. Universities and departments are
ranked in prestige, and one's own status depends upon where one
is located, both in terms of institution and rank. Rewards, such as
research funds to support time off from teaching and other
activities, are in limited supply and those who receive them
can infer a certain measure of success. In the process of "having" a
career one learns what it means to become a "good scholar" (the
criteria may vary somewhat by discipline) just as one learns how to
become a successful professional in any field. And one estimates his
success at least partially by comparing himself with those who
have not done as well. (In a peculiar form of "circularity" of
reasoning there is always someone below oneself except, perhaps,
for those who suffer deep despair.)

There also exists in the academic community an "intellectual"
morality in which one distinguishes oneself and one's "side" not
from those whose work is inferior but from those whose work is

thought to be particularly pernicious. The "bad guys" in this comedy (in the sense in which the meaning of this word was established earlier) are generally those who are looked upon as "mere" propogandists for a particular point of view, who are "ideologues," who have their minds already set, who see things only from a perspective, sometimes an "evil" perspective, but perhaps only "naïve," "old-fashioned," or "narrow." One is in more or less continuous "debate" with this other side, if not actually at least at the level of fantasy. One, in his own work, shows their arguments to be false, and attempts to set the record right. This "enemy" is the opponent of truth, of scholarship, of open-mindedness. This morality becomes a major factor in the socialization of new members and in the maintenance of standards for the profession. And from this resulting conformity, from one's intellectual heroes, villains, and fools, and from one's career one sustains himself.

The effect of all this upon students, those to whom the baton of truth is passed, is predictable enough. Students are taught to seek *the* truth and are given a multitude of "truths." In many cases they will be spared a certain amount of confusion since some teachers will simply teach "the facts" and leave the perspective from which the facts are derived unexamined. But elsewhere the tenets of a perspective will be made explicit, not for the purpose of analysis (unless the perspective is one with which the teacher disagrees, in which case it will be utterly destroyed morally), but to be learned by the student as any other "facts." Rare is the course or teacher that is critically self-conscious.

Some of this can be quite stimulating to students, as there are many perspectives which wear the charm of newness. But the cover of teaching perspectives as truths takes its toll among those who might otherwise find the products of creation exciting. The competition among "truths" becomes wearing and students "choose" perspectives (and hence what to believe in as true) on the basis of what those in society may reward and punish, their own ambitions, and what is congenial among the members of their group. Although there is a certain logic to this process which finds a home in the human condition, what is unfortunate is that such an inducement to conformity should be not only practiced but fervently applauded in an institution which might under other circumstances be a breeding ground for creativity.

And clearly one of the least savory by-products of the correct-incorrect mentality is the use of textbooks (especially in *introductory* courses) which purport to present truth. An alternative would be to present several different perspectives, in "brilliant" fashion (for although there may be disagreement about which set of books represents brilliance in any field, textbooks would not be on *anyone's* list), and taught, simply, as ways of looking at things. Students would not be encouraged to "choose one," or take sides in any way. They would, however, be supported in their efforts to develop their own perspectives—in effect to enter, painfully and unsuccessfully no doubt, the creative process.

What I have in mind would require not so much a revolution in the actual structure of education as it would a decided change in one's attitude toward what is being "learned." For it would necessitate that teachers themselves be aware of the extent to which truth is used as a label to legitimize one's own way of looking at things. One might examine what makes perspectives interesting, stimulating, or useful rather than what distinguishes the correct from the incorrect. What would be championed would not be a perspective but reaching a perspective for oneself. Such an enterprise (a good deal more anarchistic than most would tolerate) would rest securely on the explicit understanding that, since what matters is the development of one's own point of view, there would be nothing personal at stake in the rejection of someone else's. And since there is nothing to lose, there is something to be gained in the stimulation which exposure to brilliance would produce.

But I am obviously dealing in ideals, for such as this could and would never come to pass. It is, however, no less a reality for me, since it is the world in which I live.

Crete

Crete

I wonder if you are too quickly dismissing the value of scholarly work and training. The mass media are a constant source of propaganda, bad argument, bias, and support for a thoughtless morality. For most people this is their only fare. And so they come to correct one another from daily television newscasts, and cluck over a newspaper headline. It is a life made tolerable by finding support in the misfortune, selfishness, and venality of others. Contrast this with even the average academic treatise, and the comparison makes its own case. The virtues of scholarship, no matter what its faults, are a (relatively) greater honesty, objectivity, comprehensiveness, depth, and, if done well, stimulation to further thought. In order to carry out this kind of study students must be taught certain skills and, perhaps more importantly, attitudes toward intellectual discussion. Fundamentals must be mastered, research tools learned, and critical thinking encouraged.

But even more important than this, years of scholarship provide an accumulation of knowledge which others may use, whatever their purpose may be. I think you probably under emphasize the debt genius owes to sluggards. This is not to deny that there is bad scholarship—but even bad scholarship might be more useful than what is presented in the public media.

Lewis

Lewis,

We are all confronted with an "out-there," with a reality. And all of us must handle it in one way or another. How we do this is part of each unique individual history, the "shoulds" we think should be, and the occurrences we come to expect to happen. We develop an idealism and with it try to put reality down. In this there is much to be said for a comic perspective. It is, indeed, a minor triumph of man, a way of transposing threat to harmless release of tension by seeing an incongruity as non-serious. We all face a diurnal round of stimulation-flight, which cycle of life is fed by the desire for self-importance and fear of that which is strange. Reality brings us threats in the form of incongruities, things not expected nor familiar. And the struggle is endless, each man taking the world on anew, as though he alone discovered its misery.

We are all beset by troubles, incongruities which we must yet take seriously. Indeed we use our troubles to justify the very idealism which produces them, for surely what is comic and what tragic depends upon how one looks at things. Why, then, should the answer not lie in turning everything to comedy, for if the latter is a matter of perspective then it might be learned? And the answer fairly bellows at us: because reality is too much with us, because if we took more of it seriously we would soon become indifferent, because comedy demands tragedy just as self-importance demands fear, because when the world comes rushing in, as it does on occasion, or when it slowly wears us down, it is showing to us our incapacities. Reality conquers all in the end and that must be the first, and last, tragedy.

So we do what we can to shore up inadequate and weakening defenses and comedy, rather than being a human triumph, becomes cruelty. For comedy is a situation in which idealism wins—and the vanquished is often man himself, the refusal of man to accept man in his human condition. An octagenarian makes some half-alert, half-childish comment, and we smile and are touched. But what right have we to find mirth in his mutterings? What right have we to steal from eighty-year-old men the sadness of death? What right have we to reassure ourselves, give ourselves importance, as we vanquish the fear which such sights engender? We are tempted to view the human condition by flying over it— we try to conquer the night by making light of it. We feel happiness because we have to—it would be too much to bear otherwise.

Do not, then, underrate tragedy. We must accept it if we are to accept man, and we must struggle against it because we cannot let reality win. Not to think about it is a denial, a surrender, an admission that fear itself is too fearful to be called upon, and a desire to avoid the understandings of despair. Our self-importance is too easily satisfied in such flight—we could all soar even higher.

Crete

Crete,

It occurs to me that you are avoiding controversy in our exchanges. I do not know what to make of your silence—whether you accept my ideas, cling to your own, think me a fool, or what. I spoke of the importance of scholarship fully expecting, at the minimum, an elaboration of your own ideas on the subject and hoping for some "give and take" and an eventual "meeting of the minds." But instead I find a bit of cryptic philosophy about comedy and tragedy. Not that I don't find it interesting, but shouldn't we try to reach some agreement about matters we discuss before going on to others? To me resolving difference and reaching agreement are major parts of the intellectual process. For if we do not do that, we are lost. And where we do find we differ and cannot reach agreement we must know clearly what those differences are and the reasons why each of us insists on holding the views we do even in the face of determined opposition from others.

Lewis

Lewis,

Truth is agreement, wisdom is consensus, and discussion is persuasion—these are the consequences (which you would deny, of course) of the perspective from which you speak. To concur is either a social device, bringing harmony out of possible conflict and ill will, or the sharing of a perspective. But tolerances for matters out of focus depend upon with whose eyes one wants to see. Is it necessary to push and shove together, to make a common pile? To leave things unsettled may be to pay an even higher tribute to man, for where one finds heaps one also finds discussions about who contributed more, and who shall therefore win public tribute.

Further, I often find in discussion with others that they wish somehow that emotion, passion, and bias could be eliminated. And by this they mean, of course, the emotion, passion, and bias of others. Instead they would like to place pure reason, as though reason were anything other than a name for what we believe to be the case. "Reasonable" arguments are arguments *within* an accepted perspective. Then "truth" may be discussed. But what if the perspectives of the participants differ, as so often occurs when something important is being considered? The plea to be "reasonable" in this situation simply means to give up one's perspective and see things in the perspective of him who pleads. Asking for reason is to deny the existence of different perspectives. It is to pretend that there exists a truth independent of perspectives which, in the end, means that the person making such a request does not recognize his position to be a perspective, and in this sense just like anyone else's. "Reason," like "truth," is an attribution man gives to arguments he supports and believes in. Those who disagree are not reasonable, but bigoted. But one rarely includes himself in such an analysis. *We* are reasonable, others are thoughtless, unthinking, and prejudiced.

Crete

Crete,

I am still uncomfortable with your too ready acceptance of relativity. I find some solace in seeking truth, you tell me that truth is what we say it is. I wish to come to some agreement about things we discuss, you say that you are talking to yourself. I defend the scholar on the grounds of his comparative contribution, you say it all depends upon how we look at things. I am interested in getting on with it, you speak to me of comedy and tragedy. I wish to know something about you, you tell me about levels of friendship. I despair, you undoubtedly exult. I feel myself a failure, you would have me inspect my idealism. I think I will go feel sorry for myself awhile.

Lewis

Dear Lewis,

W. B. Yeats wrote the following poem on the occasion of a friend's failure. I find his view on this matter quite alien, and I have attempted to set out my own thoughts in the verse that follows Yeats's: I write this in anticipation.

Crete

To a Friend Whose Work Has Come to Nothing

Now all the truth is out,
Be secret and take defeat
From any brazen throat,
For how can you compete,
Being honour bred, with one
Who, were it proved he lies,
Were neither shamed in his own
Nor in his neighbors' eyes?
Bred to a harder thing
Than Triumph, turn away
And like a laughing string
Whereon mad fingers play
Amid a place of stone,
Be secret and exult,
Because of all things known
That is most difficult.

W. B. Yeats

An Answer to W. B. Yeats
"To a Friend Whose Work Has Come to Nothing"

For many of us grasp far exceeds
    ambition,
We inherit from the travail of others
    comforts not of our own reckoning.
And in such borrowed splendor
    we chortle at our virtue.

There are a few, like you,
    my friend,
Who cannot bear to be at
    peace
With yesterday's belongings
    and who instead
Strive to reach beyond. Like
    the gibbon who roams the
Tops of splendid trees, off
    on his own
He may come crackling down,
    not recognizing

A slender limb and mistaking
    it, nay constructing it
Into a firm haven for
    his mind's edifice.
Such a life is cruelly strewn
    with crushed bodies
Not to mention souls when
    up the line of
Monkeyhood we climb to
    bigotry and the
Cruelty of man witnessing
    defeat.

Despair as a consequence
    of sweat is indeed
Sweet misery. Better
    surely than trumpeting
The spoils of an age
    gone by.

There is a risk, of course, that
you may go over the
Brink. Despair is a
jealous lover who
Wants a constant suckle.

Do not be deceived, my friend—
do not hide behind
A mask of exultation. Failure
is its own reward—in days
To come you will wear it
proudly.
Til then, suffer the darts
of deriders who
Only exult to keep from
sulking in self-knowledge
That leaps of daring frighten
only those who

Dare not jump.

3   The Resurrection

Dear Crete,

Your thoughts were most welcome. I feel in a transition period
now, and I alternate from feeling despondent to thinking I might
make it—but I never feel entirely "there." Most of us use our
conscious life as a support for our own behavior. We convince
ourselves of our own charms and virtues, the more so that they are
called into question by others. But I am beginning to feel a new
sense of consciousness, a consciousness that exists more in
questioning than supporting, more in undermining than in
building up. There is a giddiness connected with this awareness,
for it is an unfamiliar posture which finds me higher than I am. I
think if I become used to it, it must be in terms of my climbing up
to meet it rather than bringing the awareness down to me. For to
see from the top of a ladder is to see more, partially because one is
always aware that he *is* on a ladder and he might fall. I find all
this immensely stimulating; but I am also frightened. In this state
of wonderment I am beginning to sense what it might be like to

think. Most of us wrap our lives in routine, organizing what would otherwise be a chaotic and fearsome world. Routine is a form of escape—no, that's not exactly what I want to say. Routine allows us to enter into a *staged* life in which the parts are familiar and in which we can *understand* ourselves and others. It allows us to pretend that the world in which we find ourselves is somehow ours, whether we like it or not, and not the creation of someone else which we adopt. We therefore feel we need a change of physical environment in order to change our circumstances, never thinking that "our world" might simply be a set of props which we assume is real. And in this assumption we allow ourselves to be judged in terms of how well we play the scene *as it is given*. It is in this sense that one might say that the world belongs to stage managers in whose hands we place control over our mind's furniture.

And in saying this it occurs to me that it is only our cooperation that allows certain pretenses to be established. We grant to others the right to set out what the play is going to be about, grateful, even, that this burden is not ours. We lend our belief to the performances of others, even to the point of helping them out if they seem to stumble, never realizing that by helping we become helpless to control what parts we will play. We are inclined to take our assignments from others. And that, I guess, is one reason I feel so out of sorts—I am beginning to understand how precarious the social encounter is, and how we are all accomplices in what it accomplishes, even if we feel it is not of our doing. For in such a feeling lies the acceptance as real of whatever comes our way.

And then I come to the question which lurks behind all of this. Why is there such a conspiracy to prevent other than self-flattering introspection? Is it because concern with oneself is a threat to society? Or is it because the self itself is unable to stand up alone outside of society's definition? And I think that part of the problem may lie in cooperating with others in their entrance onto a particular stage. People perform only within a structure, and we make credible this performance only when we grant them the structure itself. What would happen if we refused to do so? The first important consequence would be that routine would somehow lose its safety. Routine would be unmasked, and we would feel a sense of danger rather than comfort in playing it out. For, indeed, there is nothing so dangerous as a social conspiracy, as it literally determines what is real and what is valuable. We might pretend that we recognize only what we must recognize to be "realistic," but only a few are aware that the stakes are indeed much higher than that. By allowing ourselves to be defined we grant our lives to others. It would be difficult to think of a more dangerous game than that. And there are certainly enough "others" who would profit by our participation in such a conspiracy. For their own definition is understood only as they compare themselves to us. If we make this easy for them, if we accept their definition, then we "lose" ourselves in a way which we do not really understand even if we feel the pains of such loss in discomfiture. For others will always be willing to see their own reflection if it is someone else who is the mirror. What we must decide is whether that game is worth playing. The fact that we, at least in our own mind's eye, are usually "the winner" is answer enough, but only if one thinks about such matters in terms of one's own moral support, only if one's consciousness is a crutch upon which one's wounded ego hobbles. The mind's so facile it may even transform such halting footwork into a ballet. We show no mercy when we must justify discomfort.

But I feel now that I am rambling and am writing mostly for myself. You see, then, how dependent I have become upon you. I am going alone, but within a perspective consistent, if not quite identical with your own. But, thank God, there is still time. I want to be able to justify your anticipation.

Lewis

Lewis,

We sometimes become what we pretend to be. The crucial question, then, is our willingness to experiment with pretense, to make for ourselves the stage upon which we will perform. And it is here that society most leads us astray. Were it not for some individual's strong sense of self-preservation all would be sacrificed for the species. For the major function of society is to make things easy, which it does by encouraging, even demanding, acquiesence in a pretense that vitiates the desire of an individual to become acquainted with himself through pretenses of his own devising. And society does this for the same reason that water flows downhill, or that warm air rises.

Why, then, should anyone choose a more difficult path? The answer is that the one who does is the most driven by fear. So frightened, in fact, that even society's answer will not satisfy him. He seeks the myth of total control which, when he sees he cannot attain it, drives him on even further. Surrounded by threatening incongruities he literally fights for his life, as much alarmed by society as most of us are comforted. Some perish in this struggle, and others return to shore. But a few swim on encouraging others to believe that some semblance of personal reconstruction is a possibility, that solace may, indeed, lie in the undertaking of such a venture. The error of that assumption does not become clear until later, but by then one perhaps will not want to turn back, believing one's own dream a more worthy abode than the nightmare of "reality."

For most of us the self will find a convenient excuse to rest in society's image. Somehow if we can share our terror it becomes not a terror at all but the very cure of what seems to ail us. Until, of course, we are moved by that deep, intense, and insatiable fear that all is as meaningless as it seems. And then fear's adrenalin cannot be stemmed—the dread is too real, the incongruity too threatening. There must be meaning—chaos becomes the final challenge. And so the fear becomes so great that no other answer but one's own will satisfy, after which it may then be discovered that even this hope is ephemeral. And so one either retreats, becomes rigid, or plunges on. And a kin of madness awaits those who finally fear even themselves.

It is only those who do not question meaning who are safe. And one who is safe will never be driven to questions—he is too busy shoring up his defenses, becoming familiar with the props he finds already there. Rather than exposing himself to danger he is protecting himself from it by adapting and adjusting in such a fashion that rough edges are worn smooth and dangerous curves are provided with mirrors.

Society, however, has its own defenses. It is made strong by the example of those who tried but failed, and by its own inherent comforts, and will lure those who wish to ravage it for answers. Self-preservation for society dictates a policy of appeasement where necessary in the short run and a drive toward entropy in the long run. It is not confused, as we are, by the belief that epiphenomena are meaningful—and so it exacts from most of us our very being, an outrageous price to pay for the right to live.

Creators are the enemy of society, and so it plays the cruel trick of providing them with followers, those who wish to found a new society and in doing so continue in the cycle. Unlike creators, followers wish to implement, they are zealous and committed, not aching with awareness but aching instead with loneliness. And so society makes them its foot soldiers, carrying bayonets and instilling in others the desire to find comfort in their own amnesia. And in their countervailing amnesia there develops a hatred for the creator as well as the followers, and upon him is placed the blame for countless dead bodies. Such are the resources of society that creation itself is damned, and in the ensuing struggle there is little hope that man will win. Society cannot tolerate "excessive" irresponsibility, and certainly no morality could justify anyone or anything participating in its own destruction. The creator is, by this view, immoral as well as difficult. And it is the followers who bring on the condemnation, for it is they who transform vision into truth. The herd is a home and the herd is an army—every hero is also an enemy. But we should not thereby hold responsible the heroes of other herds. It places too great a burden on our own.

Crete

Crete,

So much of your argument turns on the process of creative activity I feel it would be helpful if I knew more about people who engage in it, and, more particularly, how I might recognize them. Does one need to have a product to be creative? Are "artists" creative? Are some people more creative than others? Who judges whether a person is creative or not? I would appreciate your clarifying these matters for me.

Lewis

Lewis,

I would like to distinguish among three concepts which are often taken to be more or less synonymous. It is quite important to make the distinction if only because one sees meaning in terms of contrasts, and each of the words will serve as such a control for the others. The three concepts are creative, original, and brilliant.

Something is done "brilliantly" or is "brilliant" from an observer's point of view. It is a judgment which each of us might

94

make of something we see or hear. We may share our judgment with others, and we may differ with others as to what is or is not brilliant, or even as to what criteria we should use to define the word. I personally call something brilliant if it captures my attention, when it interests me—no, that is really not strong enough —when it *absorbs* me, makes me think, figure, imagine, when, in short, it stimulates me to the point of my wanting to concentrate on it and to try to come to grips with it, to understand it, to see things the way I feel they must be seen from the point of view which I find expressed there. These criteria do not specify *what* is brilliant, only what feelings are produced when I come into contact with something I consider is brilliant. And, indeed, no one can specify in advance whether he will find something brilliant or not. Brilliance is something one feels and can discuss reasons for only *after* the experience.

I may also have a memory with respect to things I considered brilliant at one time but no longer do. I can discuss why I considered it brilliant then (if I was articulate about my feelings at the time) and why I have changed my mind. And in some ways it is inevitable that many things lose this brilliancy for me, since our own discussion of our feelings tends in itself to neutralize the emotional aspect and to emphasize the intellectual. And so we are constantly delighted when we find something new to call brilliant.

"Originality," like brilliance, is a judgment made by the observer, but it differs in the sense that to classify something as "original" is a less "thrilling" experience than to conclude that something is brilliant. For in order to make an argument that something is original we must be able to distinguish it from that which we would call "derivative," and in order to do this we must be prepared to place whatever it is we are discussing in some historical context. Originality is an attribute which we pretend is part of the object we judge—brilliance is much more widely recognized as being a "subjective" judgment. Our ability to label something as original, then, depends on ability to argue its comparative uniqueness. Our ability to say that something is brilliant, on the other hand, is a problem of articulating our feelings. Brilliance and originality, however, are independent concepts: something can be either brilliant or dull and at the same time be either original or derivative.

Whereas originality and brilliance are judgments made by the observer about something "outside" of himself which he experiences, "creativity" is a judgment which can only be made by the self about the self, and not about others. One is creative if he is able to come to the conclusion that what he is doing is "new to himself," if he feels that he is developing his own point of view. We can "know" this for ourselves but we cannot "know" it for other people. "Creativity," then, is to be distinguished from "construction" in the sense that creativity is a form of construction in which the ideas guiding the construction are one's own rather than someone else's. This implies that we are aware of the difference between learning how to do, say, think, or feel something which someone else did, said, thought, or felt, as when we incorporate a point of view external to ourselves, and carrying on an inner dialogue in which we develop a perspective which is ours. This is exactly why we are not able to say whether someone else is creative or not—we are not able to tell whether what we see is the product of someone who knows it is his own. Others could tell us whether they were creating, and although they could mislead us they would know themselves that a deception was taking place.

One may clearly, then, be creative without being original. One may say something "new to oneself" which others could take as derivative. Creativity is an effort to give one's own meaning to things—originality is a judgment which others may make of these efforts. Similarly one may be creative without being brilliant (and brilliant without being creative). Again the attribute of brilliance is one which we assign to external experience and which others may assign to us, whereas creativity is a particular kind of "internal" experience.

It is quite common to save the word "creative" for the efforts of "artists." Clearly from the point of view expressed here this is not the case. Artists may produce brilliant and/or original works, but we can say nothing about whether an artist is also creating. Similarly it makes no more sense to equate creativity with any particular position or activity in society than it does, say, to label as philosophers those who have a degree in philosophy. Many "card-carrying" philosophers would better be described as historians, and many of those who "do" philosophy have no academic credentials to do so. When we open a can of beans we expect to find beans—but we cannot guarantee the validity of "people-labeling" with as much assurance. Anyone may be creative —it is of no help to single out any group of people as especially likely to be so. We all know "artists" who do what they do with no pretense of presenting their own ideas. Nor is creativity to be associated with a particular mode of dress, way of behaving, or personality. "Peculiarities" in these matters are sometimes mistaken as "signs" of creativity rather than as a mode of self-expression. Creativity is indeed self-expression, but of a very personal sort.

Although creativity takes the form of an internal development, it may result in some specific, concrete form. A creative person may talk, write, paint, think out loud, construct scientific theories, practice a profession, be a mother, drop out of society, do odd jobs —there is no activity that is incompatible with creativity, nor any context which prohibits its occurring. One may pay certain costs in certain environments to be creative, but this is a different matter.

Creativity is also something we can "know" we are *not* doing or have stopped doing. One may attempt to be creative only when one is dissatisfied with the answers one finds, *including one's own.* Some believe they have found an answer and begin to tell others about it. Perhaps it is the product of creativity, perhaps it is even judged as brilliant and original. But educating, propagandizing, proselytizing, spreading the word, informing others, should not be confused with creativity. They may be no less important or interesting things to do; one's judgment of this depends upon a number of factors including whether one approves of what is being said, who is saying it, to whom, in what context, etc. It is in some ways "natural" that one share what he feels committed to. Most of us, in fact, fixate on a particular answer, whether it be our own or someone else's. Dissatisfaction may not lead to creativity, but the latter cannot take place without it. One is especially likely to stay within a particular perspective if one is "successful" in doing so. Recognition in the outside world may encourage repetition. External validation for a performance well done may substitute for internal satisfaction. Whether one is tempted into or away from creativity, then, will depend on factors we have previously discussed, like how fearful one continues to be, and whether or not the question of meaning continues to be significant.

A state of continuous creativity is unreachable. We all relax into the "known," even if it is of our own construction. Most people, then, to the extent that they would make any claim at all to creativity, would do so for only a very small proportion of their mental life. There may be a number of ancillary activities which take a great deal of time and even effort, but the actual amount of time spent creating is likely to be small even in the most creative of persons. The production of a creative idea, for example, may involve a person in a good deal of routine work in the same sense in which the production of noncreative ideas may require the expenditure of considerable time and energy. It is not "acts" or "work" or "products" which indicate creativity. Some people's "creations" are undoubtedly "lost" to others because they never become expressed or because they do not become expressed in any usable form. A creative person may keep his ideas to himself. On the other hand some creative people may work exceedingly hard to put their ideas into a particular form which may then be shareable with others. There is no particular form which is more conducive to creativity than others—again it is a matter of personal taste. But except as applied to ourselves this discussion of creativity is irrelevant. In the work of others we seek "brilliance" and perhaps "originality"; we can make no judgment at all as to creativity other than our own, if any.

Crete

Crete,

Your discussion forces me to reflect upon some of my past judgments of people and ideas. I begin to call into question the whole basis upon which I judged. In the name of "standards" I evaluated people as good or bad scholars, smart or dumb, people to be listened to or people to be ignored. But I am just now conscious of the extent to which these judgments of mine partake of the same stuff as any form of bigotry. Of course we always recognize prejudice in others, we see how *their* judgments are founded upon the "wrong" criteria, but we seem too positive that such bias is not in us as well. For bigotry is surely a product of man's thought, a mental construction which may lurk behind any opinion which he has. And, for me, this raises the fundamental question of whether man is capable of evaluating honestly at all. For if by bigotry and prejudice is meant holding a favorable or unfavorable view of something (and especially "classes" of things, but not limited to classes) because of criteria irrelevant to its evaluation, then the argument turns on what people consider to be relevant criteria. There seems a strong tendency in us all to transpose our standards into prejudice. I have heard it argued, for example, that only philosophers can do philosophy reliably.

98

This view obviously gives to a class of people, simply on the basis of membership in that class (no matter how they got to be members and regardless of other knowledge about them), a facility, a warrant, to do certain kinds of thinking. As though expertise was a matter of labeling. It is certainly true that we all need these labels in order to "know" about other people, in order to be prepared for how they will act, and to be able to react in turn. This is one of the major reasons why we want to know who people are and what they do before we talk with them. We can then treat the person as a type and we ourselves can respond appropriately. Not to know labels is to have to respond to people as they behave and to react by criteria which do not allow for precasting. Most of us, it seems, are not willing to suffer uncertainty to that extent. And so we cling tenaciously to the power of labels to give us understanding, and to deny to those who do not have the label qualities and faults of those who do. We seem, in the end, to respond to people as representations of an imputed type. We then register satisfaction, surprise, anger, or whatnot to the extent to which our expectations are incongruous with what we see, never realizing, apparently, that our expectations merely flow from the original label. We have, then, some means of adjusting our prejudices to particular instances, and we may thereby grant exceptions, but the labeling process itself is rarely called into question.

And not only do we make these judgments of others, but we also label ourselves. We are clever, unbiased, virtuous, etc., acting in a world where others may not be so. And so sensitive are we to the social requirement that people accept us as we present ourselves that we, in turn, enter the social conspiracy with others to support them in the claim which they make for themselves. For to argue such claim is to get into just that, an argument, and we will do this only with those we willingly call enemies. So we have a situation in which our labeling of ourselves and others, and, in turn, their labeling of themselves and us, becomes the playing out of a social encounter. And we all support this enterprise in the name of sociability. I would be anxious to know whether you share this same experience.

Lewis

Lewis,

Let us begin with a single and basic premise necessary, I believe, to any discussion concerning prejudice: that it is a part of the human condition. If we adopt this assumption from the outset, we will avoid the hopeless position of attempting to assert that it is possible for humans to be without bias. This latter position is bandied about a good deal, but the problem does not disappear merely by making claims concerning the objectivity of one's own position. For, indeed, we all make such claims—most of us feel that it is we who see things clearly and others who are muddled. And we are half right. Most of the time we do see things clearly. It is just that we also see them from a particular point of view. Claims for objectivity are simply claims for truth-saying power, for the right to declare what is, for the authority to determine the stage. It is the effort to banish disagreement by demanding legitimacy for one's own point of view, to establish the *actual situation as it really is*. It would be a different world, indeed, if we did not so behave, for prejudice fits admirably the twin human requirement of defense (protecting oneself against threat) and offense (asserting one's self-importance). Through prejudice we are able to discount the claims of others and at the same time justify our own claims. We can put others down while hoisting ourselves up. A most necessary and powerful device for coping with a complex and threatening world.

There is an underlying dimension to the universality of prejudice which also needs discussion. Man is unwilling to accept himself as a species. He is unwilling to see himself in others, to speak of mankind as a single class. So lofty are the claims which man makes for himself that he must deny similarity to those around him who, like himself but not recognized in himself, must violate those claims. And this is the starting point of a long series of invidious comparisons in which man distinguishes himself and people like himself from all those others who are dishonest, mad, aggressive, stupid, primitive, dirty, selfish, treacherous, cruel, bigoted, weak, cowardly, immoral, vain, diseased, and whatever else one sees in others and does not like. Our hopes for man are that he is rational, just, and capable of civilization, and we do not like to be confronted with evidence which calls them into question. Rather than reformulate our view of man, however, we proceed to reject most men who are not like ourselves. And we explain away what we see by the labels which we use: "they" are cruel (but not man), "he" is stupid (but not man), "they" are uncivilized (but not man). It is easier to reject threatening incongruities or exceptions to man's status than to assimilate them into a view of man which also includes oneself. Human dignity rests upon the view that we, and people like us, are different from others, that we do not share with our enemies what we see in them. Human dignity rests, ultimately and paradoxically, on the rejection of man as a species.

And, sadly, one can say "no wonder," "I don't blame you," "I'd do the same thing myself." Man is given the capacity to be conscious of himself in relation to others, and the ability to fear and to want to feel important. He gains his own status and significance by adopting bigotry, and in so doing he denies his identity with humanity by announcing his superiority. And in this there is much sadness, for a bigot says, in the end, that he would like men to be like himself which, of course, they are.

Crete

Crete,

I find I must make a number of comments which have been forcing themselves upon me recently. You seem to suggest that man is caught in a contradiction, rejecting most of his fellowmen so that he might accept himself. But if this is the case then there is no way out, short of some miraculous change in the nature of man, perhaps through evolutionary genetic changes. I find this view extraordinarily pessimistic and I would, myself, find it hard to live with. If the situation is as bad as you describe it, how do you manage to cope with it? How do you give "meaning" to life? For surely by "knowing" this you yourself are not immune to its logic; and if this is "the human condition" then you must accept the consequences as well as others.

In addition, it seems to me that your perspective can have only limited applicability. Most people have a stronger sense of morality than your views seem to imply. Just as most of us would not be content with the idea that there is no "truth," so would many be upset with the prospect of there being no absolute values. Human beings, after all, value judging others because they believe they have the right position to begin with. To tell them that this position of judgment is simply their point of view, and that other people may have other points of view, would produce in most of us a form of anxiety brought on by ambiguity when we feel we need certainty. The only conclusion that you seem to be able to draw is that some people are "better" than others because they are more creative, although I really don't know whether you would say even that. Since so few people are creative it gives very little scope to the natural desire to exercise moral judgments. Most of us have rather elaborate criteria of good and bad so that we might account for the many varieties of success and failure which we see before us. In many cases, as you suggest, hierarchy forces us to "discover" human differences which in turn justify hierarchy. I would guess, then, that your views are much too individualistic and, more importantly, relativistic, to be of much use to most people. Your focus on a more aware and creative individual experience is somehow remote from most people's conception of a "better" world. And you seem not so much interested in the *product* of a creative experience, in the quality of what is produced, as in the process of undergoing it. In fact, your ideas leave very little scope for judging others at all, an idea which I am just beginning to realize may not be unintentional. And further, there is very little room in what you have said for human fellowship. If I may, let me paint the picture this way. Your ideas lead me to see people who are alone, even lonely, desperately trying to develop their own way of looking at things as they wrestle with the problem of what it all means. They don't talk with each other—they talk to, or better, at each other. This talk isn't even designed to be shared—it seems to be merely a form of self-expression. I have no feeling in all of this of camaraderie, no feeling of concern for others, no sense of a desire to have a *human relationship*. But we must, after all, communicate with one another, and we must take into account the things others are trying to do. We cannot avoid the fact that, like it or not, anything we do in the presence of others is a form of communication.

We all know, for example, that there are many people who will take advantage of others, who will use others for their own purposes. Whether it is a salesman who tries to make us feel guilty if we do not buy his product, a professional man who seems more interested in his fee than in his service, a teacher who is more concerned with his status than he is with learning, these are all experiences which bring us to realize that it is possible for others to be cruel, and it is therefore possible for us, or those we love, to be hurt, crushed, brutalized by insensitive, tactless people who view life as a game of one kind or another. And because these things can happen, it is also important to develop ways of comforting those who are hurt by the manipulations of others, and to learn ways of coping, oneself, with those who seem bent on their own personal gain regardless of its effects on others.

So, now to the point. The people you describe do not act in a *social* context. They are totally individualized—they appear to be indifferent to their fellowman. In some ways they are self-sufficient and selfish, searching for meaning as though there were not others in the world who might want or need their help. There is no love, no warmth, no emotion.

I have undoubtedly overdrawn this picture somewhat. But I wonder if you are aware of the extent to which your creating individuals are not really human beings at all. What you suggest may possibly be appropriate for a very few who might be able to live that way, but could we all be like that? Could we all be what you recommend? What would the world be like if we were?

And the major reason I bring this subject up at all is that I look around me and see cruelty, indifference, and manipulation. As an antidote I feel we must try to develop compassion for one another, to help each other, to work for something bigger than ourselves. I have seen too many people concerned only with their own private lives, who always ask how things relate to them, how they will be affected, who are purely and simply self-interested. The creative ideal which you discuss may not have these implications, but it does place the self as the primary orientation. What say you?

Lewis

Lewis,

One may live in many different kinds of worlds. Many people, in fact, live in more than one. Having no articulated point of view they live in whatever world is provided them by others, which means their world depends upon the person with whom they are interacting at the moment. Others will have an explicit, single view with which they attempt to cope with the forces surrounding them. But whatever one does he cannot live in every possible world simultaneously—whichever view he has will be limited, partial, restricted by its own simplifying assumptions. It may *look* like the whole world to the person who sees through its prisms, but it will be only one among many in which we could live.

Most of us live in worlds already prepared for us. We see things as others see them, we share interpretations, ideas, opinions, even visions with others. We become a part of a colony. *What* the world really is becomes what we learn from and share with others. To the extent that we live in the world which society provides for us we give up the possibility of living in other worlds, some offered to us by other societies, some by the advertisements of other people, some by the possibility of our own construction.

You speak of the games people play. But these games are relationships and therefore require at least two people. One gets into these games only if one shares the perspective of the person enticing us to play. We can feel guilty about "disappointing" a salesman whose product we do not wish to buy only if we share the perspective which the salesman offers us. A person will be affected by the games of others only to the extent to which the "game" he plays is congruent with the game of the others, only to the extent that one grants it legitimacy by recognizing it as *the* game. If one looks at the games of others through a different perspective they simply disappear, vanishing into the assumptions of someone else's construction, bouncing off those of one's own. The world literally is the way we look at it, and in this there is both limitation and great opportunity. We are limited to the extent that we prison ourselves in a perspective; we are liberated to the extent that we see we can design a perspective of our own. This paradox is man's alone. It is a consequence of our awareness, a challenge because we are *Homo sapiens,* a species which shares this awareness. We are capable of creating the world in which we live, and to do so continuously, over and over again. We may, ourselves, participate in the act of creation. It is to such a dizzying prospect that consciousness has led man.

Not everyone, of course, will wish to partake of this opportunity although each of us has it within us to do so. We all have different reactions to fear. For some of us the solution is to join others, to take what society has to offer, to join in the games. And others will search for meaning in different ways. We share in the human condition even though our reactions to it may be different. There will be some, then, who wish to struggle with the problem of meaning itself. It is one way to live a life.

Crete

Dear Crete,

I think I now understand the implications of your discussion. You are suggesting that it really isn't possible for people to communicate with one another (in the sense in which "communicate" means "to come to understand one another" when used in a statement such as this). We should, therefore, forget about doing so and concentrate, rather, in *self-communication*. And if, in this form of communication, we can begin to create a livable world for ourselves, then we have achieved what only man is capable of achieving. The meaning of life becomes, for you, a process involving a struggle with the question itself. Because man has the intelligence and awareness to ask the question of meaning, he therefore must ask and try to answer it. And you seem to suggest we do this for the same reason the mountain climbers gave to the question of why they climb the mountain: because it is there. But because the question is so frightening, and the way easier if one does not even raise it, let alone answer it, most people will not attempt their own little creation. Almost everyone, then, is a dropout from your point of view. If seeking is everything, then not only will those who do not seek not find, but even those who do find no longer seek.

In your view we all share in a rather dire human condition, trapped in a cycle of fear and self-importance, using bigotry and prejudice as both sword and shield. Life becomes a tragedy in which the "world" overwhelms our capacity to control it, reality constantly conquering idealism. Some may develop a "comic" attitude and escape, but a comedy, if I understand you correctly, is a form of bigotry, a way in which we, perhaps only temporarily, kid ourselves into thinking we can overcome. And through all this runs a deep sense of relativism, that man himself creates the worlds which he inhabits, and that we have no absolute standard by which we can judge their ethical nature. We can perform for ourselves, and we can seek brilliance in the performance of others, but these too are subjective judgments.

But if we "accept" your analysis we, paradoxically, must *not* accept it at the same time. This is *your* creation, *your* perspective, and therefore, it too, along with everyone else's perspective, must be rejected, even by you. And this becomes, in fact, the great incongruity, the "final" threat, that keeps us searching anew: that any answer will be simply *an* answer, one world among many. Now this *does* frighten me. No one can live with an answer like that. There must be order, there must be significance, there must be beauty, goodness, and truth. The alternative simply is not bearable. Yet I do not feel comfortable with the answers others have given, I certainly do not feel comfortable with the answer you have given, and the question cannot be left unanswered. I simply must try to answer it for myself.

There was a time when I did not even think about these things. I was "committed" to society because I accepted myself as part of it. In a sense I envy that position—one simply does what he does, and there's an end to it. Yet I would not now turn back. Indeed I cannot turn back. The question seems to have awakened in me a sleeping giant, something which will no longer be at rest until I have found a solution. Yet I wonder if I will ever find a satisfactory answer.

And so I will take leave of you, my friend, and go on my own journey. I can ride with you no longer.

Lewis

4

Seeker's Apartment

Duran Seeker went straight home from his interview with Tellurian. As he enters his apartment he finds his wife in the living room, glancing through a magazine.

DURAN:

Hello, dear.

JEAN:

Hi, honey. (Pause. Jean watches Duran out of the corner of her eye while still pretending to read her magazine. Jean has clearly sensed that something is abnormal.)

DURAN:

(Walks over to the bar and fixes himself a drink.) Would you like one?

JEAN:

Yes, please. I've been waiting for you. (Duran makes two drinks, brings one to his wife, she smiles.) Thank you. (Duran chooses a chair near his wife. He sits down and looks somewhat blank. He is clearly preoccupied.) Did something happen today? (Pause—no answer.) Duran? (Pause.) Duran?

DURAN:

What? Did you say something?

JEAN:

How was your day?

DURAN:

Oh, all right I guess.

JEAN:

Duran? Something's bothering you, isn't it? (Pause.)

DURAN:

(Still preoccupied, but said as though he's getting something important out.) Who are you, Jean?

JEAN:

What?

DURAN:

Who are you?

JEAN:

What happened today, Duran? Come on and tell me.

DURAN:

I want to know who you are. (Said quietly, but Duran is also very wound up.)

JEAN:

Look, Duran, I've had a hard day. I couldn't get a cab for an hour and was late for the hairdresser. Alice didn't show up at bridge, so we had to play hearts at my table. And I don't even know how to play. Coming home I stepped in some dog-do and ruined a good pair of shoes, not to mention the mess. Jane called as I was making dinner and I burned the carrots again. Why don't we go out to dinner, by the way?

DURAN:

I want you to tell me who you are. (Said like a man who has decided to go through with something.) I need to know, Jean. And you need to know, too, if you want to know the truth. Christ, we stumble through life not knowing *who we are,* and I ask you a simple question and you make a big fuss about dog crap. (Acting.) "Oh, yes, Mrs. Seeker, I know who you are, you're the lady with dog shit on your shoes."

JEAN:

> What's wrong with you? Has Dan been putting you on again? You really should do something to him sometime, you know, like tell him to go pee up a rope. I don't know why you put up with it. You're not still hoping for Ralph's job, are you? (Said as a dig, not a question.)

DURAN:

> Jean, cut it out. Stop jabbering. Do you know who you are? Do you? You don't, do you? There you sit, smug and self-satisfied, never even glancing around to see what kind of world it is we live in, and what you're doing in it. Now, damn it, I want you to stop for a minute, put down that silly magazine, and tell me who you are. Please. Just stop and think: "Who am I? Duran wants to know who I am and I must tell him. All right. I'm . . ." What, Jean? You are what?

JEAN:

> You're serious, aren't you? I mean you're really serious. You actually expect me to answer. (Pause.) Okay, I'll tell you who I am. I'm the woman who brought up your children, who puts up with your so-called friends who smile at you as a public relations gesture, who watched you make a fool of yourself while other people stepped all over you, and who spends your money because she can't think of anything else to do.
>
> I'm the woman you married. Who went to college, was told she was smart, and who hasn't been expected, nor given the opportunity, to use her brain since. I sit around all day, playing cards and taking taxis, in order to keep from screaming. Duran, I'm bored. I'm just plain bored. I lost control of my life the moment I got married, and have been using what little brainwork I do to try to justify myself, to say it is all worthwhile.
>
> There, is that what you want to know? Is that enough? Or do you want more?

DURAN:

> You think that tells me who you are? You think bitching at me is what I want to hear? You think you can avoid the question by making me feel guilty about my own life? Well, you're wrong, Jean, you're just plain wrong. I don't want to know

who you think I am. I want to know who you think *you are*. You, Jean, who are you?

JEAN:

I don't want to hear any more, Duran. I just don't want to hear any more. (Getting up.) Let me fix your drink.

DURAN:

I don't want another drink.

JEAN:

I'll fix you one anyway. Let me have your glass.

DURAN:

I don't want one. That's not going to do me any good.

JEAN:

Let's go out to eat, then. You look tired and hungry.

DURAN:

(Somewhat absentmindedly.) Do you ever get the feeling we play at life, doing the things we do, saying the things we say, thinking the things we think, without really realizing what we're doing? What does it all mean, anyway, a life? Jesus, here we are, nearing fifty, and we can't even talk about it. I can't even tell you who I am. It's not that I won't tell you, I can't tell you. I can't because I don't even know.

If life is a stage, then who would ever produce us? Who would ever sink his money into a bunch of crummy actors who don't even know what they're doing, who'd ad lib all their parts as though it really didn't matter, but who are so involved with themselves that each thinks of himself as the star? What a funny play. I'd laugh if I didn't feel so damn depressed.

(Duran gets up, but stumbles a bit against the table next to where he is sitting. The glass falls and breaks. This is not a drunken lurch—he isn't drunk. Merely an accident because he is preoccupied.)

Oh crap.

JEAN:

Leave it, Duran, I'll clean it up later.

DURAN:

No, I want to do it now. (Duran goes offstage, brings back a broom and dustpan, and starts sweeping. He has it about half finished when he stops.)

Here we are, almost dead, and we don't know what it's all about. Worse than that—we haven't even thought about it. Maybe it wouldn't be so bad not to have an answer if you gave the question a try. (Continues to sweep. Jean is watching intently during this whole performance. Duran now has it almost all cleaned up.)

You know, it's even worse than that. We haven't even bothered to ask whether it's an important question or not. Why not? Why don't we ask ourselves? Aren't we curious? Don't we want to know? What are we trying to avoid? (Finishes cleaning up. Duran takes the dustpan and broom back offstage. We hear the glass falling into a container, and Duran comes back, sits down, and is silent.)

JEAN:

I don't really think you ought to think about such questions. That's for others to decide, not you. You're Duran Seeker, manager of the New York office of Van Allen Paper, Inc., my husband, and that's good enough for me.

DURAN:

You think that's who I am? Do you really believe that's who I am? (In great despair.) Oh my God, oh my . . . (The phone rings. Jean answers it. Duran stares into space.)

JEAN:

Hello? Oh, hi Gretchen, how are you? (Pause and listens.) What? Oh no. Oh my God, Gretchen, how dreadful. (Pause.) But he was only fifty-seven. (Pause.) Have you talked with Betty? How's she taking it? (Pause.)

What a dreadful thing to happen. (Pause.) Yes, of course we'll come. Thursday at 8:30. (Pause.) But we want to do something. We all loved Alec. (Pause.) All right. Good-bye Gretchen.

DURAN:

(Becoming increasingly attentive as the conversation progressed.) I'm afraid to ask. What happened?

JEAN:

(In a bit of a daze.) Alec Kotler died. (Pause.) A heart attack. (Pause.) The services are on Thursday at 8:30. Can you get away?

DURAN:

Of course.

JEAN:

Oh, Duran. It's so terrible. (Breaks down and begins to cry. Duran comes to her and sits beside her.) Why did he have to die? Why?

DURAN:

That's all right, dear. It's all right. Maybe we should talk about it. Let's stay in and have a snack.

JEAN:

(Looks up directly at Duran.) I don't want to die, Duran. I don't want to die.

DURAN:

I know, Jean, I know.
(Later that evening, after going to bed and not being able to sleep, Duran gets up and goes out into the living room. He starts in on the poems.)

5

Peter Pope's Poems

Hiding

How much evidence do we need? What
    would convince us?
Is it so occult or obscure that we
    must bear the burden of
Endless silliness? Are we not
    confronted daily with
Humanity? Journals thrill to the
    news: exceptions to the
Golden rule. We cluck-cluck
    and tsk-tsk,
The sanctimony game is cheap—
    like riding an
Elevator and believing that one
    ascends by virtue.

Why do we insist that what we see
    before us is
An aberration of man? Is the humdrum
    so blinding that our glasses
Let in only shadows? Is the fiction so
    precious, then, that we must
Lie about the lies and pretend to
    dream when we are awake?
The result of this is despair, disappointments
    from unfulfilled expectations
Based on false premises—a product
    surely of not believing
What is in our briefcases, of holding
    to false images.

Individualism is made legitimate by society's
    scorn, to go one's own
Way is to circle the square in the
    eyes of the collectivity.
The leaders, who must be sent by
    Satan himself, counsel
Man's perfectibility and hold out
    hope to those
Who could not face their
    real mothers, let alone
The clear vision of tragedy. It is
    what con men trade
On, which makes us into a partial
    glimpse of animality.

There are many answers, each of which is so
    threatening that all mankind conspires
To hide even the process of thought
    from the children. We live in a world
Of our own devising. Any despair, then,
    comes as a consequence of hereditary
Avoidance, perhaps by now even ignorance
    of what is true, and not from
A too pressing reality. In the kingdom
    of animals we are disinherited by those
Whom we slaughter—so we seek the
    company of man, and delight in telling
Fables around the campfire. The masterpiece
    makes us feel imperial.

Whose Life?

Attachments to pass the time,
Hobbies to keep us busy.
Anything to take one's mind
From the swirl of consciousness.

What's in it for us if we
Give to the problem of life
Our full attention and care?
Headaches perhaps, or languor.

There is a problem, I know,
And there is a solution
For some, those willing to jump
Into another's puzzle.

But there is something to be
Said for living the problem,
Though I'm not sure what unless
It be an apology.

One has to figure out the
Game in one's own way. If that
Means avoiding the whole thought
Just don't start at seventy.

Others

It's not so much that things are
    in turmoil
As it is that they aren't anywhere
    at all.
What do you do when it's not even
    important
To figure out why things aren't
    important?
There comes a heaviness, a feeling of
    carrying
A burden, and one knows there is
    no burden
To carry other than the burden of
    having
No burden to carry. It's oppressive,
    it hurts,
The world is senseless. To be engaged is
    both foolish
And the only answer possible. How
    can one
Act the fool, know he is acting the
    fool, know

Others are acting like fools, and
    still act
Like a fool? What's in it
    for people
To do that? Do they really talk
    themselves
Into believing it isn't that
    at all?
Of course they do. What utter
    fools. What
A fool I am. I might be killed
    because I
Do not defend myself. Some bastard
    will
Win. And that, perhaps, is all there
    is to
Keep us going. In a world in
    which we
Are all alike, one hates to leave
    it to
Others.

A Prayer

I sit and wonder what it's all about
knowing full well that part of what it's all about
is to sit and wonder what it is all about—

But that's not all.
There's the little things,
the getting on,
the doing what is necessary,
the involvements.
Christ!

It seems absurd.
And the reason
is that we know
it is absurd yet can't act like it is—
and *that's* absurd.

Oh, what's the use. But if I don't do
something then I'll be done to. Greed is
everywhere. At my expense. So I'm greedy too.
And there's no way out of that one,
short of living in filth and dying of disease.
And getting mad
'cause of what you see.

Sure, it's not always like this.
There is fun
sometimes,
and self-pride.
But fun doesn't last long, and
loving oneself
is not man at his best.

I want to sit in a corner and let the
world go by—but I want to feel it
doing so, and smile. And that is
why I can't do it. I want to feel
contempt. And how could I do that
if I were dead?

No, that's not right. I don't want to feel anything, really.
But I do want to observe, and feel
contempt for my own contempt, and
therefore superior because I found the
second.

It's clear, isn't it? We need help.
I can't be different from others. What
I feel we all feel—I am man, in
that sense. But who is to help,
except, maybe,
the workings of time in reverse?

Where is beauty? But Beauty is finished,
and belongs to someone else. *There's
no place to go from beauty.*
And that is all there is. And even
that is continued by long exercise and
misery. And for what?

Sleep and dream. Sleep and dream.
It could be an eternity.

Significance

How is life to be given significance? We are
    among billions, reeling in unending space
For eons—dust pulverized by weightlessness.

God, some say, and he is created for man's
    escape into the divine, shunning
Responsibility for the all too human catastrophies.

Solace for some in the facile stirring up of
    an abstract potion, drinking it down
With each meal, or before every darkness.

But we must also contend from day to day, and
    it is in these intervals that we
Gossip like little old ladies across a fence,

Like children in a playground, like colleagues
    at work, like revelers in a bar,
In never ending surgery. Patience always dies.

For ourselves, our cheap survival kits, purchased
    at scalpers' prices—consisting entirely
Of a vampire's tooth and an air pump.

We suck from our victims, and if gore is
    insufficient we puff ourselves up. Ego,
Blood, and air, the holy trinity.

But we spoil our complexions with too
    much rouge, and air will leak
In its too holey container—or burst the sides.

So we go back, searching for a high place
    to hang our names, that the
World may see we were once a visitor.

Who?

To shrivel or explode, each an
   answer to the nagging
Question of fear. One either
   hides folded and wrinkled
Within, or scatters himself, little
   pieces, a jigsaw, so obscure
That only a fellow abstractionist
   has an inkling.

A heavy price to pay, locking
   oneself up like a
Precious memory—at the bottom
   lies a mystery which needs
More than appearance to explain. I
   am what I seem only to
Those who find me unattractive—
   how frightening.

Self-imposed we carry our cages
   with us, letting in the
Wind only by the window. The
   institution is constructed
As a protection to Everyman,
   catching life in its
Own mistakes. Librarians
   and Clerks take note:

You are accomplices to the death
   of Man—especially in the
Children's corner. Appearance
   may be nothing more
Than private thoughts perverted.
   I am disposed to lick
The salt of meaning, simply because
   I need it.

Living with man as he is may
    solve the riddle of life,
For such insight might lessen
    the present need for
Mind rearranging, and make
    us act more
Humanly to death and
    destruction.

Statistics and All That

The night has come early, the day has been so
    nice I'm glad it's gone—one
Can't take too many chances. Statisticians
    are everywhere, demanding
Their tithe. They claim it's less
    than what they save you—but
By making it conscious they bury
    the whole in analysis. One is
Not dependent on them alone for
    rude awakenings, but poets
Are not strong on courage—else
    why is their song
So lovely? So they listen with
    a better ear that hears
What they don't say. If
    dreams are wishes, then
Poems are dreams. Why, then,
    can't poems shatter the
Accountants' world? Is it because
    of Gresham's Law? If so one
Simply must become an introvert.
    All the rest is
Argument—and one must be
    willing to knit-pick and
Carp in that game. Points are
    added slowly, and the game
Often goes to twenty-one.

And You Really Think They Feel?

They're moving around now, I can see them quite clearly.
And you really think they don't know we're here?
How interesting. But it does seem a waste of motion.
At least with other animals one senses that it doesn't matter,
And no need to ask how they feel about it, either.
But these, you say, have feelings? How can you be sure?
Pigs squeal, after all, when you cut them open.
But pigs don't have the range of gestures? And they
Don't laugh? No, I suppose not. But if they
Feel, then it must be terrible for them, especially
Since they don't know we're here.

Either

Is it ever too late to save oneself?
And if one does, what is it that one
Has done? How would he know? For
Arrogance would surely reign where
Timidity sat uneasily. And that is
Not so much saving as changing, from
Being a sponge to being a shark.
And is it any better to give than
To receive, when the commodity in question
Is hurt to self-esteem? Those who
Accept the arrows of others are doing
Society a good turn, even if they
Themselves bleed profusely, for
Someone must keep the malcontents
From really fighting. Perhaps this
Is why we feel so ambivalent toward
Bullies—envy for their strength, and
Hate for what we know they will do
To us. But do they have to dismember
Us with such relish? I can't be
Like that, but I can't be like this
Either.

Children

The house is closed,
The sky is gray,
The children are laughing,
What do they know?

Who can help me out?
Who can change how it is?
Who can not pretend?
Not the children.

I know someone who can hunt.
I know people who know they're right.
I know those who think it's the beginning.
It's the children.

Children cry when things go wrong—
Children exercise their power—
Children fly from thing to thing—
I don't want to be a child.

Save me from the children.

Relative Status

Being committed to a something, which
   occupies the mind
And wears one out—just the mental
   fatigue is enough
To send one into a reflective
   boredom, a feeling of
Accomplishment and rest that is
   even shown in public
In the slumped but earned
   posture of someone
Who did something today.

And what a superior position that
   half-lying-down can be.
Who can deny a blob his relaxation
   when he can hold over you
The assurance of a day in
   which something was
Accomplished? Unless your tolerance
   for tension is at an end
You'd better not leave him alone.

There is no doubt that arrogance and
   self-satisfaction are
Akin. And if the world is better
   off for the labors which
Produce a rare feeling of a done deed,
   is the price of sanctimony and
Smugness not a high one?

For beware—the line of least resistance
   will smolder the resentment of
Non-recognition and that of a dutiful
   animal to lick and sniff and
Give him homage, the devil himself devised.

For such corruption of the latter shall
   make the future bleak
Indeed, as he harks back to the

Day he was a better man than now.

Are You Serious?

I saw three men in a room questioning
   another man.
They asked him all sorts of questions,
   like where
He lived and what he did. The
   man answering
The questions became quite involved
   with his
Answers, as though much depended
   on what

Was said. He could not know,
  of course,
That his replies would make
  no difference
At all, and that he could therefore
  have said
Anything he felt. He might
  even have
Been clever, witty, or frivolous,
  and enjoyed
Himself.

But we are inclined, when threatened,
  to imbue
Ourselves with serious intent. We
  see the
World as a place where it does make
  a difference,
Or at least so we rationalize when
  we find
Ourselves becoming angry, or under
  attack.
How do we know why we do it?
  Perhaps
It's just our nature. But we
  might consider
How we could deny to others
  the ability
To make us upset so that we
  dance their
Tune. Do we really need to
  believe their
Premises?

A Mirror Into Yesterday

I had a bit of a fright today,
That made me feel depressed —
I talked with Phil who reminded me
Of how I mentally dressed

When I was young like him and frightened
Of a world at odds and
Unwieldy, when I forced my mind down
With a self-serving hand

To think thoughts that others expected.

By blocking the vision
Of a world created from within
I circumvented so
Carefully my mind's annihilation.

When one is young there is
To be done, just in terms of living,
An enormous amount
Of working out an underlying

Need to be accepted.

When I think what it cost me arriving
At where I dangle now
I feel nothing but fright that Phil might
Submit and not know how

To find his way through the exercise.
For once begun it is
Not clear where one goes—round trips are not
What one buys nor expects

And the start has many an ending.

Yet I can't but hope he
Leaps anyway—creation for him
and stimulation for
Others requires a modicum

Of disengagement from
The serious business of stupor.
The despair one finds in
The process leads to expansion or

Perhaps things worth sending.

Doctors of Humanity

There are many people who view life as
  remediable,
Who see in our condition a sickness,
  a disease,
A malaise, and who take it upon themselves
  to diagnose
The causes and prescribe a cure.

Is it part of what we are to see ourselves
  as sick?
Is it part of what we do to think that
  others need
Our help? To illustrate the point
  by example,
Are we limp and do we need a crutch?

When thought folds back upon itself
  we have reached
A stopping place, our language
  has again
Shown itself to be superior. Either we
  say things
Beautifully, trivially, or playfully.

Winning

If you find yourself in a conversation
  you don't like,
Don't complain about how dumb your
  fellowman is—
Conversations are not rooms without doors,
Nor are they the product of one mind.

There is no topic which cannot be made
  either funny
Or interesting or both. Topics are
  simply tracks
Upon which express trains run.
One can make the journey anything he can.

Conversations should be viewed as games
  in which the
Participants bounce off one another like
  tether balls.
One can always make a game fun.
Just forget it's a game and play to win.

Hope

I pick out an empty table, and
  sit and eat in silence, staring
At all the others sitting and eating at
  separate tables.
I am acutely aware of being aware of myself—
  I think about it
And grow moody. Someone sits down
  near me. Maybe this one—maybe this one.
But I doubt it. What are the chances of
  doing more than telling him about
One or two of my selves? And what would
  that accomplish?

Cycling

We all cycle in the same way.
Our responses to challenges are
Superficially different, and that
Is partially how we convince
Ourselves of our worth. Being
Different is being better,
Or worse.

Sing-song, Sing-along

De da diddle da, da de dives,
There are many who tie their lives,
Da de diddle de, de da dind,
To the betterment of mankind.

Oh if people would follow me,
How much better off man would be.
Hi de diddle de, de da do,
Why can't other men see that too.

Being

Tell me what to be,
A judge, a financier,
A chaired professor at
Some great university.

I can be anything I want,
Or so you say.
It is only in life
That I quake a bit.

The emptiness of being
Everything is as ghoulish
As the loneliness of
Being nothing.

Oh tell me what to be,
A judge, a financier,
A chaired professor at
Some great university.

I want to know.

A Man's Castle

Man erects a castle of trivia
in order not to think
of Why—to surround oneself
with details is a great
Solace and a death.

Reasons

Do we do what we do
because of
or
in order to?
The first produces tragedy—
the latter folly.

Spades for Make-Work

It occurs to me that what you
say would take
A hundred years to think
about. And even then
Who could be sure. Short
conversations are great
Disappointments—they pass for
wholes where holes
Could never be filled in.
And so we dig with
Store-bought equipment, never
realizing that in making
Assumptions about the task
of digging we have already
Dug ourselves in.

We All Tend To Think

We all tend to think that life is
  basically good—
Perhaps because the alternative is
  so overwhelming.
If we are all guilty, then none of
  us are, and Queen
Victoria and George Washington
  would have died innocently.
If this be our heritage, who then
  will not come in costume?

Deaf Ears

The world screams out, but who could
  possibly listen? The young, the
Alienated, the rebellious, the mad.

Life consists of preventing little tragedies—
  big tragedies just happen.
I must remember that sometime.

Which Way To Go?

The cave is nothing more than a resting place.
Why, then, do we give it the status of home?
If security produced generosity, that might be compensation—
But the two exist in a world touched by many other hands.
The generous are covering their bets.
The safe are squirreling their lives.
Who, then, needs to have safety when the edge of life
Is cutting off big slices for the foolhardy?

The Uninvited Guest

Do you really wish to imitate me?
Are you confident I would look good on you?
Can't you see that robbers of identity
Will never know themselves?

I come to you as I am, but wary,
For I suspect you carry a bag
With which to collect my spores.
Oh what a nasty business picking up is.

I want you strong—you come on like a
Little boy who needs a mother.
But you confuse my head with a
Tit, and think you can suck on it.

Stay away, stay away, you are not
Wanted here—if you must do these
Things then do them to someone else.
I will not provide your milk.

I will no longer play host.

Perhaps Not

Man needs his egoistic triumphs, the more they
    occur in subjective hierarchies.
When denied, the budding adversary must be
    misjudged and barred
From further intercourse,
    his purpose self-denying.
Man's capacity for voluntary withdrawals
    breaks rhythm with
His charge to victory:
    a monument to charade.

We find ourselves unable to pull away
  entirely from certain individuals.
Society meets in the court of precedent.
  Abstention, then, the withholding of
Emotional commitment,
  unless, of course, one chooses war.
Some are made for one or the
  other, but misery follows
In the trail of
  each alternative.

Man

We sing in praise, and criticize only from
  a loftier position. Man must
Be what we wish for him, for are we
  not ourselves at stake?

But good and bad are rules devised
  by those who play the game
For keeps. Spectators are afraid to
  enter the back room lest

They be enticed or forced to play
  out their hands. As they hold
So few cards the game would
  be over quickly.

And, My Good Boy, Who Are You?

One of the difficulties, surely,
  is that people *are*
Sincere, *appear* to be
  sincere, and are even
Right, in a way. But
  it still doesn't do
Any good, 'cause there's always
  more to it than that.

Sincerity is a front such that,
  the more sincere we
Appear to be, *and* the more
  sincere we in fact are
The more we could live in
  a world of pure
Illusion alone. But the
  more apt we are to
Develop nagging doubts and/or
  come crashing down
When, out of nothing, comes
  Sincerity, looking like
Sincerity, being right and
  showing us wrong.
Oh dear, oh dear. And
  this is especially
Irritating when we stop and
  think that if we
Gave up sincerity what we
  would put in its
Place as a criterion would
  be just as silly.
For don't we always live
  in a world of
Illusion even when we
  aren't being put
On, and even when the
  Put-on is our inference
And not deliberate? But
  what then? Is there
Nowhere to go? Must we
  retreat into ourselves?
And just what do we expect
  to find there
Anyway, except "mumble-mumble
  people are jerks
Mumble-mumble." And what good
  does that do
Anyone? Mumble-mumble.

To and Fro

Can you put on a performance when
   you know you are
Putting on a performance and you
   wonder whether it's
Worth it but you realize that if
   you didn't put on a
Performance you'd be left in some
   other circumstance putting
On a performance only you wouldn't
   think you would be?
Is it only a matter of
   words? But what
Isn't? And when you think
   this way you find
It helps you to go through with it since
   performances are performances,
Yet, on reflection, it makes you want
   to stay home and listen
To a Mozart string quartet, and
   you wind up going
But hungry for sound at the
   same time that you
Decide. For somehow we need
   to validate ourselves
Twice over—once for being
   and once merging
Into a language which pushes
   us back into
A selfless selfishness. But who
   knows, maybe we'll
Enjoy ourselves after all, and
   brooding can force
Us out anyway. Validation
   twice over—one after
Another. You can only lose
   toward the end
Of each cycle. But endings
   merge into old

Beginnings, so we keep on
   going. We all catch
Ourselves, sometimes on the downward
   swing of contemplation.

Reality Is . . .

How do I escape humanness? My mind won't let
   me—I bow down before
False gods, I think thoughts unbecoming to
   a Saint. Can one escape
What he is? Can one become a thing outside
   of himself? What say you?

And so I will be a human as long as I exist.
   Perhaps that is what is meant
By a peaceful death. To die knowing that one
   is not giving up all that much.
That our bodies grow old and unbearable is a
   blessing. Who wants to live
With those pains? That our minds can now
   see the indifference with which
God will greet one's death. And if we
   knew that before our time we
Would be straw men, as indeed we are.
   (It is just that some of us act
As though we were on fire, and some never cool down.)
   What am I to regret, other than
That I was a human at all, and how
   could I regret that, since
I had no choice? There are those who
   wish to convince me that I
Can be a Saint if I want to be, and that
   is one way to live a life.
People peddle illusion in order that we
   do not have to face up to
Our circumstances. In a world in which
   hope is bad faith can we not
In fact avoid despair? I think indeed
   we cannot, and so whatever we

Think is bad faith. Palliatives abound among
  language users, who need to
Construct for themselves safety and significance.
  But if we must live in garbage
Can't we at least smell it? In such a
  world illusion would not become
Reality, it would be reality.

The Other Stuff

One places his trust in his own reality,
  and gets jostled around,
Sometimes seriously.
    And one's reality comes from others
As well as one's idiosyncracies—
  How often do we think we know
Only to find out we do when in
  Fact we don't
Assuming, of course, that "in fact"
  Doesn't mean what we
Usually mean by it when
  We say it?
There is a world of directions,
  like "The bus leaves
From here" and "It's now
  8:30." Information is so
Goddamn cheap, maybe that's
  Why we all
Think everything we "know" is
  Information—and of course
It isn't—but we live in a world
  which believes that
What we know is knowledge
  Rather than
Words unbased on bus
  schedules.
  "It's time to go." What could
    that possibly

Mean? Why should we care?
  Why are we
Latched to the
  Intonations and
Intentions of others? Do we
  have to find meaning in
Everything for Christ's sake?
  Let information
Be information, and do the
  best you can with
The other stuff.

To Say Something

Different worlds, different truths, and no
  truths at all.
Are there some things we can never know, but
  only think about?
What has happened to my youth? Why must
  I seem to
Wander aimlessly when I was at one time
  going somewhere?
We have a need to know—but to know
  that we cannot
Know is a peculiar form of knowing. In
  a world where
Assertions seem like gibberish, can questions be
  asked at all?
But our minds are strung with beliefs, and we
  all love to
Play the harmonies of passionate discourse,
  where intensity
Is a substitute for wit. In our prejudices
  we carve out
Truth—pealing morality when we argue
  what is the case.
We are moral men—we are believing men.
  And when we
Wish to be the most sincere we are the
  biggest fools.

Is it possible we are in a trap, having to
    know but being
In an untenable position from which to view
    the passing scene?
When one does not ask the meaning of life
    it can be
Lived, and that's what makes it meaningful.
    But if we
Ask we have admitted a disengagement which
    cannot be
Replaced by an answer. For an answer
    will be merely
A thought, an idea, not a conviction.
    Life goes to
Those who are convinced of something, no
    matter what it
Is. To enter the treadmill of one's
    own mind is
A delight, but a separation from a life
    once lived.
And all of this is an effort to make ourselves
    different.
None of us can accept our common humanity,
    our common
Predicament, the paradoxes which do not
    allow us out
But which do encourage us to contend and
    try to wiggle
Free. We all try to go back, but
    awareness has
Spoiled it for us and we find ourselves
    acting ourselves
Or seeing ourselves trying to be ourselves
    or someone else
Whom we think of when we contemplate what
    we are.
I can't help but think that we are walking
    on our hands
And weaving baskets on the side, and
    thinking how
Difficult it is to weave without ever
    realizing

Why. Can we do two things at once?
   Can we walk
And weave together? If we walk must
   we cease our
Knitting of the brow? If we move our
   fingers in
Artful display are we then committed
   to moving
As well? How heavy is the load
   of our feet
When we are upside down. How clever we
   must be to
Carry off a pretense—either that or by
   mutual consent
We decide not to inquire into the land
   of pretend
Unless we can locate a particular
   evil. To look
At everyone's attitude would be
   to see so
Much that nothing could be said in
   particular.
It is only trite, after all, if
   we try to
Universalize. Meanings are taken from
   our fellowman
So we cannot include all of them.
   Else who would
We compare ourselves to? Cows?
   The trees?
This certainly is peculiar and must
   be cast aside.
Our meaning comes from exposing others.
   We must not
Hide in the human condition. It will
   exasperate
Those around us. For we get nowhere when
   we ask what
All of us are up to. It is only when we
   narrow ourselves
To others of another sort that we are
   satisfied that

We have said something of significance.
  Funny it
Should be that way. The clearest
  differences
Are those we cannot make. And those
  we do make
Are true to ourselves, and passionate.
  And this is
One reason painting and sculpture and
  music are
Different from the written word (except,
  of course, for
Poetry). They can say things in such a diverting
  way that we
Only feel the message but do not have to
  think about it.
A message from the arts can be beautiful
  and need not
Be considered in its onotological nakedness.
  But to say
Something in a straightforward way, to make an
  assertion, is
To trivialize by making clear that which
  can be
Beautiful but not true. That which can
  be felt but
Not thought. That which must come to us
  indirectly.
Meaning is too important to us to let what
  is important
Become a simple sentence. Such language
  games are for scholars
Except when we are made to laugh at
  the way in
Which our language puts us in ridiculous
  situations.
If one wants to say what is true, he must
  say it
Aesthetically. If one wants to be aesthetic
  he will fail

Of saying something true. A mind can go
  astray and
Think it is a leader in its field. Self-
  doubt is an
Inward necessity, a foundation for what is to be
  created,
But it is a fire hazard when looked at
  from the outside.
It is seen as a weakness, as something to be
  destroyed, as
A danger to the rest of us and the houses
  we live in.
When we see weakness we are quick to jump, not
  because we
Despise weakness but because it does frighten us.
  When others
Doubt, can we be safe? In a world where
  all houses are
Uninsurable, where the rickety, creaky
  edifice
Of mind is challenged constantly by the
  insanity
Of what we like to call others, is it unjust
  to protect
Oneself by burning down the homes of those
  who live in
Uncertainty and who talk as though we
  all do?
Do we not feel that thinking makes it so?
  That pretense
Is reality when it is our own? Our own
  self-protection
Requires that we give a show of strength, and
  so too for
Others. Do not forget that others are just like
  you. Just as
They will pick on weakness, so too will we
  ourselves.
Remember that when next you meet with
  the itch

To gossip. We all need our spooks, our
    targets of
Despair, our havens when we feel we can
    go no
Further. We seek out our spooks when
    we most need
A friend, someone who will not fight
    back or
Contradict. How comforting to revel in our hate,
    how much at
Home we feel, how safe, when we can
    exercise
Our last gasp in such a way as to undo
    others. We
Feed ourselves greatness at last—our
    lives are not
Hopeless after all. Going back to the womb is
    a strong
Desire but an ugly reality. For to be safe
    means to cause
Discomfort to our own mother, to feel the
    strength of
Someone else, to draw our life's energy
    from the insides
Of our fellowman. Why is it so pleasurable?
    Simply because
It is necessary? Why, then, is it so necessary, why
    do we find
Ourselves so warm and soothed when we are
    least attractive?
It's a lucky thing that babies are not imbued with
    the feelings
Of people, and too bad people are not
    given the
Lives of babies, for we have come to realize that
    what is
Of utmost importance to us in the one is the most
    sickening
In the other. Who will give us a second chance,
    and a third?

Only ourselves, as we pull ourselves up by our
   capacity
For inhumanity toward the trivialities of
   individual
Differences. Let us see ourselves in others, for
   truly we
Are at one with our brothers. When we feel
   low we still
Have the tension left to behave even lower
   in order
To raise ourselves up. That life is contradictory
   isn't even
Interesting any more. The obvious makes us weary
   and we
Seek out new thrills. I wonder if we will
   ever change?

Poets

Poems are a matter of mood, if by
   mood is meant
How one feels about things—but
   not really specifically.
There is, instead, a generalized anxiety
   which we all feel
From time to time, and poets manage
   to displace it
On something in particular. Lucky
   poets.

It is rare that all of us would get
   just the right
Amount of stimulation. And if
   we don't get
Enough then depression hits,
   a feeling that
Our lives are empty. And
   so we have the
Mood of heavy contemplation which
   poets know.

And we think we know what the
  anxiety is caused
By—by lack of sexual
  encounters, by
Failures of one sort or another.
  But of course
We are just guessing, and
  when we say
It's due to one thing or another we
  lose poetry.

Poets take advantage of moods—they
  are exploiters
Of human feelings, of their own
  miseries. In a
Way by taking themselves so
  seriously they don't
Take themselves seriously at all.
  For they try to
Both feel and do something about
  it. Poor poets.

6
Tellurian's Study

It is the next day, and Seeker has just returned to Tellurian's.

TELLURIAN:

Nice to see you again, Mr. Seeker. (Going over to shake Seeker's hand.) You remember, of course, Margaret Fleece?

SEEKER:

Yes, nice to see you again, Miss Fleece. (Shaking hands.)

TELLURIAN:

And Peter Pope.

SEEKER:

(Becoming quite animated.) Yes indeed. (Shaking hands.) I read your poems last night. I found them quite remarkable.

POPE:

(Laughing.) Thank you. I won't ask you in what way. I'm glad you could make it.

TELLURIAN:

Won't you sit down, Mr. Seeker? May I get you a drink?

SEEKER:

No, I think not, thank you. I have a feeling I might need my wits about me, even though I might also need a tranquilizer. I can't tell whether it would be more important for me to be crystal clear about what will happen to me or whether I should try to soften myself for the blow. (They all chuckle a bit.)

TELLURIAN:

We will do our best to make this interesting for you, Mr. Seeker, but you are right, you yourself will have to make the decisions about how all this is to affect you. I find it difficult enough to be responsible for what goes on in my own mind without having to take responsibility for others. There is, clearly, a moral question which can be raised, but I have decided it by simply assuming that it's better to be aware than not to be aware. *No matter what happens.*

SEEKER:

To be aware of what, Mr. Tellurian?

POPE:

Why, to be aware of oneself, Mr. Seeker. And to be aware of oneself being aware of oneself; and to be aware of oneself being aware of oneself being aware of oneself, if you can go that far.

SEEKER:

But what's so important about being aware? I can think of lots of reasons why being aware of oneself could be terribly debilitating.

FLEECE:

For example.

SEEKER:

It seems to me that in order to get things done we need to be involved, to be aware of *what* we are trying to do and not of *ourselves* doing it. There's a sense in which we can live a life, or we can think of ourselves living a life. And the two may not be compatible. If I sit around and become aware of myself all the time, I might not be able to get anything done. And I might not feel like I'm living, either. I may feel that I'm watching myself living, and in doing so I'm not really living at all, but merely watching myself watching myself. How can I *do* anything if I'm constantly preoccupied with myself?

TELLURIAN:

I think that's an interesting point. There is a conflict, I think, between awareness and commitment. If we are aware of ourselves being committed, rather than just being committed, then we, perhaps, undercut our ability to act in a committed fashion. But that's just the point, isn't it?

SEEKER:

What point?

FLEECE:

Whether we want to live in a committed fashion. We are all committed to things. We all believe that there are right ways and wrong ways to do things. And it is on the basis of these commitments that we judge other people.

SEEKER:

And what's wrong with judging other people? You aren't going to make the argument that we can't judge other people, are you?

POPE:

It depends, of course, on how you feel about being a bigot.

SEEKER:

Now look . . .

TELLURIAN:

(Interrupting.) I think, Mr. Seeker, that Mr. Pope is raising a general issue and does not mean it personally. I am sure, for example, that he would be the first to say that he himself is also a bigot.

SEEKER:

But what's that supposed to mean?

FLEECE:

It means, Mr. Seeker, that we are all bigots. We all give ourselves significance by denigrating other people. It seems to be part of what we are as human beings. Personal significance is of great concern to us. We have consciousness and we are capable of turning that consciousness on ourselves. This is probably what truly distinguishes us from other animals. And being aware of ourselves means that we become aware of ourselves in relation to other people. Our desire for self-importance, to see ourselves as worthy, as meaningful, means that we spend a good deal of time evaluating others. One of the ways we can puff ourselves up is to knock others down. And that's what Mr. Pope meant by bigotry: the natural human tendency to see some people as less worthy than oneself.

SEEKER:

But you make it sound like people derive their satisfactions solely on the basis of being mean to other people, in treating some people as inferior.

POPE:

Not at all. Prejudice is merely one strategy that people pursue in their quest for significance. But, as we all know, people are very complex. It's very unlikely that a single assertion about them will realistically interpret all of their behavior. For example, people discriminate in all sorts of ways. One of the most interesting is the way in which people treat great creative achievements. Those who produce these are labeled geniuses. Now, this is very convenient. Obviously people who are capable of such achievements are very threatening to the rest of us. How can we possibly justify ourselves in the face of such great achievements? The answer, of course, is that we don't even try. What we do is to get rid of the danger by describing these people as "geniuses," as people who are superhuman, who have been given a gift, a talent, who are somehow naturally endowed with more of something. And so how can anyone expect the same from us? You see how the game works?

FLEECE:

And that's not all the story. People also like to give themselves status from time to time. They will flatter themselves, refer to their good points, show how they are necessary, take credit for happy consequences of activities in which they participate.

SEEKER:

Yes, but they also criticize themselves. It seems that you are not accounting for that.

TELLURIAN:

That's easy enough to do. We often take great pleasure in despair and sorrow. So much so, in fact, that we sometimes make up things to be sorrowful about. St. Augustine pointed that out fifteen hundred years ago. We have a tendency to think of happiness only in terms of what we think of as "being happy." But what we want is not so much happiness as meaningfulness. We want to be aware of ourselves as being significant. Sadness can contribute to that awareness every bit as much as happiness.

SEEKER:

I'm afraid you people are catching me off guard. What you say seems to make a lot of sense, but I'm not at all comfortable with it. I'm afraid I'm not very good at thinking on my feet. I'd really like to give it some thought.

TELLURIAN:

I agree with you. Thinking is something which is not done easily on the spur of the moment nor in the presence of other people. As an old college professor I can attest to that. The classroom is a place where you can give students material to think about, or where you can let them express themselves, but it is not a place where one can expect actual thinking to take place. In fact, thinking would undercut the very foundation of the classroom, which is to keep up a constant chatter about things. We often confuse spur-of-the-moment reactions with thinking. No wonder professors often win that game. Whatever else you may say about them they have probably done somewhat more thinking about a subject than a typical student. Which means that they are ahead only with respect to *prior* thinking. This is why some of the best professors view their job as stimulating students to think rather than, say, to memorize or to "learn." The classroom is ideally suited for stimulation or expression, but not learning or thinking. That must take place later.

SEEKER:

You know, you people are really depressing me. It's as though my whole world is fraudulent and cockeyed. That's a terrible way to feel.

FLEECE:

> There are people who will insist you live in a world which everyone recognizes. But the point is you must live in a world. So why not a world of your own?

SEEKER:

> What do you mean, a world of my own? (Beginning to get agitated.)

FLEECE:

> I mean that we have a good deal of discretion about what the world we live in may look like. Outside of physical objects we construct the world, we determine of what it will consist and what value each object shall have. We can let others do this for us—we can simply adopt the world as it is presented to us by others—or we can do something about constructing the world as we ourselves would like to live in it.

SEEKER:

> But what you're saying is fantastic. Crazy people live in a world of their own. You want me to do that? (Becoming increasingly upset.)

TELLURIAN:

> Mr. Seeker, *we* don't want *you* to do anything. It is true that if one tries to live in his own world there is no guarantee that it will be beautiful, or that one will still look and act like other people. But for some people the world as it comes is no longer acceptable. Many are not capable of constructing any other world than a safe shelter. But not all—by no means all.

SEEKER:

> Stop it, will you! Just stop it! (Seeker jumps up and begins to scream.) I can't take this anymore. For Christ's sake, lay off and let a man think. How am I supposed to handle all this stuff anyway? (Begins to sob.) How can I cope with these things you're talking about? My world is flying apart and you people just sit there. (Sobbing heavily. The three simply observe and do not move.) Jesus, I feel awful. You people are talking me right out of my life. (Sits down and buries his head in his hands and cries. Tellurian, Fleece, and Pope merely

watch. There is a long pause. After a minute or so Seeker begins to come out of it.)

I'm sorry, I guess I'm making a fool of myself. Please excuse me.

TELLURIAN:

Not at all, Mr. Seeker. May I get you something?

SEEKER:

No, no, thank you. I'll be all right. Just give me a minute or two. I'm really sorry about this. I'm usually fairly composed. I don't know what came over me.

TELLURIAN:

Don't worry about it. Just take your time.

FLEECE:

If you don't mind my saying so you are bucking up under the strain quite admirably. I think you're well on your way, Mr. Seeker.

SEEKER:

On my way where?

FLEECE:

Wherever it is that you're going.

SEEKER:

(Letting out a big sigh, taking out his handkerchief, and blowing his nose. Seeker then gets up and paces a bit.) I hope you're right, Miss Fleece. But I must confess I don't know what the hell you're talking about. (They all chuckle at this, and Seeker does so, too.)

TELLURIAN:

I suggest we all have a bit of refreshment. What will you have, Mr. Seeker? Same as yesterday? (Goes to his desk and rings.)

SEEKER:

Yes, that will be fine.

TELLURIAN:

And you, Peter?

POPE:

A beer please, yes.

TELLURIAN:

It won't take a minute. (The butler arrives and comes over to
Tellurian, who gives him instructions. He then returns shortly
and serves the drinks.)

SEEKER:

Do you mind if I ask you people a question?

TELLURIAN:

No, not at all. Go right ahead.

SEEKER:

Does the world have any meaning?
(Tellurian, Fleece, and Pope all look at each other, each hiding an expression.)

FLEECE:

It depends, I guess, on what you mean by that.

SEEKER:

Well, what I mean is, does the world have any meaning? (They
all smile.)

TELLURIAN:

I think each of us is equipped to give you a long-winded answer to that question, Mr. Seeker . . .

SEEKER:

(Interrupting.) Please, call me Duran. If you don't know me
well enough to call me Duran, I don't know who does.

TELLURIAN:

Thank you, Duran. Each of us could give you an answer, but
it wouldn't really be an answer to the question as you phrase

it. We all have to think about it, and one's answer is the very thing which makes asking the question unnecessary.

SEEKER:

You're saying, then, that this is a matter each person has to discover for himself.

POPE:

I think, Duran, that Lewis is saying ever more than that. He's saying that it's something that each of us must *create* for ourselves. "To discover" makes it sound like there's an answer to be discovered. I don't think that any of us would want to imply that.

SEEKER:

But life is meaningless, then. There is no meaning that you can direct one to, is there? (Each looks at the others.)
    No, I didn't think so.

FLEECE:

That doesn't mean, Duran, that each of us might not have an answer for ourselves.

SEEKER:

Then tell me.

POPE:

Why should we? Why should we let you off the hook by giving something to you that you won't take anyway?

SEEKER:

What do you mean by that? (Becoming slightly hostile.)

POPE:

I mean, Duran, that one does not share an answer to that question with someone who obviously won't accept it. People like you, in the mood you are in right now, can't accept it. You must figure it out for yourself. So—go ahead. Just don't ask me to provide ammunition to blow me to kingdom come.

SEEKER:

I'm afraid I'm going to have to go now.

TELLURIAN:

> That's fine, Duran. (Getting up as Seeker does. Fleece and Pope then also rise. Tellurian is first to shake Seeker's hand.)
> Good-bye, Duran. Good luck. Let us hear from you from time to time.

FLEECE:

> Good-bye, Duran. (Shakes his hand.)

POPE:

> Good-bye. I assume we'll be hearing from you.

FLEECE:

> I know you may not feel like looking at this but we thought you might like to read a play I've written. Would you?

SEEKER:

> Of course. I don't see how I could feel any worse. (Seeker takes the play.)

TELLURIAN:

> You won't know very much until you do. Good-bye, Duran, and good luck.
> (At a later time Seeker did manage to read Margaret Fleece's play, as follows.)

7

Margaret Fleece's Play

Phillip Markings is in his study, working behind his desk. There are lots of papers around, and Phil is writing. There's a ring at the doorbell. His housekeeper answers it (offstage), and we hear a muffled sound of voices. There's a knock at the study door. The caller is Lyman Pierce, Phillip Marking's publisher and moderately good friend.

MARKINGS:

Come in.

PIERCE:

Good morning, Phil. How are you?

MARKINGS:

Well, good morning, Lyman. Come in, please. (Phil gets up and shakes hands.) It's nice to see you. What brings you here so early? Has the publishing house decided to take back my advance?

PIERCE:

Just the opposite, my friend. You tell us what you want and it's yours.

MARKINGS:

Now that's something of a temptation. What have you in the way of beautiful, terribly smart women who are devoted, witty, excellent conversationalists, extraordinary in bed, and good chess players?

PIERCE:

No, no, you have it wrong. I'm a publisher, not a wizard.

MARKINGS:

But aren't publishers in control of what pens become mightier than what swords?

PIERCE:

You mean we're like a five and dime, peddling the latest styles in ballpoints?
(Both are obviously having a good time in this conversation.)

MARKINGS:

Well, the least you could do, it seems to me, is to find me what I'm looking for. Then I'd stop bothering you.

PIERCE:

No bother, really. A couple hundred thousand dollars is no bother.

MARKINGS:

Before I ask you what that's all about, how about a cup of coffee?

PIERCE:

Fine. Black for me.

MARKINGS:

(Goes to the door and shouts for Betsey, the housekeeper.)
Betsey — two black coffees, please.

BETSEY:

(From offstage.) Yes, sir, Mr. Markings.

MARKINGS:

(Returning to his desk.) Come and sit. Now, what did you mean about several hundred thousand dollars?

PIERCE:

Well, you know what's been happening, don't you.

MARKINGS:

About what? Don't tell me World War III has started?

PIERCE:

It undoubtedly has—we just don't realize it yet. No, I mean even more important things than that. You know what has happened to you.

MARKINGS:

No, what? Am I alive and well in Austin, Texas?

PIERCE:

Have you read any of the newspaper and magazine clippings I've sent on your latest book?

MARKINGS:

You know I haven't. I gave up reading the newspaper long ago—when I realized that I couldn't learn anything about man from the paper, just the nitty-gritty about what he's been up to lately.

PIERCE:

Oh, for Christ's sake, Phil. It turns out that you have become the greatest living philosopher in America, and you don't even know what's happening. Did I say living? They're beginning to compare you with all sorts of people, including Socrates. Your book has brought the intellectual world to its feet, and it appears to be a wild, standing ovation. People are beginning to talk about you and your system like Frenchmen, and later the world, used to talk about Sartre and existentialism. You are fast becoming a movement, Phil.

MARKINGS:

You don't say.

PIERCE:

Yes, I do say. And I think you ought to know it.

MARKINGS:

What would you say if I told you I don't want to know about it?

PIERCE:

I think you have to.

MARKINGS:

You know how I feel about these things. You've read my books, haven't you? If you have, and you think me honest, then you'd know that I might feel good that people like my work but, fundamentally, it doesn't make any difference at all whether they do or not. It couldn't make any difference. I'd write the same thing if they did or didn't. I am not writing for other people. I like the idea that I can make a little money and do what I would do anyway—but that's about as far as my interest goes. (Betsey comes in at this point with a tray with coffee, cups, and cut up squares of toast. She sets the tray down on the table.)

Thank you, Betsey. The toast is very nice. (Phil smiles and Betsey smiles back. She leaves. Phil walks over, pours two cups of coffee, takes one to Lyman, along with the plate of toast. Lyman takes the coffee and places a couple of toast squares on his saucer. Phil then takes his own cup, with toast, back to his chair.)

PIERCE:

Thank you. It smells very good.

MARKINGS:

(In his normal, pleasant voice.) Betsey makes a darn good cup of coffee. I wish I could have her more than twice a week.

PIERCE:

You can now, you know.

MARKINGS:

Oh, I really didn't mean it. A comment out of my penurious past.

PIERCE:

This latest book has really done it for you. And we are now reissuing the three earlier books. They should have quite a sale.

MARKINGS:

I'd just as soon you didn't do that.

PIERCE:

What do you mean?

MARKINGS:

I'd prefer that people forget about my three earlier books. They're not really saying very much.

PIERCE:

That's not really for you to determine. Perhaps they say more than you think.

MARKINGS:

Thanks. But I wrote them, you know.

PIERCE:

You're going to be asked to do a lot of things now, Phil. What are you going to do about it?

MARKINGS:

About what?

PIERCE:

About invitations to speak, for example, or requests for articles on current topics. Will you do any?

MARKINGS:

What do you think?

PIERCE:

I think if you did, it would help the sale of your books. Does that interest you?

MARKINGS:

No.

PIERCE:

But you do want people to read them?

MARKINGS:

I want them available for people to read if they want to. I get no kick out of lots of people reading what I write—only having what I write published.

PIERCE:

But we could get your ideas to many more people if we pushed a little.

MARKINGS:

If anyone wants to read them, they can.

PIERCE:

But don't you want people to know of your ideas?

MARKINGS:

Only if they want to. To tell you the truth, I don't really like to hear my ideas come from other people.

PIERCE:

But you do want people to think, don't you? And how will they be able to think about your ideas if they don't know about them?

MARKINGS:

People do seem to know about them.

PIERCE:

But more could.

MARKINGS:

Maybe. I'm rather more convinced that word of mouth and general discussion will give people the idea to read them.

PIERCE:

But there are lots of people who need encouragement.

MARKINGS:

So what?

PIERCE:

Don't you want them to know of your ideas, too?

MARKINGS:

Why should I?

PIERCE:

Because your ideas are important.

MARKINGS:

No more important than lots of others.

PIERCE:

That's not true.

MARKINGS:

So you say. Look, Lyman, I don't want to argue with you. No, I'm not interested in merchandising my books—no, I will not help peddle them—no, I will not engage in lecture tours and speaking engagements. There is no reason why anyone should read my ideas. I enjoy thinking and writing—no, that's not quite right. I don't actually "enjoy" doing these things—but these things are what I do, what I seem to want to do. That I can earn a living doing what I want seems just fine to me. Earning more doing what I don't want to do and cutting into time I could be doing what I do want to do sounds absolutely ludicrous, don't you agree?

PIERCE:

But surely you must have some desire to change the world, to make it a better place.

MARKINGS:

What makes you think so?

PIERCE:

We all do, don't we?

MARKINGS:

We all have hopes and dreams—but that doesn't mean we all think the world could be changed. We don't change the world by changing our way of seeing it. We simply change our way of looking at it. New incongruities are exchanged for old. The world goes on as before.

PIERCE:

I don't follow you.

MARKINGS:

Look—the world is as it is. We see the world in different ways. We can change how we see it, but that's not changing the world, is it, at least not really. And I don't want to change people's ways of looking at the world. And I certainly have no idea about how to change the world itself.

PIERCE:

Now I really don't follow you.

MARKINGS:

How about some more coffee?

PIERCE:

Yes, thank you. (Phil pours more coffee for both Lyman and himself.)

MARKINGS:

Someone once said that it's a mark of maturity to make distinctions. And the Bible tells us to become childlike. There's something interesting about the juxtaposition of those two ideas.

　　Let me give you an example. Someone you are speaking to calls someone else sanctimonious: "What a sanctimonious son of a bitch he is." What does that mean? "Sanctimonious" means something like "righteous indignation," and righteous indignation means puffing oneself up by putting someone else down. And so the person labeling the other as someone who puffs himself up by putting others down is puffing himself up by putting him down. "What a sanctimonious son of a bitch" said the sanctimonious son of a bitch. Or, "That man is self-righteous," said John self-righteously. And this is one of the consequences of our making distinctions. And it's also why we must not pass ourselves off as truth-sayers, but must do what we do aesthetically as well. Many self-reflective statements would be avoided if we tried to say things beautifully.

PIERCE:

Well, it sounds very interesting, but I'm not sure I know what you mean. But, if you don't mind my saying so, it seems to me that what you are doing is making distinctions. And that, I thought, is what you are railing against.

MARKINGS:

Exactly. And now you know why I don't care if people read my stuff or not. How could I possibly make a claim that somehow what I am doing is different from what others are doing? It isn't. And I know it. But others don't know it. And that means that I claim I know something they don't. And that's a contradiction too.

PIERCE:

Wow. No wonder your books are doing so well.

But you're not saying that what you are saying is just a bunch of words, perhaps said well, are you?

MARKINGS:

Why not?

PIERCE:

But where does that leave us?

MARKINGS:

Right where we were before? Or, where did you have in mind? Or, do we have to be left anywhere?

PIERCE:

I'm getting very depressed. I've got this overwhelming sense of . . . of being overwhelmed. I feel like I'm choking. (Looks at Phil but Phil doesn't say anything. They sit in silence for some moments.)

MARKINGS:

How about some more coffee?

PIERCE:

No thanks, I really ought to be going. I do hope, though, that you'll change your mind sometime.
(They both get up and walk toward the door.)

MARKINGS:

I change my mind all the time.

PIERCE:

I mean about this.

MARKINGS:

Yes, I know what you mean. Well, old friend, it was good seeing you. Come by again sometime. I seem to be especially good at depressing people—at least some people.

PIERCE:

Yes, well, you will think about this, won't you?

MARKINGS:

No, I won't, but thanks for your interest.

PIERCE:

(As Phil intends to show him to the front door.) Don't bother. I want to thank Betsey for the coffee anyway. Be seeing you.

MARKINGS:

Yeah, Good-bye.
(Phil comes back, puts the dishes together on the tray, and goes back to his desk. After he sits down, a "person" dressed in black comes in and sits down. This "person" is not a person at all, and Phil never looks at him, nor addresses his conversation to him physically.)

OGE:

Why do you depress people? You really did make Lyman feel quite uncomfortable, you know.

MARKINGS:

Because I think people ought to be depressed. If they're not close to depression then they're not very interesting.

OGE:

Now what in hell do you mean by that?

MARKINGS:

It's simple. People who aren't close to depression have no idea how precariously the world is put together. And those who think the world is "solid" are simply naïve. And naïve people really haven't much to say that's interesting.

OGE:

Hmm. But don't you find the gloominess overbearing?

MARKINGS:

Depressed people don't have to be gloomy, at least not all the time.

OGE:

Right, but when they're not gloomy they're not depressed—or else you're using words in funny ways.

MARKINGS:

Maybe. But I think one can be depressed and *not take everything seriously*. In fact one of the saving features of depressed people is their sense of humor about other people's problems. Just as long as they don't talk about their own problems they don't have to be gloomy. They can be quite playful.

OGE:

Most depressed people can't get involved in other people's problems.

MARKINGS:

That's right. That's why they can be playful. But don't get me wrong—I'm not saying that depressed people are automatically interesting. But those who have learned to be playful about other people's problems certainly are. To some people—like those who aren't depressed—they can be quite a pain in the neck. Most people want to be taken seriously. They don't want to joke about what they think is serious. But to another "depressed person" such repartee can pass the time quite interestingly.

OGE:

So you take it as your mission to depress people.

MARKINGS:

No, not really. I apparently do depress people because I make them aware of the precariousness of what they took for granted, of what they thought was solid. But I don't think of it as a "mission," no.

OGE:

Why do you do it, then?

MARKINGS:

I don't think that's a very interesting question.

OGE:

Oh?

MARKINGS:

To answer why is to provide an interpretation—that's fine, but you are now asking me to provide an interpretation of the reason I have a particular interpretation. That implies that the reasons I just gave can be explained—meaning, of course, *explained away*. And I won't be an accomplice to that.

OGE:

Very clever of you. (Long silence.)
    You obviously throw people off their guard when you do that.

MARKINGS:

Yes, I suppose I do.

OGE:

And you obviously "win," therefore.

MARKINGS:

Yes—I suppose that's true. But not with people who are already in the same state I'm in—only with those who feel no sense of precariousness.

OGE:

But there are lots of people like that.

MARKINGS:

In a sense we are all like that.

OGE:

What do you mean by that?

MARKINGS:

We all feel depressed sometimes. And we all feel the world to be solid sometimes.

OGE:

Do you like to win?

MARKINGS:

I'm not sure. I'm not even sure I would know how to find out. I find "losing," for example, very depressing and very stimulating. I get some of my best thoughts about people after I've lost.

OGE:

And how about after you've won?

MARKINGS:

After I've won I get somewhat stopped. I don't know what to do next. I seem to have no reason to do anything. I don't even care about the loser. But I rationalize all this in supposing that people are better off the earlier they develop a sense of precariousness. If it happens when one is too old, it can be very sad indeed. But I don't claim that's the *reason* I do it—just the way I excuse myself if I hurt someone.

OGE:

But don't you find yourself depressed most of the time?

MARKINGS:

Of course, but now you're trying to make me feel bad because being depressed is generally thought of as a bad thing.

Oge:

Well, isn't it?

Markings:

I've just been trying to give reasons why it isn't.

Oge:

Yes, but if you had your druthers I wonder if you'd really settle for depression.

Markings:

Any more of that kind of talk and you'll really make me feel depressed. (Laughs.)

Oge:

What do you think Lyman will do?

Markings:

I think he'll get over it in a couple of hours. People have a way of curing themselves. If it happened to him often enough that might be a different story.

Oge:

That strikes me as being dangerous.

Markings:

What does?

Oge:

Depressing people.

Markings:

You mean it could lead to suicide?

Oge:

It might.

Markings:

Life is more complicated than that.

Oge:

What do you mean?

MARKINGS:

> I mean there are lots of plausible interpretations of suicide. Placing the "blame" on someone is one way of explaining it.

OGE:

> So you wouldn't take responsibility.

MARKINGS:

> I sure wouldn't. I'm not that powerful.

OGE:

> You're not even a factor?

MARKINGS:

> We're all "factors" in something.

OGE:

> But we can avoid some of the more obvious.

MARKINGS:

> Can we? I wonder.
> (Betsey knocks and opens the door. The "person" in black gets up and quietly leaves the stage.)

BETSEY:

> I've made you some lunch, Mr. Markings, do you want me to bring it in here?

MARKINGS:

> Thank you, Betsey, that's lovely of you. No, I'll come to the kitchen. (She starts to leave.)
> Come on in a minute, Betsey, I'd like to talk about a couple of things.

BETSEY:

> All right. (Betsey comes back and Phil gets up and shows her to a chair.)

MARKINGS:

> First off, I'd like you to call me Phil. Seems a bit silly for me to

call you Betsey and you to call me Mr. Markings. Is Phil all right?

BETSEY:

(Somewhat puzzled.) I'll try.

MARKINGS:

Fine. Also, I want to double your salary. It seems I've just come into a lot of money. No reason why you shouldn't share in it too.

BETSEY:

Gracious me, Mr. Markings . . . I don't . . .

MARKINGS:

Phil—please.

BETSEY:

That's very generous of you.

MARKINGS:

Well, to tell you the truth, Betsey, I've become somewhat successful recently. And I have an idea that those who become successful should share their good fortune with the people around them. So, that's settled.

BETSEY:

You're very kind.

MARKINGS:

How about that lunch now?

BETSEY:

I'll set it out.

MARKINGS:

I'll come with you.
(Both exit. The curtain falls.)

8

Seeker's Apartment

This scene takes place in the Seekers' living room, two years after his first visit with Tellurian. The furniture is changed around, and the room is cluttered and messy. Duran is sitting at a desk with books, papers, and a typewriter. He is in slacks and an open shirt, unpressed and himself unkempt. Jean enters, quite cheerful. She is a working girl now, and her spirits are obviously up. She is well dressed.

JEAN:

Hello.

DURAN:

(Not looking up from his desk.) Hi.

JEAN:

(Takes off her coat and goes into the kitchen [offstage]. Duran is busy writing. After a minute Jean sticks her head out the door into the living room.)
Would you like a cup of tea?

DURAN:

(Without looking up.) Yes, that would be fine. (Jean ducks back into the kitchen and in a minute comes back in with a tray for tea. She hands a cup of tea to Duran with a tea bag in it. He does not immediately acknowledge it. Jean then pours herself a cup, takes it and sits. She begins to thumb through a magazine. Duran finally finishes what he is doing, glances at Jean, and picks up his tea.)

DURAN:

I wish you'd take the damn tea bag out. What the hell am I supposed to do with it? (Said as a man who has worked hard all day but has nothing to prove it—but he expects to be treated as someone significant. He takes the tea bag out and puts it in his saucer, then puts the cup on a book.)

JEAN:

Sorry, I keep forgetting. (Pause.) How did your writing go today?

DURAN:

Not bad. I finished revising act 2 of my play—and I had a good thinking session this morning.

JEAN:

Hinkle came in drunk again after lunch today. He's been doing that quite frequently. He's such a nice man, too. I wonder what's bothering him. The customers must wonder, too.

DURAN:

Oh, and I did manage to write a poem, today. Do you want to hear it? (Duran begins to rummage around on his desk, picks up a folder and pulls out the top paper.)

JEAN:

If you want to read it to me. (Without much enthusiasm, but enough to show it's false.)

DURAN:

(Reads the following poem, with great emphasis and meaning. When he reaches the end he breaks out laughing. Jean laughs too, only hers is an embarrassed laugh, as someone who hasn't quite seen the importance of it all.)

Oh How Exciting

Do we all ask the same questions?
And do we all reach the same answer?
Why do we ponder the ways of
Whatever-it-is?

The box is empty at the moment.
It need not be that way always.
People do put things in boxes—
Lots of things. But boxes are

Surprises only for those who
Don't expect them, or
Who, at any rate, underestimate
The chances they will get one.

A box has a top which one may
Lift up and peer under.
Assuming, of course, a crowbar is
Handy if it is nailed shut.

Who is it for? Who is it from?
What is in it? I can't wait.
Let me open it. Quickly, quickly.
Oh shit, it's only handkerchiefs.

DURAN:

I think that's pretty funny.

JEAN:

You know I have no sense of humor. (Pause.) It's kind of interesting, though.

DURAN:

(Looking at his poem again and chuckling.) Yes, well . . . I guess I'll put it away for awhile. That makes about thirty-five poems I've written. I wonder what I'm going to do with them.

JEAN:

Why don't you save them and put them in a book?

DURAN:

Yeah, maybe I will. Who knows? (Pause. Duran puts the poem away.)

JEAN:

Did you know that Carolyn is getting divorced?

DURAN:

Carolyn who?

JEAN:

You know, Carolyn Riley, the girl I have coffee with at work. Poor thing, her husband is off on trips most of the time and apparently has girl friends all over. Anyway, he came home the other night and announced he wasn't going to live with her any more and that he wanted a divorce. They have two young children, too. Just out of the blue. Said he really never has liked living with her. She was really crushed.

DURAN:

Sounds like a swell fellow.

JEAN:

The thing is, she gave up her college education for him. Worked to put him through school and still works to keep extra money coming in. She really doesn't make very much. God, I really hate men like that. Here he just ups and leaves, probably to marry some young thing who is just looking for a ready-made home—and she gets stuck with lonely nights. (Pause.)

DURAN:

Do you think I did the right thing? (Becoming very serious.) Some days, like today, it goes really well. But some days it doesn't go at all. And who's to know whether any of this stuff is any good?

JEAN:

I thought you didn't care.

DURAN:

> Well, I don't, I guess. But I have enough vanity to want to have people tell me that what I do is good. I keep telling myself that the important thing is that I like it—but some days I get awfully frightened. Like I was just sitting here turning out a pile of crap.

JEAN:

> (Getting a little testy.) Look, you said you wanted to try to do something interesting. So you quit work and here you are. I'll admit the last couple of years have been strange, but I've enjoyed getting back to work, and you're beginning to write now. What do you expect, to be a genius overnight?

DURAN:

> I don't believe in geniuses. Pope said something interesting about geniuses. He said a genius is what you call someone who is so good that you have to put him in a special class. Think how threatening it would be to believe that an ordinary human being could write *Crime and Punishment*. We make Dostoevsky a genius because we can't stand the comparison. Dostoevsky isn't human, he's superhuman. Well, I don't want to believe that. I don't want to protect myself by making someone else superhuman. Dostoevsky was tremendously creative—and so can we all be. At least that's what I've got to think. 'Cause if there is such a thing as a genius I know I'm not one. And then what chance do I have? (Long pause.) But Jesus, this not knowing. This having thoughts which are your very own, and wondering whether other people will find them as interesting as you do. I wish I could get something out.

JEAN:

> You worry about it too much. If you're going to do something then you'll do it. Would you rather go back to selling paper?

DURAN:

> Touché. But it just takes so long. And I don't know how much time I have left. I'm fifty years old now, and time is running out. And I don't have the stamina I had when I was a kid. I read in a magazine somewhere that there are two life processes, anabolism and catabolism—building up and wearing down.

Before twenty-five everything's great. But after twenty-five catabolism goes faster than anabolism, and it's all downhill.

JEAN:

God I hate that kind of talk. If you worry about something like that you can forget the important things. You're alive—you've found out you didn't like what you were doing so you changed. What more do you want? Some people never have what you have.

DURAN:

There's a quote from Montaigne that seems appropriate here: "To philosophize is to learn to die." I think Montaigne is saying that when you're young you can't be a philosopher. An activist, a propagandist, a liver of life, yes. Committed, passionate, impatient. But it's only when you know what death is that philosophy becomes possible. And I don't just mean to know that you're going to die in the sense that we learn that men are mortal. I mean to know in the sense of to *feel* it.

I also think Montaigne is saying that Philosophy is about the meaning of life and you can't know much about life until you know about death.

JEAN:

I don't agree. I think one lives life. I don't think you have to sit around and think about it. Life is doing, not feeling sorry for yourself because you're going to die. Haven't you anything better to do? (Jean bolts up and goes into the kitchen. Duran just sits where he is, staring at the wall. Eventually he lets out a sigh and goes back to writing.)

9

Seeker's Philosophical Notes

During the following few years Duran Seeker put together his own way of looking at things, which he called Philosophical Notes.

Meaning

Man is an ontological being: he must believe that something is the case, even if this means that he believes that nothing is the case—nothing is "something" as we are using the words here. And this, it seems to me, is the essential feature of man, the basis of his predicament, and the reason for his meaning-giving.

If one says that life has no meaning, could the person asserting the statement be giving meaning to his life? Life is obviously "meaningless." And that is just the point, isn't it? We give our life meaning in order that it be meaningful. It is in this sense that one might say: the meaning of life is to give meaninglessness meaning.

There is a very common way to handle the question "What does life mean?" which is not to think about it, to slough it off as uninteresting or even nonsensical. And indeed unless one is willing to become a philosopher he must either have an answer or ignore the question. To search is to be consumed.

If two fundamental questions concerning man are what is he and why is he doing what he is doing, when we answer these questions we give man meaning even when we appear not to and/or attempt to avoid doing so.

We might limit ourselves to the description of man and his activities, but it is not clear that we can do so successfully. But

177

even if we could in principle we would not do so. We want to know what these things mean.

Assuming that there are many ways in which we can give ourselves significance, and assuming that we cannot do all of them simultaneously, when we engage in one it may always be observed that we are doing so at the expense of others. And so we must learn to defend what we do as valuable—or else be subject to the feelings of emptiness which some others may be willing to impose upon us in playing out their own significance.

And from this comes a reason for conflict: its use as a source of significance as one defends his own sense of significance against those who are defending theirs. And what is noteworthy is that the parties can share the same way of gaining significance as they add the significance-giving of conflict to their own significance-giving ways. And we reach the conclusion that because of this potential for sharing, conflict may be popular.

Knowledge

To know that something is chaos is to know it in an orderly way. In order to impose order we need not see order—although to see order is certainly one way to impose it.

What kind of "knowledge" is man seeking when he seeks knowledge about man? Is the knowledge he seeks of the same kind as the knowledge he seeks about nature?

Man, by virtue of being able to raise ethical questions at all is caught in an ethical world. For even to deny ethics is to act in a way which can be judged ethically. Everything we do, and don't do, may have ethical significance.

Similarly man can be thought of as having a purpose or purposes. And to assign purposelessness to man is, in a way, to speak to the question of purpose itself.

It is easier to explain behavior than it is to describe it. And this is one of the reasons why our descriptions often contain explanations.

Similarly it is easier to evaluate behavior than it is to describe it. When called upon to describe what someone has done, therefore, we will often evaluate it.

And when asked for an explanation of behavior we often find the easiest answer to be an evaluation.

What we want to understand about human beings cannot, even in principle, be verified. It is not even a question of its being verifiable, although many people who adopt the paradigm of science for human analysis think so. It is a question of whether it seems right.

When we attempt to describe man's behavior we confront two difficulties: 1) the words we use as descriptions may also contain, implicitly or explicitly, explanations, in which case one would be doing more than "merely" describing; and 2) if we "merely" describe, especially at a level very close to what we see (for example, "his arm moved"), we are likely to be trivial. And the more we attempt to avoid the latter, for example, by describing with words "further away from" what we actually see, the more likely we are to do the former.

If I describe a person as going to the office, taking five drinks of water, etc., etc., one wants to know "so what?" Even if we could purely and simply describe behavior (without, for example, also interpreting it and evaluating it) we would not be satisfied—we would want to know why, what does it mean?

And this is why we do not "purely and simply" describe behavior.

It is also of interest to note that what these paragraphs say about others is also true of these paragraphs: that is, what the paragraphs "mean" and the reason for the paragraphs are the same thing. Put another way, the paragraphs are themselves an example of the meaning of the paragraphs.

What would it mean to describe? Clearly we cannot describe all of something—so we describe part. But what does that part mean? Clearly, again, it means what we say it means—and if we don't say, it will mean what people who read it think it means. Information is a form of ammunition; the battle, ceaselessly waged, is to give meanings to parts.

What is a difference between the statements "his arm moved" and "he moved his arm"? The first is "truer" than the second in the sense of being closer to what one sees. If one sees an arm move and one reports that he saw someone move his arm he is adding to what he "actually" saw. One does not, strictly speaking, "see" people move their arms. One sees arms move. "He moved his arm" might be an answer to "why did his arm move?" but in this case such an answer would be an interpretation of what one saw and not what one "in fact" saw.

To the extent, then, that we wish to describe behavior we should avoid words and sentences which ascribe "action" to others.

Some explanations of human behavior are in terms of the meanings which things have for people. And because we are meaning-makers our descriptions of these meanings give meaning.

Perspective

The world is as it is. There is nothing more to say. Unless, of course, one wants to say *what* it is. And to say what it is is to take on the task of saying what we do when we say what it is as well as to say what it is. And, presumably, we might also say what it is we do when we say what it is we do when we say what it is. The fact that this could go on for quite a while is a hint as to what it is we do when we say what the world is.

We need not assume that we can "know" everything in the same way that we know some things. It would be simpler if we could—and that is why it is so tempting to do so.

A "perspective" is a way of looking at things, a "point of view," an "outlook." It probably cannot be a very precise term and one could, presumably, discuss to boredom just what it "meant" or might mean.

People "have" perspectives in the following sense: when they analyze something they may be said to do so from a perspective. There may be disagreement about what precisely the perspective is, and how "coherent," "consistent," "logical," "useful," "important," "real," or "true" it is. There may also be disagreement over whether it is *the* perspective, or whether it is "complete."

And under these circumstances, and others, we come to "understand" the world.

To say that someone "has" a perspective is very frequently to be misleading. Explanations of human phenomena "imply" perspectives, a fragment of which has been expressed by the explainer.

The explainer may himself not be aware of the "logical" implications of what he is saying, or what he is "committed" to. Very often, then, when we say someone "has" a perspective we really mean that we have *given* him one.

If one assumes that *any* analysis which one gives for something is simply that, an analysis, then one can point out "weaknesses" in any such analysis and provide a different one to take its place.

Part of what is involved in our significance is to see things from our own point of view. And it is more important that some people disagree than it is that some people agree (more important because it is possible in some situations to want no one to agree). Hence we inevitably have a situation where people derive significance from not seeing things in the same way. And as long as this is the case we will not only always have people with different perspectives, but people will devise ways of insuring that different viewpoints are the rule.

To see something from a perspective is not so much to see things as simplified and/or distorted as it is to understand them from one point of view rather than from some other point of view. Even if one's perspective could include "everything" it would still be a perspective—to see things from all points of view is a point of view.

To conclude that another person has a way of looking at things (a perspective) is to put that person in perspective.

Explanation

In some perhaps mysterious way our significance is involved in our being "more than" a physical object—that we have meaning which goes beyond how we might be assessed biologically, chemically, and physically. When we ask why man does what he does we are asking more than why do stars do thus and so. The kind of answer which would satisfy us about the latter would be quite different than for the former. And for this reason we deceive ourselves when we believe "why" questions in human analysis are the same as they are in astronomy.

Let us illustrate how the question "why?" is different in the world of physical objects only, and the world of man.

If a man falls from the top of a tall building to the cement below, to answer the question: Why did he fall? with the law of gravity would be thought to be inadequate. We do not find it sufficient to speak of man as a physical object. "Why did he fall?" is meant to include: was he pushed, and if so, by whom and why? was it an accident and if so, how did it happen? did he jump and if so, why?

And one could "know" the answer—he obeyed the law of gravity—in a different way than he would "know" the answer: he jumped because he was despondent.

When we are asked to explain something we give a reason. And although some people might ask us to explain why we gave that particular reason, would anyone ask why we gave a reason at all?

It is not enough for us to describe what we see—we must give it meaning as well. We must say "why" an accident occurred. We must give reasons for dreaming. But there are no "real" answers for things like these. People can be more or less interesting, plausible, and/or persuasive. And these things have nothing whatsoever to do with "why" in the sense of "really."

Some people say that explanation is either "because of" or "in order to." The former is related to fate and determinism; the latter to intention and free will. But it turns out that each may be translated into the other. Does a person eat because he is hungry or in order to satisfy his hunger? Will a man seek a new position in order to advance himself or because he desires status? Clearly which mode one employs is a matter of style. But not merely a matter of style, as the choice may set a tone for one's whole mind. Each can become a separate perspective. And frequently this is the extent to which things are thought of as being different.

Often when we "describe" things we simultaneously explain them. For example, if we described an accident as "two cars collided" we might have been asked why they collided and answered "because the blue car ran into the red one." But we might just as easily, when asked "what happened?" have answered "the blue car ran into the red one."

Some words both describe and explain, simultaneously. For example, if I say that Johnny is "anal" I am saying that he acts in a manner which may be described as anal and that he does so because he has an anal personality. Being anal is both a description of behavior and an explanation for it. One might ask why someone is anal, but one need not ask why someone who is anal is behaving in the way that he is. His behavior (which is anal) is anal because he is anal.

And this is true of all words which are said to represent a generalized mental state. Mike's behavior may be called grumpy. What is Mike doing? He is being grumpy. Why is he doing what he is doing? Because he is grumpy (or because he is a grump).

Alice is a very clever girl. She does what she does (which we shall call clever) and she does it because she is clever.

When we use adjectives for people we characterize their whole person. John is intelligent (he is an intelligent person); Peter is angry (he is a person who is angry); Mary is pretty (she is a pretty person). It is possible for John to be intelligent sometimes and/or about some things but not necessarily always and/or about everything. And this is clearly the way "angry" is used. But when a person is angry, pretty, or intelligent he is so as a whole person at that time and/or as that thing. And this is why the words are both descriptions and explanations. An intelligent person does intelligent things because he is an intelligent person.

Truth

For most people truth is a certainty. The important thing, however, is hidden in a sentence of this kind, for it is not truth as a certainty but the *existence* of certainty which "really" dominates the sentence. That there is no truth is just as much a certainty as the reverse.

People who do not believe in "the truth," the way that is usually meant, will be difficult people with whom to deal for those who do believe. For if one is not searching for truth then what could he possibly be searching for?

Truth is the assumed standard against which people measure one another's "talk" when that talk is "serious." And if someone does not cooperate in this then how can he be taken seriously?

If one believes there is truth where there is none, then success will be closely tied to truth. Those who seek success will learn the "truth," and those who are revolted by the "truth" will attack the truth with truths of their own.

Those who do not believe in truth will see behind the glitter, and this path may lead to many things, including silence. In a world where assertions are assumed to be claims on truth it is difficult for nonbelievers to make assertions.

If in one's discipline there were no truths (other than obvious and trivial ones having to do with physical objects), then one might wish to promote the saying of interesting things. And if in one's discipline there were no truths, but one believed there were, then it is highly likely that in promoting truth-saying one would inhibit the saying of interesting things.

What would happen if we substituted the standard "interesting" for the standard "truth" in discussing human behavior? Presumably we would all agree that we could not agree on what "interesting" was. And the question is whether we would be better or worse off under these circumstances.

To say that something is "interesting" is to say that it is intellectually stimulating. If there were no "truth" of human behavior in the same sense of truth we use when we talk about physical objects, then what "errors" might we fall into and what might we be missing if we believed in truth?

When we say that someone is not serious we say that what he says should be given no, or little weight. Yet we would not also agree, abstractly, that things are true or false depending upon how they are said. We even have maxims to the effect that "there is much truth in jest," etc. In order to engage in truth-saying in any given situation we must act appropriately, a conclusion about which one can reason conclusively only after one finds that he himself is or isn't doing so.

If we do not believe in truth or falsity within certain kinds of realities, however, one can more readily see how people who believe in truth in realities in which we do not, substitute form for content in judging whether something should or should not be believed. In the absence of other clear-cut criteria, to act sincerely is evidence for the validity of what one is saying.

One can say some things about physical objects and be incorrect, but that is different than saying some things within another reality in which true or false in the same sense is not at issue. To be capable of being incorrect is an advantage in some ways. For one thing it means that one may speak straightforwardly, fearing only contradiction by the very reality about which one speaks.

Reality

What it means to say that something is true depends not only on what one is talking about but also in what reality what one is talking about is presumed to lie.

Since what we say "reality" is makes reality what it is (even if we say that reality is "out there"), there will be a minimum, irreducible reality in any given situation only if people agree to say so at any given time, in any given situation. And it will be so until someone changes his mind, unanimity is breached, and persuasion fails.

A most intriguing aspect of our analysis of human behavior is not that we fail to see *the* reality but that we think in terms of *a* reality at all.

Is there, in any given situation, an irreducible, minimum reality on which we can all agree? Part of the answer obviously lies with how perverse people are. But perhaps the "real" question is, is it not true that all of the answer lies there?

Man might be said to be an ontological animal—he sees things as real. A question, then: in what sense is it the case that what man sees as real is real in different ways?

The nature of "reality" is very complex—and this is partially because there is not one reality but many.
In order to understand human behavior we must understand what it means to understand. And part of this is to understand what is knowable and in what ways in the various realities.

It is confusing to speak of "facts" as though it doesn't make any difference whether what one is talking about "is."

"Dr. Jones is a good doctor" is a sentence of multiple realities. Different parts of it will be true or false in different ways.

When we say that a man has courage we are dealing with a concept which may be thought of as belonging to multiple realities, even simultaneously. For example, it could be argued that "courage" is a mental state (in the form of a "character trait"), a position in social reality (a member of a group of people called courageous), a term in formal reality (a good person on this sub-dimension), and a certain kind of behavior (anyone who behaves in the following way under the following circumstances will be called courageous).

Here again the determination of which reality discourse about courage will take place is itself of primary significance in defining, for any group of people, what courage is thought of as being.

If we are interested in explaining, or coming to grips with, or giving meaning to man's behavior, then man's behavior is the "reality" which serves as our "starting point." We can then "describe" it, "interpret" it, "evaluate" it (along several dimensions). We can do these things using *other* realities. And many of our difficulties lie in just this: that giving meaning is a multiple-reality enterprise. Meaning-giving is never simple.

Physical Objects

Can we explain why science is successful? Yes—what scientists talk about exists.

It is sometimes said by those who suggest that the science of physical objects should serve as a paradigm for the study of human behavior that the use of words in physics such as "gravity" and "force" shows that science uses concepts which are as "elusive" (or even "illusory") as some of those of social science (for example, "intelligence," or "ego"). And whether or not one wants to take this analogy seriously is partially determined by his position on the following question: Is the motion of physical objects qua physical objects to be considered the same as the behavior of animate objects? Clearly gravity is to motion as personality is to behavior. But if "motion" and "behavior" are not considered conceptually identical then neither should "gravity" and "personality" be. The concepts may perform equivalent functions *within* their own "realities," but if the realities are different (as I argue they are) then the "reality" of these concepts is different as well.

When one says that personality "accounts for" some part of the behavior of human beings, what one is saying is that performances of one kind or another (and, presumably, non-performances as well) are due to a mental state of one kind or another (and, interestingly, perhaps the lack of a particular mental state as well).

If one says that gravity "accounts for" some part of the motion of physical objects what one is saying is that a relationship between objects obtains.

The explanation of the behavior of two people with personalities is not the same as the explanation of the motion of two bodies with gravities. People are said to *have* personalities and the behavior is the consequence—objects are not said to have gravity with motion as a consequence.

Gravity is one of the relationships which exist among physical objects. It is not a physical object but it is "real." To say that gravity exists, however, is no license to say that therefore one may say ego, personality, and intelligence also exist in the same way. It turns out that one may say that these latter do exist, but when one does he is speaking quite differently.

The existence of gravity is no proof of the existence of other things one cannot directly see. Not being able to see intelligence may be one of the features "intelligence" has in common with "gravity," but it is only one, and it certainly says nothing about the difference.

Surely all the things that one cannot see are not the same.

"Gravity" is "really" there in a way different from "personality" being "really" there. That is, they are "real" in different senses. Gravity accounts for some part of the motion of physical objects— and it is said of personality that it accounts for some part of the behavior of human beings. And in this sense they are thought of as being functionally equivalent. But they are not the same in that not only are they not "completely" functionally equivalent (gravity "does" account for the motion of physical objects—personality does not account for the behavior of human beings so unarguably), but even if they were, gravity is a relationship between physical objects and personality is a mental state. It would be most peculiar to call mental states and physical object relationships identical. To describe a mental state is to try to construct a "structure" of the mind—gravity is not thought of as a structure.

There is no isomorphism for "gravity" as a concept in the explanation of human behavior. In fact, of course, people as physical objects do "exert" gravity itself. It just so happens that gravity is thought to be irrelevant in explaining human behavior.

Because two "things" are similar in some ways does not make them similar in general. Much discussion centers around comparison of parts as though such comparisons were of wholes.

For example, when one discusses whether social science is a "science," to counter the difficulty of doing social science with the difficulty of doing physical science, and thereby conclude that they are the same, is to commit a part-whole error.

Science and Man

Man has a "sense of himself" to which science can only be peripheral. The findings of science may affect man's sense of significance, but they will not *substitute* for it. For even those who may believe that all we are is what science tells us we are are deriving their significance from saying this. Man's significance may be thought of as an independent entity but may be connected with anything.

It is difficult to divorce man's significance from things like thunder and lightning, coal fields and forests, disasters and buffalo. We would like to think that natural phenomena are for our benefit —that what we do or what we are somehow causes or has caused them. Science proceeds under the assumption that this is not the case. And so we must be content with deriving significance from the *consequences* of naturally occurring events rather than from the fact that they happen at all. Births and rainbows may be admired, and human slaughter is not meant to teach us a lesson.

If we describe a mountain scientifically we are giving meaning to the mountain, but this is not the same meaning of "meaning" as when we say that when we write a poem about a mountain we are giving meaning to the mountain. In the latter sense we also mean that the mountain is giving us meaning as human beings; in the former sense to say the mountain is giving us meaning is not meaningful. In science, mountains give information—they do not give meaning. Some people need not find meaning in mountains in the nonscientific sense. But this is simply to say that not everyone finds everything equally meaningful. And some may find that through scientific description one is given meaning. And in this sense science can be like poetry.

There are probably very few poets who are not meaning-givers. There are many scientists who are not. Many take meaning from *being* a scientist, but not from the things they study. Science is both a human activity and a study of physical objects and their movements. And as the latter it may be different than as the former.

When we speak of "science" we mean, generally, the study of physical objects. The study of man, then, can be "scientific" to the extent to which such a study is concerned with man's "physical objectness." If we wanted to study a stone we probably wouldn't say, "but what more is it in addition to its being a physical object?" Clearly we are not so confined when we study man.

The study of man can be "scientific," then, up to the point of describing man's material nature (chemical, physical, and biological). And one can always say, "But there is more to man than that."

As an example of the way in which man's sense of his own significance and his ability to be scientific are related, if man believes that he is a result of special creation, the scientific study of man as an evolved species is impeded. If scientists themselves believed in special creation, then evolutionary theory would at best be an underground movement. The progress of science has been related to the withdrawal of man's significance from more and more topics. Since man seems flexible enough to gain significance from feelings of insignificance, however, science, rather than having narrowed philosophical discourse, has merely guided its content.

Science is facilitated when man's significance is disengaged from the topics which it studies. If man feels that he himself is threatened if certain lines of inquiry are pursued, he will adopt means of obstruction and sabotage. One could, presumably, learn a good deal about man as a physical object were man not so involved in his *own* significance. For this reason man has barred most potentially dangerous, painful, and/or cruel experimental treatments of man from scientific inquiry, although often investigations are conducted in ongoing, "natural" dangerous, painful, and/or cruel situations such as wars, accidents, man's everyday inhumanities toward his fellowman, and other circumstances when the treatments are justified on other grounds, or possibly in medical situations when such treatments, although contrived, are viewed as part of the cure.

There is no particular advantage, at least to scientists, in referring to some stars as "bad," or to call some storms "crazy," or to put some insects down. And words used in these discussions can usually remain relatively unattached to the problems of human significance. It is all the same to a scientist that electrons have a small mass. And when it does matter to scientists (as it might if a hypothesis is about to be overthrown) the resulting human conflict might not be recognizably unlike conflicts in everyday life. But we do have a stake in what we call people—all people, and all of the time. And for this reason our "people" words are fraught with meanings. And so it will always be.

It is neither good nor bad to be an electron—that's not what we want to know about them. But to say that one does not want to know good or bad about people is to be a person who has taken a good or bad position from one's own and others' eyes.

If one says that something is like something else, this does not mean that it *is* that thing. To argue that physical science should be the paradigm for social science should not be construed to mean that they are "the same thing." I would argue, incidentally, that the science of physical objects not be the paradigm for human behavior—but this is not to say that if one suggested that it should be that one had to argue that the contents of the two domains are even conceptually the same. To the extent that science is a method of thinking and bringing evidence to bear on one's assertions it can be kept distinct from the contents of the things being studied. If one applies scientific reasoning to human behavior it should not commit one to believing that the things talked about in physical science are identical in nature to the things talked about in social science.

Human behavior is not more complex than chemistry. It's just that the latter is basically understandable and the former is not, in the usual sense in which we understand "understandable." We do not, then, simplify when we speak of human beings. Rather, we literally do not know of what we speak. For example, one might describe a dream and someone might say "but what does the dream mean?" But if someone described a tree one would not say "but what does the tree mean?" unless, of course, the tree being described were a dream tree.

One can understand how scientists, in order to distinguish themselves from others, might spend a lifetime describing a corner of reality. And one can understand how human analysts, for similar reasons, might spend their time saying things about human behavior. One can even understand how human analysts can describe human reality in the same way that physical scientists describe physical reality. And if one understands all of these things there are few places he can go, save creativity.

Behavior

Science is concerned with describing the structure and movement of physical objects. Movement may be of three kinds, motion, life processes, and behavior. Inanimate objects have structure and may have motion; animate objects have structure and may have motion, life processes, and behavior. Physics can tell us about structure and motion—chemistry and biology about structure and life processes. The question is, assuming that biology and botany will tell us about the behavior of plants and nonhuman animals, who is to tell us about the behavior of human beings?

A physical object "has" motion. Does a person "have" behavior?

We may say, with equal ease, the boy's arm moved or the boy moved his arm (although the latter is not identical with the former) ; we do not say, with equal ease, the comet's tail moved or the comet moved its tail.

We speak of the motion of physical objects passively. Animate objects may have motion—but they may also *do* behavior.

Some physical objects have structure, motion, life processes, and behavior. To some extent each of these may be discussed separately from the others. Just because a physical object has structure, say, and behavior, does not mean that the way in which its structure is studied is also appropriate to its behavior.

Certain products of man are both physical objects and examples of his behavior. It is useful to know when we are speaking of man's behavior as a physical object, and when we are speaking of the physical object as man's behavior.

Those behaviors in nonhuman animals which we are not able to account for physically (such as homing in pigeons) we continue to see as mysteries. But most behaviors in humans we do not even try to account for physically.

When one describes the structure or motion of a physical object the amount of description which is "required" is very small. And, as one talks about it, as one "explains" it (in the "how" sense of further description) it can become progressively more complicated.
And we also try to do this with people and their behavior. The difficulty, however, is that we have no "simple" descriptions of what people do. The explanations become complicated, but in a different sense. In science, explanation is description elaborated. It is *continuous with* the original description. In human behavior there is a "break" between description and explanation. What is being described and then explained is not continuous. It is actually "easier" to give a "meaningful" explanation than it is to give a meaningful description in human behavior. This assertion would not even make any sense in science.

In science when we explain something we describe it further and/or we tell how it works; in human behavior when we explain something we tell why someone did or did not do something. Explanation in human behavior is meaning-giving.

If there is a difference between the process of doing something and the content of what is done, then to say one is "objective" because he is not talking about content is as dubious as saying that one is subjective because he is not dealing with process. The "laws" of human behavior as process are not less interpretive because they are meant to be applied to any content. In fact, even such an assumption, that is, that process is invariant, is clearly an interpretation.

We can try to describe the behavior of man with a minimum amount of meaning-making, but only if we are primarily interested in the physical objectness of man. Interest in man's behavior as behavior opens a whole new world.

We have a stake in the earth being at the center of the solar system—galaxy—universe only if we believe that to be at the center gives us significance. Think, for example, how startling it would be if we "really" were at the center of the universe (whatever that might mean, especially if the universe is viewed as being infinite). Human beings are capable of "seeing" all kinds of signs of their election.

But humans also believe in their own significance, if only to make themselves significant by calling themselves insignificant in relation to God, the universe, or nothing at all. To study human behavior as though the question of significance does not exist is to try to separate from the study of man that which makes man man.

One of the things from which we infer structure, process, and content of thought is behavior. But to infer a structure of behavior from behavior is not the same thing as inferring a structure of thought from behavior.

We must stop asking ourselves why people do things if we wish to know about the structure of behavior.

Mind

All discussion of mind processes (but not necessarily mind phenomena) is pure speculation.

We could take the position that thought does not exist, but if we did, it would make it impossible to talk about "it" at all. Interestingly we couldn't say "thought does not exist" without stating a paradox in which we would have to assume that "it" exists both as something that we could then say wasn't and as something which contradicts itself. The former is illustrated by: if "thought does not exist" says that "thought" does not exist, then is "thought" like a unicorn? Clearly not, but "unicorn" appears to be a certain kind of thought. But what kind of thought is "thought"? The latter is illustrated by asking: is "thought does not exist" itself a thought?

It looks, then, as least by some criterion of "exist," that we might *have to* assume that thought exists. But if we do, what do we mean? If we assume the statement "I have thoughts" is meaningful, what is "thought" so that it can be said to exist?

Thought exists, and if it exists it is real—it's just that it is not real as a physical object is real. We can treat some manifestations of thought as having physical objectness, for example, speech and words, although not all of what we mean by them is as physical objects. But we can also think to ourselves. And when we do, or when we are interested in the nonphysical object properties of thought, what exists when one says he is thinking?

The problem is what words "stand for" or "represent," not only specifically but in terms of a class of things that one might claim represents a reality in which one can then say that something exists. The word "true" may stand for the existence of a physical object; the word "unicorn" stands for an idea of a physical object that doesn't exist as a physical object; the word "thought" stands for something that is not even an idea of a physical object; and the words "stand for" stand for " 'represent' in the same way as '2 + 2' stands for '4.' " If we can call a tree a physical object, what can we call a thought, besides a nonphysical object. It is common to call such things "ideas." A "thought" represents an idea, which is what nonphysical objects are when we speak about them as existing. Except that "thought" represents "idea" as "2 + 2" stands for "4," or as "represent" stands for "stands for," and in the same sense that in talking about what anything is we must use other words with which to talk about what it is in ways which assume, for some purposes, that those words are already understood. This does not mean that we cannot talk about them further for other purposes. Words might be assumed as "primitive" in some situations but not in others. "Thought" and "idea" are equivalent in the sense that "I have a thought" and "I have an idea" are equivalent. And both stand for nonphysical reality.

If thought is a reality, how do we talk about it? The answer is that we talk about it in many different ways—and the answer is also that we will never "really" know what the reality is, not in the sense that we don't know thought is a reality, but that we will never know its "structure." And to say this is different than saying we will never know what physical reality is. Clearly we will never know everything about physical reality. But we can know "enough" about some parts of it; and we can know in the sense of "really" know. And both of these are also true of thought only if we think so (as we do in our everyday lives). And this is to mark off two peculiarities of the subject of thought: what is "true" of it is what we are willing to see it as; and what we think about it is the same thing as it. It takes thought to deal with thought. We use what we think to talk about what we think. Thoughts about thoughts are thoughts, "data" in the same way that the original thoughts are data. Unlike words like "true," we have no independent check against our thoughts about thoughts, except, of course, as speech and writing have physical-object properties.

We do have thoughts. And to the extent that we are interested in the reality of thought as separate from the reality of physical objects, we are left with the problem of dealing with a reality which lacks the "usual" (that is, physical science) criteria of organization. And the way we solve this problem is to assign meaning to thought. We want to know not so much what the thoughts we or others are having are, but what they are in the sense of what "having them" means. When we "describe" our thoughts we talk about them in terms of their meaning—either as already implied or interpreted by us or as analyzable by someone else. But the meaning of thoughts is the meaning we give to them with other thoughts. And in this way the "reality" of thought is constructed. If we describe a tree it does not "mean" anything in this sense. Nor are we compelled to ask what a "tree" means. And if we do ask what a tree means we are no longer studying its physical objectness.

When we study the mind we make plausible interpretations, which is not the same thing that science does. Science checks its descriptions against a physical world. We check our descriptions against a description. The mind is already a fiction which the "mind" has invented.

The mind devises its own structure and a description of its own processes.

A physical object may have motion. Can thought have motion? Perhaps, but how would we know and, perhaps more basically, what would it mean? We could say thought had motion if we wanted to. And of how many other things about thought is that also true?

A physical object has structure—in fact several structures. Does thought have structure?

Thinking is "the process" of having thoughts, always remembering, of course, that to call it a process is to give it meaning. Thinking is also something we think we do. We think that during our "process" of thinking we have thoughts. And if we think this, that itself is a thought. And if we write that thought down it is behavior, and in some ways a physical object, which means what others think it means.

So we don't really think out loud. We are undoubtedly doing something in our heads, and we are also saying things and behaving, changing, embellishing, etc., as we respond to ourselves and others. But in lots of ways we are "thinking" about behavior as well as what, presumably, our thoughts are about. Equally as clearly we are responding to thought as behavior by others in the guise of responding to thought. People have conversations, thoughts don't.

We have thoughts, but when we say them the thoughts are also behavior. And one of the shadows in which we all lurk is to act as if this were not the case. We want our sayings or writings "to speak for themselves." But we give meanings to the "thoughts" (thought as behavior) of others with our own thoughts. And we ourselves behave by telling our "thoughts," which are not necessarily the thoughts we "really" have but which even if they were would still be behavior. Our telling and our thoughts are not the same things.

Behavior is characteristic of some animate physical objects, including people. Thought may be viewed in many different ways, one of which is as behavior. But as behavior it is most peculiar— only the person doing it knows he is. And the problem is complicated by the fact that people also look at behavior as a consequence of thought. But, strictly speaking, thought does not behave, people do.

Writing and speech are thought of as being thought. It might be more useful to think of them as behaviors which people do. But writing and speech also have physical object properties, and one may describe these properties. One may then infer that a description of these properties is also a description of thought. This assumes that such behavior is thought itself, or at least that thought behaves. Intelligence tests, poems, and the like are in part physical objects themselves, and behaviors of physical objects. They are, at best, manifestations of thought.

One might argue that when someone says a thought that the thought says something (or is said not to say anything). But to say a thought is to behave—and what the behavior "means" is what others think it means. And for this reason we can try to pretend. One way to pretend is to behave in a way which is calculated to have a desired effect. And usually we can tell whether it does or not since the desired effect is often expressed in terms of some behavior by others. It is only when we want to change "thoughts" that it makes no sense to speak about "desired effects."

If someone describes someone else's thoughts to others, he is telling others through his own behavior what someone else's behavior means to him. And this will be given meaning by the others.

Feeling

Feeling, like thought, is a reality *in* a person. A person alone "knows" his feelings. And, in a sense, even he knows "them" in a very limited way—it is never clear, for example, just what "them" consists of. How many feelings do we have? What are appropriate names for "them"?

Others may infer feeling states in us—inferences based on how we look, how we act, and on what we say. And it is certainly no less difficult for others to "label" our feelings than for us to do so.

I think we may reduce feelings to two fundamental kinds: comic and tragic. All other "types" are labels which fall into either one or the other of these two. We may feel either that we are (more or less) triumphant, or (more or less) overcome.

All feeling is a form of stimulation: in this sense both comedy and tragedy are stimulating.

When I "feel" hunger what do I feel? I feel a general sense of uneasiness, but is this hunger? When I eat it may go away, but was it hunger? It was a general sense of uneasiness that went away when I ate. If it hadn't gone away could it still have been hunger? Does hunger mean food deprivation, or a feeling? Or does it mean a feeling brought about by food deprivation? Can one feel hungry when one "knows" he is not? We can "know" we feel uneasy with a good deal more precision than we can know our uneasiness is hunger.

Part of the difficulty in identifying the sources of feelings is that we are likely to have many sources operating at the same time.

We must distinguish between feeling and the supposed source of a feeling. We say we feel hunger when we believe our uneasiness is caused by hunger. There is no reason to believe that hunger uneasiness is any different as a feeling of uneasiness than any other uneasiness.
Uneasiness is uneasiness, no matter what the source.

If someone says, "I am hungry," there are, then, two questions involved. First the person says that he has a feeling, and second he identifies his feeling as hunger. Whether or not he has a feeling will always be unknown except to the sayer. Whether or not the "feeling" is "hunger" anyone can argue about.

A good part of the time we are all in an apparent state of unfeeling—that is, relative to great feelings of uneasiness and satisfaction we are somewhere in between. Most of us play the game of identifying small changes from unfeeling as having the property of what we think has "caused" the change.

When we feel stimulated it is tempting, given man's ontological nature, to identify the "name" for the stimulation. This may involve us, at least some of the time, in suggesting what we think are inappropriate labels for feelings, the "source" of which is unclear. We have a tendency to think that feeling-states are caused, usually by a single source. What occurs is that we feel stimulated and then assign a cause. Whether we are right or wrong in our reasoning is separate from whether or not we feel stimulated. This is not to deny that it is possible to look at feeling states as caused by "situations." It is, however, to raise the possibility of difficulty in "knowing" what the "cause" might be. Knowing a cause and knowing that one is stimulated are not identical.

It is difficult to speak of feelings for another reason. We ourselves can "know" whether the way we feel is positive or negative, uneasy or satisfactory, tragic or comic, but what of the possibility of others believing, for example, that we *enjoy* negative feelings? Clearly we may get positive feelings from things which look negative to others—but can we feel positive about negative feelings? No, by definition. But we all harbor thoughts of this kind about other people.

I can "know" I feel, and I can think I feel a particular, labeled feeling, such as love, hunger, pain, joy, sadness. The former is a feeling—the latter a thought. When I "feel" a feeling I am feeling. When I think I have such-and-such a feeling I am thinking a thought about a feeling.

I can say I feel, and I can say that feelings are fundamentally of two sorts, and clearly these are thoughts as well. A feeling is a feeling, and a thought about a feeling is a thought about a feeling.

Feelings are neither true nor false. They either are or aren't. Statements about feelings are said to be true if the speaker and the hearer agree that a stated feeling should be called a such-and-such.

Constructed Reality

There are some things which are "something" regardless of what we call them, and regardless of whether or not we call them anything, for example, a tree. But there are some things which are something because we say they are and would not be anything if we did not say so, for example, anal personality. And those things which are of the latter type are what I will call "constructed reality."

Realities

1. Experiential Realities
   A. External
      1. physical reality
         a. structure
         b. movement
   B. Internal
      1. thought
      2. feeling
2. Constructed Realities
   A. Representative
      1. mental states
      2. emotion states

B. Devised
   1. social reality
   2. formal reality
      a. goodness
      b. beauty
      c. truth

Constructed realities are "devices" we use to give meaning to things. We *take* meaning from physical reality, feeling and thought, or, perhaps more simply, physical reality, thought, and feeling are what is "there." We then construct other "realities" to give meaning to physical reality, thought, and feeling.

Social Reality

What we name people in social reality modifies them, and in this sense: if before we call someone something he may be described as a person, then what we name him modifies him as a person. To call someone a plumber, or Ph.D., or insurance man gives him a meaning different from "person." And this, in a sense, is what is meant by social reality: when people are thought of as credentialed we actually believe them to be an "X," whatever that X might be.

The world does not come populated with things called Ph.D.'s, as it does come populated with things called trees. "People" made Ph.D.'s and, if "they" wanted to, could do away with the category. Although we might say "X is a Ph.D.," people are not Ph.D.'s, they "have" Ph.D.'s, and they are "called" Ph.D.'s, and when asked to "prove" it they may refer to a document received from a Ph.D. granting institution. But the document is not a Ph.D. in the same way that a "tree" is a tree. The document, which has physical object properties, confers what may loosely be called "status," but is not itself a Ph.D. For example, if one "had" a tree presumably he could give it to someone else. If one has a Ph.D., he does not have it in this same way. Ph.D.'s exist because "society" created them. And this is what I will mean by "social reality," a type of constructed reality.

One can tell whether a tree is "real" by examining the tree now. One could not do the same with any socially constructed reality (like a Ph.D.). "Obviously" (in a sense), with the latter one must reconstruct the construction.

Ph.D. does not designate anything *inherently*. There is no Ph.D.ness. Trees do designate something inherently; it does make sense to talk about something one could call treeness. For this reason, paradoxically in some ways (or at least surprisingly), when one says a person is a Ph.D. one has modified person in a much different sense than elm modifies tree. To be elmlike is "clear." To be a tree is also "clear." Each designates something independent of the other. To be a person is like being a tree. To be a Ph.D. is not like being an elm. Ph.D. has no distinct properties. People may think it *means* something, but it "really" doesn't. And, interestingly, because it doesn't designate anything independently, it is presumed to modify person in a *major* way. Elm trees are expected to be different from non-elm trees, but trees are trees. Ph.D. people are expected to be different from non-Ph.D. people because people aren't people when modified by a term which is not inherently anything.

To know whether someone is "really" a Ph.D. one would have to know whether he "actually" received a degree, and whether that degree is still considered legitimate, that is, one had not had it revoked because it was given, say, under false pretenses. One could "be" a Ph.D. and have that status taken away. And it is not that it was not clear at first whether a person was a Ph.D. or not—one could actually be declared one in the most legitimate circumstances and later have that status revoked. Could a tree, which was a typical maple tree, be declared not a maple tree because it had violated a rule along the way? And if one answers that a person who violates a rule "really" isn't a Ph.D., how do we know that those with Ph.D.'s might not inadvertently have violated a rule and therefore aren't really what they think they are and what we think they are? And could *this* be true of trees?

There are some things which we "are" because we are credentialed to be. Yet we would have no way of knowing other than knowing about the credential. Anyone may do what a Ph.D. does, yet not "be" a Ph.D. And anyone may do plumbing without being a plumber. Conversely one may "be" a credentialed thing and not do it. Ph.D.'s need not do what Ph.D.'s do. Plumbers need not plumb. And so with credentials there is nothing which "exists" except a sense of legitimacy.

To be a father is not the same thing as to be a Ph.D. A person is a father in the sense of "really." There is a person, X, such that the sperm of X fertilized the egg of Y producing a child for whom X is the father, regardless of his later behavior and even if someone else plays the "father role" (and in these two respects "fathers" and "Ph.D.'s" are similar). It is not, as with Ph.D.'s, a question of legitimacy, but a question of a physical object sort. One can "really" be a Ph.D. and have it "really" rescinded. One cannot be "really" a father and have it rescinded "really." If one thought that "father" were like "Ph.D." then one would also think that the label "father" could be rescinded "really." And the point is that what can be done "really" depends upon what reality one is talking about.

There are terms like "father" which have many things in common with social reality except the underlying reality. I will call these "physical members" of social reality. A claim to be a father rests, "ultimately," on physical reality, not legitimacy. A father is he whose sperm fertilized the egg.

One would find, however, that in reconstructing whether someone were "really" a father one would normally accept the evidence of social reality (that is, legitimacy) as satisfying the meaning of "really." A birth certificate, for example, would be equivalent to a diploma for a Ph.D. A doctor and/or hospital would be the credentialing agent rather than a university as with Ph.D.

Nevertheless one can "really" be a father in a way different from really being a Ph.D. With the latter, for example, one is "really" a Ph.D. if it is found that one is legitimately credentialed. One is "really" a father, however, only in a socially constructed sense when one finds out about credentials. One can still be in error in the physical sense. And this is not true of Ph.D. And second, one can have the social reality aspects of fatherhood rescinded but not the physical. If one is the father in a physical sense he will always be in a physical sense. This also is not the case with Ph.D.

There are some things we designate people as in social reality which more completely modify the person than do other designations. At one extreme are those credentials which, if given to a person, practically exclude seeing that person in any other way. Illustrations come from both highly credited and highly discredited credentials, for example, priest and criminal. These credentials tend to be so "meaningful" that a person who "is" one is seen as *nothing but* one.

Social reality is made "believable" in two ways: by attaching to it physical objects; and by performing "appropriate" behavior.

Social reality has physical objectness—a Ph.D., for example, is also a person. But there are often physical surroundings and technological instrumentations as well which might be said to "harden" social reality. A Ph.D. in a university classroom presents something like the following "believability" situation: "a Ph.D. must be something, or else why would we have these buildings and facilities?" Similarly a doctor is "really real" in a hospital with a stethoscope around his neck.

Costume may also be considered as part of the physical objectness of social reality. A television repairman in a uniform with "T.V. Repairman" printed on the back "must be" a television repairman. When one walks into a doctor's office, if one sees a man in a white coat in an inner office he is likely to be "the doctor." A policeman in a uniform is more recognizable as what he "is," although the costume is clearly not the definition of what a policeman is. The credential is the definition. Uniforms and markings are ways in which those with credentials announce themselves as persons to be taken as those who are to be considered legitimately what they present themselves to be. And obviously to the extent that anyone can wear a uniform there may be possibilities for those who would not be considered legitimate, if it were possible to find out, to look exactly like those who would be.

Some costumes are more complete than others in making it clear who the person wearing the costume "is." A person dressed as a "clown" is likely to be thought of as a clown. A person dressed in a business suit, with white shirt and tie, leaves open a larger number of possibilities, although "Australian aborigine" is not likely to be among them.

Dress, then, becomes a way of limiting alternative descriptions of who one is.

Props are less complete than costumes. A cigarette describes very little about what a person is—a mustache perhaps more. Most props are designed for mental reality rather than social reality.

Social reality is also made "believable" by behavior. Credentialed positions have routines to be performed. One can, "obviously," learn the performances and do them and not "be" what someone doing the performances as "one" is called. A person may even try to pass on the basis of performing like one.

These possibilities in constructing "false" identities are made available by the very nature of social reality, that is, that it itself is a construction. To construct "falsely," then, is to pretend *illegitimately.*

Occasionally we may find ourselves questioning the credentials of someone on the basis of behavior which we consider to be inappropriate for a person who is apparently an X to be performing when, given what insiders know, the behavior is unexceptional. And one possible consequence of this is that those who "are" legitimately X's may have to engage in behavior under "true" pretenses.

To say that a man is "courageous" may be to give him a position in social reality, the credential for which is some past performance which becomes recognized by someone as warranting the label "courageous." This may then be validated by institutions and/ or social agencies (for example, the army, or news media). Like other labels in social reality, because the label exists on the basis of people giving it legitimacy, it may be revoked. And, because there is no specific position in society for courageous people (although courageous people might, for example, receive requests to be bodyguards) over time people may forget. One might then be confronted with the following situation. On meeting a person whom one knew had been cited for courage, but having forgotten, one might, on being reminded, say: "Oh, I'm sorry, I forgot you are courageous." One might even think of asking, "are you still courageous?"

Mental States

A second type of constructed reality I will call "mental states." This reality is derived from our inability to escape treating thought in terms of thought. Written and spoken words have some physical-object properties, but thought "in the mind" is known only to ourselves and only as thought. Yet we are compelled to understand why people do what they do, and why they are what they are, and we find it useful to discuss people's mental states. It is these constructions which constitute the "reality" of mental states.

What can we "know" about human behavior without talking about mental states? To the extent that we do not want to know everything we can say some things without reference to mental states. But in another sense this question is beside the point. We must talk about mental states because we "know" they are important, and we "know" that we have "thought," and that "thought" is real. To ignore mental states, then, would be to refuse to take into account something we know is "there." On the other hand just because we know it is there and must take it into account doesn't mean that when we do we will be doing anything else than being inventive and creative. Let us not presume that because we take it into account we do so for any other reason than to try to be plausible.

When we speak about mental states we "describe" what we think is "true" about a "reality" which lurks underneath what we see "naturally." And in this sense the procedure is no different from that in science. Except that what lies underneath in the reality of mental states is not a physical object nor the property of a physical object. And this is not true of science. Clearly we "make up" mental states and talk about them as though they were real. But to be real in mental states is not the same thing as to be real in science.

We do know that thought exists. The reality basis of mental states rests on this. But because we know thought exists does not mean that what we say about it exists (except in the sense in which we have already discussed thought as existing). Thought exists in a sense that we can not "know" about "it" in the same way that we know about other realities. The construction of a "reality" of "mental states" obviates this "difficulty." With our thoughts we construct thoughts about what thought "is," what it is "meant" to "be."

The designations we make in the reality of mental states are what I will call "heterogeneous distinctions": they are not "universally" believed in, and if they are believed in by any given group of people there will still be disagreement as to whom the designation applies. (This is in contrast to social reality where the designations do tend to be universally believed in, a factor intimately involved with the possibility of passing. We might call these "homogeneous distinctions.") For example, "intelligence" is a term which most people (who are acquainted with the term) believe "exists," but there is no strong agreement as to whom it applies. "Anal" is a word for which there is less agreement that it "exists," and also disagreement as to whom it applies among those who agree it exists. Ph.D. is homogeneous in the sense that, among those who know the term it is universally agreed to exist, and there would be (for all practical purposes) universal agreement about who is one and who isn't.

One would not say "I believe in Ph.D.'s," although one might quite commonly hear "I believe in Freudian psychology." And the difference is not that people do not believe in Ph.D.'s. It's just that it isn't necessary to say "I believe in Ph.D.'s." Who doesn't? But there are people, many people, who might say, "I do not believe in Freudian psychology." When one professes belief in something, it makes sense only if there is some question as to whether what one professes belief in is "real."

If you say someone is authoritarian, and you ask why he is, it is obviously presumed that when you say he is he "in fact" is, as though if you say that something is a mountain and you ask why it is a mountain that it is in fact a mountain, that that is the same thing. And of course it isn't. Mountains *are* mountains. But authoritarians are not authoritarians.

To say that a person committed suicide because he was despondent is to assign a frame of mind from which one of the possible behavior alternatives is suicide. That a person could commit suicide without being despondent is not necessarily a contradiction—but it would probably require special explanation. "Despondent" means to be in a "frame of mind" in which one feels pain and hopelessness. An act of self-destruction makes more sense from that state of mind than from one of joy and promise.

People who are thought of as being intelligent are expected to act intelligently. What constitutes such behavior varies somewhat with what people themselves are willing to evaluate as intelligent behavior, but the category of intelligence is "hardened" by such physical reality evidence as report cards, grades, tests, evaluations, and the like.

Most inferred mental states are simply congruent with behavior "descriptions" (interpretations). An intelligent person is someone who does intelligent things—a rigid person is someone who does rigid things, an authoritarian personality is someone who presumably behaves "authoritarianly." Hence most statements about mental states, especially in "everyday language," are redundant.

There is no reason why the structure of behavior we find on the "outside" should have anything to do with the "structure" and/or "processes" of thought we infer to take place on the "inside." Properties of the product need not be properties of the producer. In fact, on most other matters, we would not make such an inference. Why do we do so with thought and behavior? Presumably when the producer isn't "seeable" it is a parsimonious method of description.

In the absence of other criteria, discussion of what the mind is and how it works might be evaluated on the basis of how "interesting" it is.

To say that something is true in the reality of mental states is to be "dogmatic-because-one-misses-the-point." To say one isn't sure whether what one says is true or not is to be inappropriately tentative.

To "get the point" is not so much to avoid speaking about such matters, because in some senses we cannot, but to "know" that why we speak that way is a problem.

Once we "understand" a person's mental state we can then talk about the person in terms of what can be said about the mental state. And this, in effect, *changes the topic of conversation*. We no longer talk about the person—we talk about what we have called the person. And in doing so we think we know and understand.

When we assign mental states to people we give people or their behavior meaning—it is one of the ways we come to "understand" why people do what they do and are what they are. And in this way we satisfy our own need for meaningfulness. We give meaning in order to get meaning.

In a sense to evaluate something and to assert that something is the case in the reality of mental states is the same thing. Very few words about mental states do not also have evaluative connotations.

To be an authoritarian is not generally thought to be good; to be permissive, however, may not be good either. To be understanding or intelligent are good things to most. And I have a feeling that if given his druthers a person would not want to be an anal personality, although he might be willing to attach that label to someone else.

One attributes mental states to people—such gifts are gratuitous, acts not only of generosity or spite, but of simplification.

Social Reality and Mental States

Both social reality and mental states are constructed realities, but they are constructed differently and they have different properties. Social reality is defined in terms of the presumed legitimacy of a label. Performance is an expectation of a label, but it is not the definition of it. For example, anyone who knew how could take out an appendix, although those who do are usually presumed to be doctors. Also, one could be a doctor without doing any of the things doctors are usually thought of as doing. But in mental states performance, rather than what a credentialed someone might do, is the criterion one uses to make the inference about the existence of the mental state itself. If one performs intelligently he is usually considered to be intelligent.

One would not argue that "Ph.D." does not mean that one has a degree, and that it really means something else. But one can argue that intelligence means something other than a score on an intelligence test.

If one is described as being an anal personality it is not normal to ask: "but is he a good or bad anal personality?" But if one is described as a doctor it would not be unusual to ask whether he were a good or bad doctor.

Mental state words, like social reality words, are more or less pejorative and evaluative. When one infers a mental state from behavior he labels a person as being someone whom he and/or others may think of as being good or bad. Because of this evaluative aspect there will frequently be disagreement about who is who, a possibility encouraged by the inferential nature of the reality of mental states.

And this is one of the features of constructed reality, as well as some categories of physical reality when applied to people: to label people as something, to modify their whole person, is to give them meaning. And to give people meaning is to, among other things, place them in an evaluative context.

As an example from physical reality, to have leprosy is different from having measles. The greater the modification of the whole person, the more "potent" the word.

One interesting phenomenon with respect to the relationship between social reality and mental states is the extent to which they appear to merge under certain circumstances. There are some, for example, who attempt to harden intelligence as a mental state into social reality. Performance of a certain kind, a score on an "intelligence" test, is viewed as the "credential" for intelligence. And those giving the test then assert the right to act as certifying agents, at the minimum implicitly by making the claim for legitimacy. This is also the case with mental state categories of "mental illness" in which agents in institutionalized settings transform inferences about behavior from mental states into social reality. Anyone can call someone "crazy," or even a "paranoid" or "schizophrenic," but a person becomes "legitimate" through being certified by the "proper" authorities. It is then made to appear that one *is* mentally ill in the same way that one *is* a Ph.D., even though the definition of being mentally ill is an inferred mental state from behavior, and the definition of being a Ph.D. is the credential. No one, for example, would say that a person is mentally ill only because psychiatrists in a hospital say so. The doctors say so *because* the "patient" *has* a mental illness. A Ph.D., however, is a Ph.D. because someone gave him a credential.

And, interestingly, one can also notice this phenomenon in reverse: social realities being transformed into mental states. For example, a person can be credentialed as a criminal and one might then speak of the "criminal mind."

Formal Reality

There are three realities which are related to feelings: the good, the beautiful, and the true. We will call these realities formal realities—"formal" in the sense that they are *forms* of expression, creations, which may be thought of as related to feelings in several ways.

Anything may be thought of as in formal reality. Anything may be imputed to have truth, goodness, and beauty dimensions. This is, in some ways, part of the "game" of formal reality: the establishment of the relevance of a formal reality dimension and its *dominance* as the dimension most appropriate for discussing the question at issue.

Words are one form of formal reality, but so too are names, ideas, and constructions (social and mental states). Formal reality is a way in which all other realities may be discussed.

We may view the "things" in formal reality in terms of the feelings they are imputed to "represent," or in terms of the feelings they do or do not elicit in us, or both. And we may have discourse concerning the extent to which feelings represented and feelings elicited are congruent. Much of the discussion in the various fine arts and literature, for example, involves these matters.

In comparing our statements in formal reality with our feelings we may do one of two things: represent or misrepresent. To represent is to say "elation" when we feel elation, and "uneasy" when we feel uneasy, and in about the right measures. Clearly this is not an easy task—especially since our "feelings" are only one of the factors involved in our assertions in formal reality. Others are social contexts, individual "intentions," and abilities to articulate.

We may ask of any statement, object, idea, institution, or, in general, "thing" ' (meaning anything at all), whether it is good, true, and/or beautiful. And when we do we are in the world of formal reality. Take, for example, the statement "Thou shalt not kill." We might discuss it in terms of its goodness, truth, and/or beauty. So too with "she must (or should) go to school" and "dominoes are black blocks with white dots." Each may be considered on any or all of the three dimensions. And each may also be considered in realities other than formal reality. For example, "the person who said 'she must go to school' is compulsive" is a statement which might be thought of in the reality of mental states.

A statement in formal reality, for example, "the picture is beautiful," may be given many interpretations. "What does 'the picture is beautiful' *really* mean?" is a not unexpected question in an inherently ambiguous situation. An answer to the question of what is really meant by statements in formal reality depends upon what one is satisfied with as an answer. It is useful to note, however, that people do give answers, and frequently their answers lie in a reality different from formal states. For example, "what he really means when he says that the picture is beautiful is that he is flattering the person who painted it since he is addressing his remark to him" is an answer primarily in the reality of mental states. The import of the original remark is interpreted to concern someone who is imputed to have a purpose rather than, say, the picture itself.

It is difficult to say why something is beautiful—and for this reason it is easy to say *that* something is beautiful (or ugly). Ultimately, when we defend our statements in formal reality, we can refer to our own personal internal states: "I *feel* it to be beautiful" (good, true) —"that's just the way I feel." And no one knows one's inner experience better than oneself, although others may claim they do, a claim which gains some credence from the fact that one has difficulty himself in determining the "meaning" of one's own internal states. Help from the outside, then, is sometimes welcome.

In aesthetics, if we say "that is a beautiful picture" it may mean that we are moved by it, that we "feel" something. The reason "may" is used is that, in a formal reality, we frequently say things which seem appropriate as taught to us—that is, in a sense, we speak formally *only,* without feeling underlying what we say.

It is not easy "to say what you feel," and for two reasons: we may not feel anything (and there is a good deal of pressure not to say this—it makes one appear insensitive and uninvolved, cold and unemotional, apart from one's surroundings); and we may feel something but not know how to articulate it. If it is "true" that we "feel" only uneasy or elated, then to say anything else, more "complicated" than that, would require a facility for stating things in some kind of formal reality.

To say that someone is honest is to assert that one *feels* "right" about someone on certain dimensions of his behavior, unless, of course, what one says in formal reality and one's feelings are not congruent.

We have an expectation that most people will be "honest" most of the time. This expectation is undoubtedly based on how we would like the world to be (how we think it ought to be) every bit as much as how we think it "really" is. The statement "he is honest" is somewhat different from the statement "she is beautiful." We do not expect most people to be beautiful.

A general translation for statements in formal reality is: Of all the X (that is, the X with which I am familiar), Y is unusual, where Y is a class of X. People may differ, however, on what they say X is. For example, "this is a good book" might mean: given my life, reading this book has been exciting; or, given the way books are usually written, this book is unusual; or, given books about Z, this book says more than most; or any other comparison between Y and what Y is thought to be a class of.

When one says "he dances beautifully" such a statement in formal reality might be interpreted to mean: "given dancing that could occur this dancing makes me feel elated." This implies that a good deal of dancing that could occur would probably strike one neutrally, and that some might make one feel uneasy. It also implies that one is not misrepresenting his "true" feelings. Because one could so misrepresent, and no one but oneself could know it for certain, statements like "he dances beautifully" are inherently subject to multiple interpretations.

Expressions in formal reality have to do with what may be called drama. People's feelings are aroused on the basis of what they find unusual. Hence they are moved to utter, for example, "he dances beautifully" when they find an incongruency between what they have any reason to expect people to be able to do and what they see. This is one of the reasons why the appreciation of artistic phenomena is learned: one needs to know what people are capable of doing to recognize something unusual.

We might also account for the existence of popular arts and entertainments. A particular novel might be widely read because the comparison is: given my life, this book is unusual. It might be called "common," if the comparison were: given books, this book has the following features.

Whether something is appreciated has to do with what one learns is unusual. To hit a home run in a major league baseball game is "known" by many boys and men, especially, to be a difficult task. But it may not be clear to most boys and men that to dance like Nureyev is also difficult.

To men in general, men dancing in ballet may be thought of as unusual, but not in the same way as hitting a home run in a baseball game. Given what men do, ballet dancing is unusual. Given what baseball players do, hitting a home run in a major league is unusual. Clearly the basis of comparison is different. In the latter the comparison is internal to the subgroup of baseball players. In the former it is the activities of men in general. *How* something is unusual, then, is the basis of one's appreciation of it.

Refinement in taste has to do with the ability to appreciate narrower and narrower differentiations. "Good" taste and "bad" taste is another matter, having to do with what one thinks is interesting to have refined tastes about.

Statements of preference, of likes and dislikes, are a class of statements in formal reality which may be ambiguous concerning which of the categories of formal reality is being referred to. "I like logic" might mean: logic is beautiful; or it might mean that logic is a good thing; or it might mean that logic is truthful.

To say that one likes or dislikes something is simply to say that one has a feeling about that thing. In order to know on what dimension or dimensions of formal reality one has feelings it may be necessary to ask further.

Truth in formal reality can be a multiple thing. For example, if one says "I like orchids" one could ask "is it *really* true that you like orchids?" That is, are the public statement and private feeling congruent? But one may also want to know with what dimension of formal reality the statement is about, and how refined the dimension is. For example, if "I like orchids" may be represented by "orchids are beautiful" then the translation would be something like "of all the flowers I know, orchids are unusual," or, "of all the things in the world, orchids are unusual." One could then argue as to whether the person is "correct." That is, ought he to feel that way given one's own feelings. One could, for example, attempt to show in what ways orchids are not to be thought of as beautiful. And one might be persuasive. If one were persuasive it would no longer be "true" for the original utterer that he now believes that orchids are beautiful, and it may also be no longer true that he likes them.

Discussion in formal reality may concern feelings, and feelings can be played upon and changed.

"Definitions" are statements which are meant to be taken as true. Clearly, in some senses, definitions can be false (for example, dominoes are small glass balls of different colors). Clearly, also, some definitions are true simply because a person declares he is going to use a word in a particular way (by "strunk" I mean a skunk with a trunk like an elephant).

When one asserts a "definition" one is dealing with "truth" and hence formal reality.

Everything is something. A "thing" does not have to be a physical object to be thought of as "real." When we say that a "strunk" (a skunk with a trunk) does not exist we mean it does not exist as a species of animal.

Formal reality offers one the greatest flexibility and opportunity for creativity. There are few guidelines—and the criteria for judgment are highly variable.

Formal reality is a devised reality, a reality of forms, of words, created to express, mask, or simulate a feeling. It is also an ambiguous reality, inherently, hopelessly ambiguous.

Explanation or Meaning

Human beings have given themselves the task of accounting for their own behavior. We want to know why we do what we do. We can never "know"—we can only "understand."

When we explain behavior we assume we know what the behavior *is* that we are explaining. This is usually assumed to such an extent that we don't even bother to find out what it is.

A second difficulty in explanation of behavior is that one has some control over the "reality" in which one discusses the "behavior" to be explained. If one is trying to explain why someone is "unintelligent" is he trying to explain a social reality, a mental state, or, as is likely in everyday conversation, a physical object?

(A person is usually assumed to be stupid, "he really is stupid," in the same way that a tree is an elm.) And what constitutes "evidence" depends upon what one thinks the "thing" is.

The third difficulty in accounting for human behavior is that we also have some "choice" over the reality we use for explanation. Will intelligence be explained by man's physical objectness, by mental states, by social reality, by formal reality?

And is there any criteria by which we could choose one reality as a "better" locus of explanation than another?

We "understand" why people do things because we must. "Why did X do that?" "Because . . ." "Why did Y's child do that?" "Because . . ." And this is the way we cope with the world as it passes before us.

Is there any reason to think that people would not try to come to some conclusions about human behavior? Is there any reason to think that people might not believe someone else's analysis, if not their own? Is there any reason to believe that people wouldn't believe that there is an answer?

It would undoubtedly be surprising if people didn't try to understand and explain their own and other people's behavior, and for at least three reasons: (1) understanding is a way of making one's surroundings safer; (2) we give ourselves a sense of ourselves by giving meaning to others; and (3) it gives us something to say.

People give reasons for things, they explain why things happen so that they and others may understand them. What constitutes an "acceptable" explanation? What is defined as "meaningful"? What is accepted as being "right"? The answers to these questions lie in human dynamics, not in philosophy. And philosophers are people. What constitutes a "really" good explanation of explanation is an exercise in formal reality. And this may also be "decided" by people.

Reasons ("causes") which people give to explain behavior have two dimensions: (1) plausibility and (2) justification. To ask whether reasons which are given are plausible is to ask whether something "really" happened that way. To ask whether reasons are justifiable is to ask whether they are "determining."

One can explain something by giving it a "cause" in a particular reality. The cause may be believed if others share the sense in which that reality does determine things and whether it is plausible in this case. If I ask why A killed B and you answer because A needed money, to make it plausible I might want to know some details about whether B had money, what A needed money for, etc. To make it justifiable I would have to believe that "desire for money" is one of the things which could determine such an event.

By making something appear plausible one can make it appear determining, and by making the reasons appear determining one can make it appear plausible.

A justification (that which gives determination to an explanation) may also be called an unjustification. People are as impressed with immoral reasons as being determining as they are with moral ones.

One difficulty in our accounting for ourselves is that we do not "know" what we are accounting for. "Explanation" of behavior is an easier type of assertion to make than "description." We are capable of thinking we understand an explanation without "really" describing the behavior being explained.

We "explain" labels which "stand for" or "represent" behavior.

When we give an explanation of something, very frequently we give a "single" reason. One can then see "behind" that reason a "logical" structure "belonging" to someone. People are not unaccustomed to labeling others. And so we become Freudians, Marxists, conservatives, moralists, and whatnot. If we resist being so categorized then we have a conversation about whether we are or are not an "X." This is one of the hazards of explanation.

But one may also find himself accumulating "realities" "yes, X is involved, but Y is important too, don't you agree? And perhaps we must also take into account Z." Explanations, then, become a matter of how many separate "fields" or "variables" one can think of as relevant. To be "eclectic" means to be good at addition.

One way of disagreeing with the explanations of others is to give reasons for their reasons and then give the "real" reason for the phenomenon for which they had offered the initial explanation. By providing discrediting reasons for the explanation one may also discredit the explanation itself. Given the nature of "truth" in realities other than physical reality it is not surprising to find that an explanation of an explanation becomes evidence itself vis-à-vis the veracity of the explanation.

The reason we can never *know* why people do what they do is because we have no basis to distinguish one among the possible realities in which the answer is presumed to lie as being "better" than another, and within some of those realities no basis to choose among some of the possible answers. We give reasons for things because we quite literally give things reasons.

What would it mean to give an explanation of human behavior which suggests that explanations of human behavior are efforts to give meaning in a way quite different from how we usually think of explanations—different in the sense that by giving meaning to things "outside" we give ourselves meaning (*not* in the sense of giving that meaning to ourselves) as well? Part of what it might mean is that the meaning of the meanings given and the meaning of meaning-giving are not the same thing. Meanings can be explanations; but meaning-giving can also be an explanation.

When people explain human behavior they tell you how they look at things, what they think is real, how they view things as "connected," and in what ways they cut people down to size.

Commitment

Granting someone the opportunity to exercise a superior moral position is like giving a person a chance to be born anew: the cleansing effects of self-righteousness appear natural and species-determined. And refusal to admit an inferior position forces us to improvise shaky stratagems and justifications, mere *ad hoc* pursuits barnacled to irrelevant principles and devised for pure self-defense. For there is nothing so powerful as a clear moral advantage—and nothing so senseless as to fight against it.

What *is* important after all? And does the reason we can't answer that question with other than things like "happiness" have anything to do with what we settle for as actually important? Things like a misplaced check, having to clean the garage, being late.

A person may be thought of as having a waning and waxing sense of himself. When "waxing" he is "full of himself," with a

strong sense of his own importance; when on the wane he is frightened, and "self-poor."

People who are "full of themselves" are frequently repugnant
to those who are not, at the time, sharing in that person's involvement with himself. Outsiders see those who are self-rich in a detached way, and the enthusiasm of the self-rich seems somehow
false and/or inappropriate. Anyone who is "involved" with himself
to a greater extent than we are is threatening—they are perceived
as not showing the proper ambivalence toward life, as not being
properly aware of the ambivalence of others.

Those who are on the wane are also threatening, but this time
for their surface weakness. When self-poor, a person will often seek
an "instant self," a familiar and safe sense of himself. Smoking, for
example, is such an instant self—it is an image of oneself which is
familiar, and it gives one a sense of being there.

When we are "doing good" and providing ourselves and/or
others with self-improvement, what we are saying is that we *need*
to do what we are doing in order to bring about the improvement
we foresee. Man, when optimistic, justifies what he does because we
are what we are but need not be.

But when pessimistic, man might say we do what we do because
we will be what we are.

Those who appear to lack commitment simply fail to show an
obvious one. We think of people lacking commitment when they
seem to believe in nothing. But belief in nothing may be a commitment. Or, more likely, we are just "wrong"—they do believe in
"something" but what it is is not on the surface, or is more difficult to articulate because it is generally not accepted.

To be "obviously" something is a way in which one can determine for himself that he is. It encourages stereotypical behavior
both from the person himself and from those who respond to him.
And this is the case whether the "obviousness" is conventional or
unconventional.

A "deep" person is someone who is not "obvious." To be deep
is not to behave in different ways at different times or to be "un-
predictable"—but to be someone who is "hard to figure out," whose
"game" is not clear, who appears to have a good deal "in reserve,"

who does not let one settle comfortably on a label, whose exterior is not consistent with the usual presumption of a simple or easily understandable "interior." It is someone in whose presence it is somewhat "upsetting" to be, since one does not "really" know in whose presence one is; there is always present a sense of possible incongruity. Deep people give a feeling of a complicated inner life, a high degree of mental activity and feeling which belies a somewhat blank or noncommunicative exterior.

People, of course, aren't "really" deep—they are thought to be so by those who think so, including, possibly, themselves. What some people may find deep, others may find easy to label conventionally. "Cruel," "evil," and/or "brilliant" are sometimes terms which are applied in place of "deep."

People like to think that other people are thinking either the same or the opposite. Two "poles" are easier to handle than three, etc.

When I ask you to tell me who you are I am asking for help. Not to know entails risking the development of a bad impression of myself. How I perform and what I say is partially determined by your answer as to who you are.

When one believes the world is precariously put together he is likely to be a good deal more indifferent to the "troubles" of his fellowman. It is when we view the world as "solid" that we show we care.

When someone calls someone else a cynic he normally means that the way in which the "cynic" describes the "realities" of any given enterprise violates commonly shared values. For example, a cynic about man would be someone who argues pessimistically about the viability of man as an animal.

But we may also mean something else when we describe someone as a cynic: we might mean that we feel the person "knows better" but does what he does anyway. For example, we might call a politician a cynic if we felt that although he knew that what America "is" is very complicated he hides that complexity in simplifications, distortions, and rhetoric. And so, in this case, a cynic could be one who upholds what many people feel the values ought to be.

A cynic, in the first sense, then, might call some of those who call him a cynic naïve, but he might also call some of them cynical.

We all do some things in such a way that we are disappointed when others do not realize the sacrifices we have made for them. Bitterness is the inevitable consequence of unrequited sacrifice.

If it is our lot to construct meaning, and if we feel safer when meanings are thought to be shared, then there will be great pressure to pass on old meanings to future generations. And when old meanings are rejected there will be fear and spite.

Indifference is great power. If we care more than others about something we must work out together, the burden rests squarely on those who care.

If one does what he wants to do and what he considers to be valuable, he cannot be made to feel guilt or shame, except as he blunders away his advantage.

Any position can be made morally defensible—*any* position. The rest is argument. And this is why we are often thought of by others to be merely conventional.

Prejudice

It is threatening not to know. And that is one of the reasons we put labels on things. Another is that it is pleasant to be a labeler.

One can know what one is, in some senses of "know," by knowing what one isn't. If others can be referred to as people different from oneself, and those people are undesirable, then the implicit assertion lurking underneath requires little sophistication to grasp.

If one needed a sense of justification for a tenuous existence the creation of classes of "peculiar" people would take the edge off the need to provide it.

A feeling of who one is is partially provided by reminding oneself *that* he is—in rediscovering that one exists, in getting a "feel" of oneself. Excluding others from one's notion of community helps provide this sense of being.

We give people a "wholeness." The act of giving anything might be viewed as gratuitous. That what we give is so complete is clearly a basis of man's folly.

We understand the "whole" of a person by giving him parts which, individually, stand for him wholly. We then discuss these parts, part by part (that is, "whole" to "whole"). And in this sense the whole is less than the sum of its parts.

There are some people, "different" for all of us, who have styles of interaction which require of us a mobilization of energy and resources which we are unwilling to muster. We "see" what is necessary—but we are unable to bring ourselves to do it. These people are our "bugaboos." They make clear to us the *performing* nature of our interactions in a way which leads to our failure to perform at all, and we thereby, to boot, give a "bad" performance since we are left to "perform" our inability to perform. We are "drawn out" badly—we are shown to be incapable of playing a particular role—we are disappointed in ourselves—and we conclude that we do not like the other person.

Everyone "has" a "spook," someone, or group, or thing that "really" bothers him, consistently and intensely. This spook can change, and there can be more than one.

A spook provides a base, an absolute, a point of reference which energizes the self. One feels he (himself) is there when one feels it (the spook) is there.

A spook is one of the sources of a "quick self." If one needs to know he (himself) is there, it is sometimes convenient to think about or talk about one's spook. A person then "comes alive."

We are all bigoted; some of us more conventionally than others.

The reason we become bigots has to do with our believing that people "are" what we call them. People become not people who have acted in one way or another—*they become particular kinds of people*. And in this sense they become "less" than people.

If we view Negroes, for example, not as black people but as

people whose skin is black, or anti-Semites not as anti-Semites but people who are acting anti-Semitically, we would not have a problem of bigotry.

To believe people *are* what our adjectives and nouns modify them to be is to make bigotry easy. But this is not meant to imply causality: one of the things that people do is to modify people into *being* what the modifiers say they are. Bigotry as a process is merely a part of the human condition.

When we say that people should not discriminate on the basis of irrelevant criteria (like race and religion) we assume there exist *relevant* criteria for discrimination. *Any* criterion is a basis of bigotry—we simply find some justifiable and others not. If one does not like bigots, for example, why would one want to assume that this itself is not bigotry? And in this sense, of course, "I don't like bigots" is not only a bigotry but also inaccurate. "I don't like bigots" means "I don't like people of such-and-such a sort," not that all people are disliked.

A criterion we sometimes use to distinguish bigotry from preference is "reasonableness"—is it reasonable to discriminate on the basis of X or Y? What is reasonable is what we believe to be reasonable. To pretend that bigotry based on "reason" is not bigotry is to pretend that reason has an independent and "real" meaning.

And it is in this way that we legitimize our own bigotries. The content of bigotry may differ from person to person, but the process of bigotry remains the same.

We tend to judge others from the point of view of our own significance-giving devices. And judging the epiphenomena of others is undoubtedly the most important significance devices we have.

Significance is giving meaning to oneself as a person. We are equipped with many devices to do so—and we learn more all the time, discarding those which no longer serve.

By modifying others into being negative *kinds* of people, we give ourselves status by comparison. If X's exist, and are "less" than people, then being an unmodified person is valuable. We, in a sense, become "real" people by pointing out the "less thans."

Significance by invidious comparison: differentiating ourselves from those who are exactly like us.

One of the things that we all have in common is that we think some others are different from ourselves. And we will engage in many kinds of activities, especially verbal and written, to show that this is the case. People, then, are different because they are the same.

Can you imagine being able to tell others why someone did something, what the other person "has in mind," what *kind* of person he is? We all buy labels and try to stick them onto people. And the price is our humanity.

Interaction

Tension management is a major preoccupation of people: it is part of what it means to interact with others. Most of our interactions involve tactics of avoiding possible tension escalation—and occasionally we increase tension in noticeable ways.

Games are an organized way to interact with people—one does not expect to have to "get to know" the person—in fact it is often clumsy to do so. Which makes even more apt the analogy of games to life. Interactions with people are "game like"—even those games which are designed to "get to know the other person."

If one takes something seriously he will find it extremely frustrating to deal with someone playful—especially if that someone takes his playfulness playfully.

Our lives are so interrelated with others that unless we are willing to lose (which we are not, at least continuously) we must ourselves exercise power. Most political activities in which we engage are anticipatory—we have learned that winning or losing is itself an issue.

All phenomena may be said to have political consequences— just as such phenomena may be said to have economic, moral, social, or aesthetic consequences. The case may be more difficult to make in some seemingly obscure circumstances, but this is simply an additional insight one gains from an essential generalization.

"Losing one's temper" indicates a lack of respect for the other person's intellect—it is saying: "you are not up to talking about this since you are so ———" (stupid, emotional, young, tired, etc.) .

And, of course, it is precisely that itself: it shows oneself to be a person who is unwilling to "talk it out" intelligently and unemotionally. Losing one's temper is a form of attempted coercion—it indicates that one is what one thinks the other is.

We withdraw from an interaction when it looks like it will be "too much" of a hassle to continue. But what happens if someone likes hassles?

Withdrawal is a response produced by fear. A person who backs off from an interaction is frightened; "smart" persons sometimes find themselves quite frightened.

"Lonely people" want significance—and people can't give it to them. They can only substitute for the feeling of loneliness.

The *absence* of people is itself stimulating. Loneliness is as distracting and preoccupying as other stimulants.

"Lonely people" will fall in love easily, since love is a form of selflessness which permits the person an escape from being himself with others. Those who call themselves lonely are also uncomfortable with people.

Language

It is one thing to say that the mind helps us in how we see structure in aspects of human behavior, for example, language—it is quite another to say that the resulting structure mirrors the way the mind runs.

To some extent words may be studied as physical objects. But words are also behavior. And what we say about words as physical objects will not be the same as what we say about words as behavior.

If we think of "motives" as being classifiable into "because of" (pushed, fate, determinism) and "in order to" (pulled, intention, free will), then what is to prevent us from saying that "I went because of my 'in order to' motive," or "I went in order to satisfy my 'because of' motive"? And to answer that it would violate the "spirit" of the distinction being made and is therefore a word game is exactly the point. One source of word games is to look at something in its own terms. But many would go further and say it is "just" a word game. Clearly this is not the case, although to violate the spirit of the rules of a game in order to generate another one is often annoying.

Distinctions of this sort are also taken "seriously," with the pretension that one is not only not playing "just" a word game, but that one is not playing a word game at all. But clearly distinctions themselves constitute another source of word games.

We might speak of two forms of language: information and interpretation. A trick is to distinguish when we are engaged in one as opposed to the other. Another trick is to determine whether one wants an interpretation to distinguish information from interpretation. What is information within a perspective may be interpretation from another, since information exists within interpretations. We share information, then, when we share perspectives. But we also share information if more than one perspective encompasses the information, even when we don't realize that the perspectives are different. The fact that we agree on something, for example, may be a piece of information because we share the perspective that we are seeing things in the same way even when we are not "really." And this is one reason why we can have conversations which are trivial: what we share is the idea that we are sharing.

Can one describe something without also interpreting it? It seems to depend somewhat on the "distance" the words are from the physical movement one actually sees. We want to say things meaningfully, and the more we interpret, the more meaningful what we say becomes. Meaning is had in this sense by adding to a stark reality.

But meaning comes also by describing unusual or frightening events. If we say "the man walked down the street," it, alone, wants embellishment, such as "the tall, harried-looking figure picked his way down the street as a man apart from his surroundings." But if we say "the tiger ate the child" that may be enough. Sometimes we are privy to "naturally" exciting events—but more frequently we must devise meanings.

And this is why "pure" information can be so highly valued— "facts" may be embedded within ready-made frameworks of meaning which allow one to talk importantly about naturally unimportant events without effort. Knowing that the bus leaves every two hours on the even half-hour can be very meaningful, quite without embellishment.

That paradoxes exist should come as no surprise to us. Why should we think of language as something outside of ourselves? Do we do so because talking about ourselves in such a way avoids certain paradoxes? But are we not also left with paradoxes if we think that language is external?

Philosophers think that paradoxes should be eradicated. One could go about his business trying to "fix things up" so they did not exist—one could treat paradoxes as language (and/or thought) diseases. A question arises, however, as to the "proper" parallel. It would appear that medical doctors can "cure" diseases of the body. And if we think of "mental illness" as behavior which is considered deviant and better hidden from view, are paradoxes like physical diseases or like mental illness?

In order to say anything one needs a point of departure, a reference, an "absolute," from which to measure and contrast what one is saying. And one needs this even if he does not believe in absolutes. "There are no absolutes" is itself an absolute.

We have, then, two senses of absolute: the philosophical and the psychological. And the most interesting position of all is when one professes philosophical relativism absolutely (psychologically). The one melts into the other, and is simultaneously schizophrenic.

Talk

Let's assume that people talk because they talk. The question, then, is: how does one talk in a way which makes it appear as though he is not "just talking"?

Conversation is a game, and should always be taken more seriously than what is being conversed about, unless, of course, what one wants can't be achieved through conversation.

Evaluation is a way of treating things wholly. What is being evaluated becomes an "it" which can be dealt with. And this is one reason why we evaluate. We can think we are conversing with someone about "the same thing," the "it" being evaluated. But evaluations change the topic. What one talks about is his own preferences rather than the "it" 'which is presumably being discussed. And so we have a system of "parallel play."

We all try to make the world safe for ourselves. Part of the way we do this is to encourage other people not to push us in particular directions. It may be observed, for example, that we try to "manipulate" (regulate, perhaps) conversations through evidence of approval and disapproval. We try to make others responsible for our state of mind, as a way of getting what we want and of not being pressed further. Few of us like others to scowl or be upset—we are all intimidatable (meaning the "environment" has reached "fear" levels and safety becomes a haven from possible further difficulties). Those who understand that they need not give way just because someone grimaces have learned the way of obstinancy. If done "good-naturedly" there is a possibility of joshing others out of their posturing.

We can often feel "unsafe." We might then try to feel "safer" and to avoid feeling even less safe. One way to try to do this is to "control" an entire situation. And one way to do this, certainly the "easiest" and "quickest" way, is to control the "mood" of the situation. And to do this one might raise the tension level to a point where other people will visibly "back off." Being "domineering" is an effort in this direction. Many who try it will, (1) fail, and (2) give it back to the extent that they succeed. To gain a mood is much easier than to maintain one. It takes a lot of work and skill, but especially energy, to keep control of something one has set up to control in the first place. Intimidating people is an "artificial" control system requiring much effort to sustain over long periods of time. In fact most people find it more trouble than it is worth. Which is why we all do it only selectively, mostly with those with whom we can get away with it, but occasionally in situations where we will "lose" and feel bad about it.

If one intends to have his position prevail over others then he must be ungracious. Part of the art, perhaps, is to be ungracious graciously.

Talk is a way to make life interesting. And the best way to guarantee that is to be interested in talking and to say things which are interesting to oneself. Others will simply have to fend for themselves.

If a person sets out to dominate an interaction, and the other person doesn't want to, the person who sets out to do so will do so.

If the "submissive" member becomes aware of what is happening, he may continue to take the submissive part, withdraw, or fight back. In most of our interactions, explicit attempts to dominate are not present.

If one doesn't believe that anything is worth talking about then the only way he can carry on a conversation is jokingly, satirically, ironically, etc. One pursues a belief in nothing seriously only at the risk of self-contradiction. Similarly, one must not believe too passionately that nothing is worthwhile. One finds, as well, that people soon tire of anyone who is never serious, if only because they themselves want to be listened to seriously.

But the most difficult thing to do is to believe in only a few things which are the opposite of commonly accepted ideas about truth. One is then frivolous when others are saying serious things, and making other people laugh when one becomes serious.

Sometimes, when we try to say a great deal, it is necessary to pretend that we are saying something (which is almost always nonsense) in order to carry on the sorting out which may be required preliminary to working ourselves into the possibility of saying something which we would *know* was important and which, if others didn't find interesting, would be no concern of ours. Our reluctance to recognize our own pretense at the time obviously makes difficult the acceptance of rejection by others in whom we have faith. Others know this and are, therefore, likely to validate what we have done, a consequence which maintains confusion about what is "good" anyway.

If we feel uneasy about what we are saying in the sense that we are not sure if we are saying anything at all, but we wish to establish, especially to ourselves, the idea that we are indeed saying something, then it is probably the case that our inner uneasiness is a "better" test of the hypothesis than our outward demeanor or even the reactions of others.

What someone says, and *how* someone says it, affect people. There is no doubt of that. But that is not the end of what a person is doing when he says something in a particular way. We may also *interpret* a person's behavior as having some intention—he may be seen to be playing a part in a larger context which may be consistent with what he says and how he says it, but which is different from both. It is an interesting strategy, in conversation, to focus on what one thinks the other is "really" doing, and to put less reliance on what is being said and how it is said. One might then make his own case on his inference as to what he thinks the other is up to—not what the other says he is up to or how he says it.

There is simply no substitute for having a position. If one has a sense of what he wants he can then make relevant what others are talking about and can himself make a case of one sort or another. Otherwise one is constantly being polemicized by others. The only defense to this is to polemicize back. Unless, of course, one wishes to follow, or to be bored.

There is a great trick in conversations which avoids all possible put-downs and feeling-bads connected with someone who asks you to account (for anything) : *you don't have to tell him.* And if you are jolly and use your wits you can hold out forever, getting the other angry, of course, if he is insistent. But it is the *other* who will become angry, and not you. And *that's* something—since, of course, the game being played is to call *you* to account.

To be spiteful is to say or do something which probably hurts someone it makes no sense to want to hurt (although we can understand how we might try to hurt them). Sometimes we are surprisingly spiteful, surprising to ourselves, and, perhaps, even to others. There is a sense of betrayal in spite—it is, in a way, inappropriate nastiness. Clearly we are working out with people things we don't know about until after we humiliate ourselves. We all know how vicious we can be if we want to: it is frightening and disappointing to discover how vicious we can be without even trying.

How often do we find ourselves in conversations giving reasons for situations which if asked, "what is it that you are giving reasons for?" we could not answer other than to say, perhaps, "why things are what they are" without specifying what "what they are" is? So anxious are we to give meanings to things that we frequently give meanings to things which are not yet things. Meanings, then, become a conversation without referent, other than to an unspecified condition with which the parties have reason to believe they should be dissatisfied (which if they weren't they wouldn't be able to have a conversation) .

If part of what it means to talk about something is to "make assertions" (and especially in the sense of having those with whom one is talking believe that one is asserting something, even if they don't "understand" it), then one device for assertion-making is comparison. One can say, or imply, that one thing differs from another. (One could do this, of course, simply by labeling something as "X" when it is generally believed that "X" is not characteristic of all those things which are of the same sort that one is labeling.) And think of the possibilities when one is labeling people in the reality of mental states where the dimensions on which comparisons are made are not "really" real.

This, then, becomes people's "easiest" opportunity to make "meaningful" talk. Assertion-making becomes one's "description-interpretation" (label) of another. And people won't argue about whether the talk is "real"; they will argue about whether it is true.

There ensues, then, a conversation, perhaps even a "heated" conversation, in which people believe they are talking about something. And *both parties* are accomplices in this construction.

We attempt to understand things wholly, even when we know we can't understand everything. When we talk about people we label them and, unless a conversation ensues, the label stands for the person wholly, even if only publicly (as opposed to people's private thoughts), and even if only at that time. A dispute about what a person is, then, is sometimes a dispute about *what* he "truly" is, and sometimes about how many things he is.

Talking is a form of self-stimulation. It gives us a sense that we are there. And this is true no matter what happens: if we win we are triumphant; if we lose we are crestfallen; and if we are bored we can complain. How nice for us.

If someone asks you why you believe what you are talking about he is changing the topic of conversation.

Assume that at a cocktail party person A asks person B what he does. Person B then says he is an "X." Person B's behavior may then be evaluated by A in terms of "X." And B "knows" this.

One comes to "know" and "understand" the world in particular ways as a consequence of picking up labels and dispensing them as the "occasion" seems to "allow." One gets into trouble doing this only when someone is ungracious enough to challenge him and sophisticated enough to beat him at his own game. If one is "careful" he can get along quite nicely most of the time.

There is safety in repeating someone else's argument. For one thing, if we get into trouble with it we can always reveal whose argument it is.

There is also comfort in having the arguments of others at our disposal: it gives us something to say.

We can look at things in terms of "content"; and we can look at things in terms of "form." All communication has both. And in some senses the content is the form and the form the content.

Content is form when content is ritualized. Form is content when something is being communicated in addition to the meaning of the words themselves. "Go fly a kite" is both content in form and form in content. Talk about talk should be very unsatisfactory.

People don't have to have a "reason" to talk. Talking is one of the things people do. One could just as well say people should have a reason not to talk.

We might, then, find talking fun. Trivial? Of course. A waste of time? Of course. Leading nowhere? Of course. But all of this is beside the point if it's fun.

Art

Art does more than describe—it interprets. Art is descriptive explanation, or explanatory description. "Good" novels don't tell you what happens and then why things happen. Things happen, they seem dramatic, and they also appear to have a "natural" logic.

One can describe what he sees as the human condition. And one can try to explain it. But "pure" explanation is almost entirely the purview of nonfiction prose writers who may, incidentally, also be artistic. Explanation in painting, sculpture, music, poetry, drama, and fiction would be considered didactic. And "pure" descriptions are boring and/or trivial. Art does not say what something is, it says what something means.

One of the characteristics of artistic forms is to show why people do what they do by what appears to be description alone. The
subtlety with which this is done is part of what distinguishes "great"
from "other" art. And this has two aspects: not explaining explicitly, but not "merely" describing either. "Poor" art is often
either purely descriptive or didactic.

What we have to say about man is either arguable or trivial.
It is the function of "art" to hide this.
To say, for example, that man is starkly naked may not be
saying very much. But a sculpture by Giacometti is something else
again. To say that mothers are ghouls is not the same as a painting
by deKooning.

Surrealism is the way the world would "really" look if "the
Freudians" were "right." Psychoanalytic theory is creative explana-
tion—surrealism is "creative" description based on that explanation.
It is what "nature" would be if nature imitated art.

The major component of art is tension; this is what we "feel."
And this is true of all "good" art. But one must feel the tension
before he knows "why"; the greater the difficulty in explanation
(assuming the same amount of feeling) the more "profound" the
experience. If one sees a poster of a naked woman and is aroused
one "knows" immediately why he is aroused. If one sees a painting
of a woman by deKooning one may feel tension and puzzle about it
for a long time.

A picture of a naked woman which creates tension in a man
who is sexually aroused by pictures of naked women but who is
puzzled about why he "feels" tension over this particular picture
would be an interesting picture.

Art which arouses no feelings is one form of "bad" art. Art
which arouses "obvious" feelings is another.

Feelings have direction as well as intensity. Some art may
arouse negative feelings as a consequence of the style and/or the
content of the art. Most of us, most of the time, however, have no
or only superficial feelings about most art. We react negatively
because we can gain a sense of significance by doing so. Many con-

versations, for example, undoubtedly take place among people who try to explain feelings they do not have. In addition, social situations often induce us to exaggerate our feelings. This is one reason why we speak of "bad" art when we probably should, more accurately, speak of "indifferent" art. We are also, of course, prone to respond to things by what we know about them. A picture by Rembrandt will often be spoken of as a masterpiece because we know of Rembrandt as a painter of masterpieces.

Incongruity

We are all idealists in the sense that we all have our hopes and dreams, expectations of what ought to be which may be violated. Similarly we are all realists: we have our beliefs about what the world is like, beliefs which may also be violated.

Incongruities are the consequence of the existence of our "ideals" and/or our "reals" as they are "felt" to contrast with what we believe to be events or possible events.

An incongruity is a violation of an expectation of how the world is thought to be or ought to be. We sometimes "know" what our expectations are only after a violation occurs. We then can say, "that surprises me, I would not expect the world to be like that," or, "that disappoints me, I had hoped the world would not be like that."

Incongruities provide threats which are associated with fear (simultaneously—it's only language that is sequential). An important question, then, is what people find incongruous—another important question is how people respond to incongruities.

In threat situations there are three major variables: one's belief about its seriousness; whether one thinks he will win or lose; and the extent to which one feels trapped.

There are three major classes of incongruities: 1. Something can violate one's sense of "ought to be" without violating one's sense of "what can happen": "I understand how things like that happen, but they shouldn't."

2. Something can violate one's sense of what can happen without violating one's sense of ought to be: "I don't mind that it happened—I just didn't think it would."

3. Something can violate both: "Not only did I not expect that to happen, things like that shouldn't happen."
And, of course, something can violate neither.
These incongruities are the source of life's drama.

When one believes that things *should be* settled, and things are not settled, there will exist "uncertainty." Such an incongruity between what ought to be and what is does not "produce" uncertainty, since one might also say that a belief that things should be settled may itself be a consequence of uncertainty—these things are merely the way one chooses to speak about them. "Uncertainty," then, is a less personal way of talking about "generalized anxiety" —a pervading discomfort in one's situation.

When one is uncertain he will pursue "offensive" strategies. What he is expressing is his discomfort with how he feels about himself in his world—vaguely defined. To be offensive, then, is to take the initiative in attempting to put things right because one is uncertain about one's capacity to tolerate his present circumstances. An offense is a defense against acute depression.

Incongruities produce "defensive" strategies—but this a consequence of how we use words. A defense is a reaction—a form of protection. And this is exactly what people do when faced with incongruities. That it is also possible to speak of people contriving incongruities simply makes it clearer how offense and defense are useful only when they are redundant. It is the process of making them congruent with what they mean that we come to "understand" the nature of some people's behavior.

Generalized anxiety is a difficult thing with which to cope in others and oneself. When one "has" it it is consuming, providing its own energy for its own sake—and when someone else "has" it we also notice how it consumes them. We are left to act out or to watch, helplessly. And if we get involved in someone else's generalized anxiety, we become either close and supportive, or an enemy—or both at different times. To be standoffish is to be free.

Life itself is a vicious circle: just that you are offends and frightens some others; and you, in turn, can be offended and frightened. There seems no way to break out of this, collectively.

Individuals can attempt to "control" their own feelings of fright and offense, but they cannot control, totally, the offense they give to others. We offend some people simply by being *whatever* it is that we "are." We might regulate, to some extent, to whom we give offense, but not *that* we will give offense.

Drama

Incongruities provide the drama of life as contrasted, say, with routine. Drama is tragedy (man loses), or comedy (man wins), and has to do with idealism, realism, and the presentation of how the world comes at us.

We sometimes *submit* ourselves to expected incongruities: we would do this to "liven" our lives, to reduce routine and boredom. Play, contests, theatre, rites are examples.

Man also has ways of prolonging or foreshortening drama: anticipation and money, imagination and fantasy, and forgetting and ignoring, overlooking and misperceiving.

The question of incongruity is highly dependent upon expectations of what one believes the world is like and should be like, but fundamentally the former since what the world should be like is most relevant to incongruity when the world isn't as it ought to be. We are impressed again, then, with man as an ontological being: his participation in comedy, tragedy, and laughter also rests on this base.

Vicarious drama (watching something happen to someone else) can be a source of real drama. It is not as intense as "really" real drama, and that's because it's safer.

There is safety in routine—but also "boredom." And so we manage small dramas to "break" the routine, to put an *edge* on things. We then feel it right to scurry back to safety. We want to peek—but we also want to hide.

A "drama" takes place in two circumstances: man triumphs over adversity; and man succumbs to adversity. The former is comedy, the latter tragedy.

Our lives are "full" of adversities—but if they are not there "naturally" we can merely create them (self-stimulation). For example, to complain of a lack of excitement in one's life is to create a little tragedy.

We make our lives dramatic through *private* stimulations, akin to the child's lonely game of "step on a crack and break your mother's back." We each, then, have private triumphs and private tragedies, seemingly embarrassingly idiosyncratic and therefore seemingly non-sharable. Our public triumphs and tragedies (awards, deaths in the family) are easily shared since they are socially defined. But they are also, for most of us, too far apart to give us a "satisfactory" level of drama. Hence we revert to private dreams.

One can go down in defeat so nobly that it appears to be a victory. In the face of the inevitable, dignity and heroism can offer a minor, last-ditch triumph. And afterwards, as people look back upon what happened, some may be ashamed that adversity was accepted in such a manner. But man needs his triumphs. And those who are critical are creating a drama for themselves. It is *their* way of coping with tragedy.

Tragedies are inherently unsatisfying. Those of us who witness them must rob them of their sting—we must triumph not over what produced the tragedy but over the tragedy itself. A death becomes a lesson for the living—an atrocity, an example of the power of evil. We cope with tragedy by putting it in its place.

When man loses, those hearing about it must win. Tragedy, therefore, involves two struggles: adversity besting man and man besting the ensuing adversity which comes at him in the guise of tragedy.

How better to prevail than to create a tragedy to prevail over?

If we wait for natural adversity we may lose.

Adversity is not the same as tragedy. A tragedy is an adversity, but so are lots of other things.

There are two kinds of adversities: obstacles in which the outcome is in doubt, and struggles which man has already lost. The former is "real" in the sense that the drama is ongoing and risky; the latter is a convenience to man, an opportunity to show his worth without risk. Man always triumphs over tragedy—he frequently loses to other forms of adversity.

Comedies are less thought-provoking than tragedies. We are left with nothing to overcome—the job has already been done for us. This does not mean that comedies are any less satisfying. When man triumphs it fills us with our own sense of importance. But they do require less of us afterward.

Even a "bad" performance is not wasted on us—man becomes significant by invidious comparison. But as in most anything, how much of a challenge it presents is of some consequence. We may feel cheated if the tragedy gives us too little to overcome—we may also feel overwhelmed (and a bit puzzled or mystified and perhaps put out) if it gives us "too much." In either case we are likely to reject out of hand, to be somewhat depressed. We win, in a way, but unimportantly. Similarly we may feel bad about a comedy which does not give us a sense of ourselves sufficient to make us bubble over at its success. We have lots of ways of being "a little happy." Comedies should be extraordinary.

Incongruities make life stimulating. All incongruities invoke fear—but there are many responses depending upon the situation. For example, comedy is based on incongruities which are not to be taken seriously, tragedy on incongruities which are. When we respond to a situation with "anger" we are treating incongruity seriously. Panic is a response to an incongruity under pressure of time. And an interesting feature of incongruities is the extent to which they are "manufacturable" by the person himself. Clearly many situations invoke fear in almost everyone—but we also have many private comedies and tragedies, angers and panics.

Laughter is an *overcoming* response to fear—it is a way of showing that one does not take an incongruity seriously. Laughter *itself* turns tragedy into comedy: man prevails over a situation in which it appears that "reality" prevails over man. The clearest example of this is slapstick. *If* laughter prevails in the situation the *whole* situation, *including* the laughter, is comic. We usually say that we laugh at comic situations—but we are not using the words that way here. What most people call comedies are actually non-serious tragedies. We cry when incongruities are serious—even when they are "happy" ones.

And this suggests a fundamental distinction between laughter and comedy. In a comedy man prevails; but farce, for example, is not comedy. It is tragedy in which the audience prevails. One must distinguish between what happens "on the stage" and what happens "in the theatre." After a serious tragedy we try to prevail by talking about it. During a nonserious tragedy we prevail by laughter. During a comedy we "feel good" about man—we feel a sense of importance. Tragedy makes us fearful for our sense of importance, even nonserious tragedy. Laughter is a way of expressing that fear when the situation seems nonserious. If, "on the stage," man prevails, the audience may feel good. If, on the stage, man loses, then the question is whether the loss is to be taken seriously. If seriously, then tragedy and efforts to overcome by thinking and discussion— if non-seriously then laughter. In both situations tragedy (what happened *on* the stage) was transposed into comedy (what happened on the stage plus overcoming strategies). We may not laugh at a "nonserious" tragedy—it is too "real" for us. We may not "see" a "serious" tragedy—for us it is a farce. People can appear idiosyncratic with respect to what something *is* and therefore what their response is compared to what it "should" be as defined by what others think appropriate for the occasion. Laughter at a funeral is to say that the incongruity may not be the appropriate one—a lack of feeling an appropriate incongruity may itself be an incongruity which one wishes not to take seriously. Anger at a wedding may mean, for the person feeling anger, the situation is a tragedy and not the comedy it is "supposed" to be.

All laughter is "nervous" laughter—it is just that it is clearer in some situations what is appropriate. Sometimes we force laughter because we think it appropriate to laugh (for example, when someone tells a "joke" which doesn't come off and we do not want to hurt his feelings). In this instance, interestingly enough, we may be "laughing" at a tragedy—an inappropriate response which is appropriate because the drama is not supposed to be the failure to tell a joke but the joke itself. Sometimes we force laughter when we don't really want to take the threat seriously, or are afraid of where it might lead. And those "watching" the "inappropriate" response might feel a sense of tragedy—that is, they take the incongruity seriously. It is, for them, not the *occasion* which is the source of tension, but the way the "actors" respond in the occasion. One must conclude for himself just *what* the drama is—it need not be what others think it is nor what oneself or others think it ought to be. A person can have as *his* drama two other people who are responding to a drama occasioned by another person acting "inappropriately" in a situation. And we might feel this to be a common phenomenon: private dramas at public occasions.

Why are some incongruities taken seriously and some not? When does fear dissipate into laughter? When, from one's point of view, it would be silly to take it seriously. Sometimes we do not recognize that we will be "silly" to take something seriously (when we are being "put on," for example) and we become a source of amusement to others by being "taken in" and responding "inappropriately." (Interestingly, we are actually, in these "intended" situations, acting "appropriately" by being gulled, and then told our appropriate behavior was inappropriate—setting up another "crisis" which may be "mishandled.") Others can then continue with "can't you take a joke?" Perhaps one cannot, but that is a separate question. When a "joke" is disguised it may not be recognized.

Incongruities in man's sense of his own importance are the source of drama, both comedy and tragedy. When man's importance is given a "twist" tension (fear) occurs. The resolution of that incongruity is the task of drama or the "theatregoer."

Why do we feel an overwhelming sense of pride, of goodness, from sentimental, romantic comedies? Man triumphing is of great emotional significance even, apparently, when we feel uneasy about how we are moved. If we are all subject to such easy self-indulgence, why man does what he does becomes, perhaps, somewhat clearer.

Laughter is the consequence of a nonserious tragedy. But not all people need view the same things as non-serious. And this is why some people do not find some things funny.

Similarly, comedy to some may be tragedy to others. Comedy depends upon man prevailing over a situation. But might not we disagree as to what constitutes a triumph? For example, marriage is thought to be a sign of a happy ending to a drama—but may one not view marriage as a tragedy?

The basis of drama, all drama, is fear and self-importance. Incongruities invoke fear—we must resolve this fear in favor of our own self-importance. Each of us does just that, although how we go about doing so may be variously described.

10
Seeker's Philosophical Notes (continued)

Considerations

Significance

We are, more or less, continually at battle for control over what we perceive to be stimuli (whether internally or externally generated). For a person who deals in thought and knowledge to have a position from which all subjects may be touched is a keen source of control. Philosophers seek not so much truth and wisdom as an ability to better others, whether present or not doesn't matter, in argument, to be on top. The history of philosophy is a history of thrusts and parries, of wounds and counterwounds, of heroics and villainies of the mind. That the subject matter is such as the nature of truth and reality serves only to allow the battle to progress uninhibited, and to permit the victor, if there be a victor, to be determined by the argument itself, the arguers, and the listeners and readers, each of whom may have different perspectives of the outcome. It is one of the things men can do, men who have the desire to pursue a contemplative life, and who are dissatisfied with a specialty.

We commit two very frequent mistakes in human analysis: the first is to believe that things could be different from what they are; the second is to believe that some other way of doing things would be better. In the first, of course, things may be said to be different in the future than in the past, but the past and present are what they are, and so too will the future be when it is present and past. In the second, we discover a way to make the present bad—to contrast it with a hypothetically better future. And in each case we then have some way of trying to save human dignity. How much more unacceptable it is to realize that the dignity of man is not an outcome at all, but a way of legitimizing our less than dignified doings.

It is important for us to hide what we do in a lofty context— or else it would strike even ourselves and our comrades that what we do is as petty and filled with human failing as our enemies know it to be. Stripped of its symbolic content, what is left of the whole of a human existence?

Who has ever seen a creative child, and who has ever seen a child who was not? Each of these is an attribution, a gift or a torment, from the beholder. It is one of the ways we can magnify the possibilities of man and associate ourselves with those magnifications. To speak of creativity, to fondle it with our wordy caresses, is a form of species stimulation, a vicarious participation in what we would like to think man really is capable of.

What is solid is that we gropingly attempt to establish something solid.

We are looking for ways to be successful as a consequence of our need to be self-important. What we will settle for as success is partly determined by what we will settle for as self-importance— "partly" because the reverse occurs as well—what it is we settle for as self-importance is affected by what we achieve as success.

There is happiness in self-discipline. One gives order to one's life, illustrates the existence of power through its use, gains power over others (through denial), and feels a base from which to approve himself. It is the form, if not the content, of morality.

Happiness provides us with a sense of significance—so too does unhappiness. And when we have an opportunity to be either we may find either better than insignificance.

We devise goodness so that we can differentiate among people. We then root out evil in the belief that we are doing good. With our sense of goodness and badness we conquer the unconquerable.

Perhaps the most meaningful times of our lives are tragedies—not only to ourselves but to others. When man is conquered, how powerful a sensation that is.

Those who say that man seeks happiness have missed an important feature of man's existence: that happiness is not meaningful enough—it is not, as it turns out, a very deep emotion.

Happiness is a consequence of comedy, when man conquers reality. It is the feeling of having done something, of having overcome, of being safe after have been in danger. Comedy is one of the ways in which man derives significance.

Sadness is a consequence of tragedy, when man is conquered by reality. It is the feeling of being puny, of being wretched, of being less than what one would want to be. And sadness, too, provides man with a sense of being someone, of "being there."

Safety is a middle ground between happiness and sadness, comedy and tragedy. People live most of their lives in this safety zone, fear pushing them there and self-importance milking deviations from it for their significance. But what we are likely to remember are the larger dramas, when we prevailed and when we were done in. We are never happy nor sad for long.

Like all behavior, talk is a way of demonstrating to oneself and others that one is there; what happens in talk sets off one's self-importance. And so, too, is one's significance affected by silence. We may feel, for example, that we should participate but do not, and so we come to think about ourselves and give ourselves meaning.

A "difficulty" may arise when our sense of significance as judged by ourselves and others is perceived by us to be incongruent. And so we turn this to our advantage by differentiating ourselves from others, for example, by placing others in a category which reduces their granted capacity to make such a judgment, a feat which, incidentally, increases our own status thereby. Another "difficulty" may occur when we find ourselves less significant than we thought. Upon such a difficulty is based our internal capacity to construct a world to rectify and/or justify such a conclusion. We may even, for example, view ourselves as less significant in a rather permanent way, thereby giving ourselves a sense of significance by explanation. We all do this, for example, with relation to geniuses (except the few who place themselves in this class) .

Life may be viewed as meaning-testing. And what is at stake, ultimately, is our own sense of ourselves.

Life continually presents us with problems (or so we think anyway). It is convenient, frequently, to blame these problems on something. But most of the problems we have are problems because having them is a way of trying to make it clear who we are, mostly by helping us to explain why we aren't someone different from who we are—which is usually an adequate paraphrase of our problem to begin with.

How available many of us are, especially the young and enthusiastic, to do other people's work. I suppose that's primarily because we have none of our own.

We rely to a large extent on those others doing the same thing as we to justify our own efforts. It is the company we are in (or ask to be in) that makes what we do appear reasonable. Even one who breaks new paths is doing the same thing as those many others who also did so.

Youths are preparing to be people—and should be dealt with with that in mind. Let us not expect youngsters to think and act like people. But when someone is no longer a youth, he is old enough to be shown no mercy—he is ripe to becoming a human being, nor will he fast become one unless sufficiently broken down.

People with specialties amaze and delight themselves as they come to see that the whole world (as they see it) may be seen in terms of the more general concepts of their own specialty. Thus the economist, criminologist, linguist, experimental psychologist, literary critic, etc., all talk of the world in the language of their own metaphors (which, for them, are not really metaphors at all but the finally acknowledged and now explicable absolute from which everything else begins to make sense). There may be only a certain amount of the world which groups of us who are accustomed to speaking to each other can talk about and understand, and any relatively complicated metaphor (appropriate for the group) can cover about the same amount.

When we talk about human behavior we use the words and ideas in the perspective we more or less take to be the case. Problems, then, are problems which the perspective suggests. And so too with answers. And this is what it means to reach conclusions. Without a perspective one would merely "see," "hear," etc.

A perspective, any perspective, will run into its own boundaries. All perspectives treat some "phenomena" as mysteries and/or nonsense. Distinctions will be made (for any perspective must have diversity) and diversities that others see will be denied (since a theory must also have unities). Some questions will be relevant, and some questions not.

A perspective must have a base from which to view what it views, and this base is fixed. And this fixing, this absolutizing, makes some things sayable and others not. Part of elaborating the perspective is in discovering what is and is not sayable. And it is just as important for the theorist to say what is not sayable as the reverse. The "prizes" go to those who most plausibly cover what appears needed to be covered, and exclude what plausibly needs excluding. One needs to be comprehensive at both ends. All perspectives, therefore, have faults from the view of other perspectives. Constantly enlarging and making one's perspective increasingly complicated is part of what is meant by intellectual growth.

Most of what we say of an "empirical" sort is neither true nor false. Within the category "empirical" one needs a further breakdown: something like fact and interpretation, or knowledge and perspective. Facts or knowledge can be true or false—interpretations or perspectives cannot be.

Since, in human affairs, not much of what we say will be other than interpretation (and that part that is will be information), we must have some criterion or criteria to distinguish between "good" and "bad" interpretations. Such criteria may include science, beauty, what is interesting, morality, what one thinks is practical, and doing for its own sake. What kind of human analysis one does and supports, then, will depend upon what criteria he has chosen to justify his way of doing things.

Description

A feature of the world in which we live is that people disagree about what is knowable and what is not. Some argue that everything is knowable; some that only some is; and some that none is. And those who argue that some is find themselves disagreeing about what that some consists of. There are also interesting variations on these basic positions. For example, if nothing can be known then one might believe there are no differences in what cannot be known, between, say, physical objects and human behavior. But one might argue that all things which are not knowable are not the same. And the argument now takes a new twist: that some things are not-knowable in ways different from others.

Knowledge is contextual—what we know (as fact) occurs within time and place. When we give information, therefore, or base arguments on knowledge, we should be aware of whether we do so in the proper contexts. For example, "findings" from a psychological experiment are knowledge in the context of the experiment. To treat such knowledge as true in other contexts is a (more or less) risky assumption.

The same constraint, however, is not operative with respect to interpretations. One can make assertions of interpretation (as opposed to fact) which are meant to be about man in the context of an experiment, but also about man in general. Whether they succeed or fail has to do with how complicated they are and how well one can argue them. We should always assume that someone can show us up—and that how "good" our interpretations are have to do with how many people we ourselves can best.

The things which we most want to know are things which we can only understand.

Are there some things about life that we cannot know because to know them would require that we go one step further than we have just gone? There is at least one position between mysticism and science such that one can say some things will remain mysteries without committing oneself to spooks or real ethereals.

It would make more sense to assume that most words about human behavior are ambiguous and fuzzy and that a few are not, than to assume the reverse. When we speak, then, about human behavior, even when we describe it, we are ambiguous and fuzzy. And if we know that about ourselves, we must also know it about others no matter how authoritatively they speak.

The words we use to interpret the behavior of human beings are not to be taken as descriptions of behavior. A person, for example, is not creative—nor does he even do something creatively. He presumably did thus-and-so and for so doing he may be called creative by some. But he *did* thus-and-so (and even that is arguable). We call him creative.

People do what they do. When anyone does something we can ask what he did. But we are never told what he did. We are told both less and more than what he did. And if, by some peculiar stroke, someone does set out to tell us what he did it will undoubtedly turn out that that is not what we wanted to know.

If we are to say anything, we must absolutize something— something must be fixed. A theory of relativity as most people think of it, then, is impossible. Not everything can be relative—only those things which are not assumed to be fixed.

What happens is behavior (or absence of behavior). We then (usually) *interpret* what "happens," providing what happens with meaning. If pressed about this, however, most of us would not "know" what we are doing, we would assert that we are simply describing what we "see," and that what we "see" is what "happens." We make our (meaningful) interpretations real by calling them descriptions.

Seldom, however, do we actually give descriptions since "real" descriptions are "meaningless" (what happens devoid of meaning). We wish to show others (and they us) that we know what what happens means. Sometimes, but not often, we can give a piece of information which we know the other person will instantly recognize as meaningful (and because we know this, it is meaningful for us as well). In these circumstances we can stay close to description. More frequently, however, we give interpretations because most of what we are able to describe is, curiously, meaningless.

And this initial situation is (frequently) further complicated by bringing in additional layers of interpretation. If someone asks "why is he doing that?" chances are that "that" isn't a simple description of behavior but is itself an interpretation. What one is being called upon to do, then, is to give meaning to an assertion which already "contains" meaning though not understood. We find ourselves explaining interpretations as though we are giving the reasons why something happens when what we are doing is providing additional meaning to something which was not meaningful to someone else although the language was such that it could have been. When we ask "why" we ask for meaning—we imply that what was said was in the nature of a description, and that we have, ourselves, no ready-made meaning context for it.

Most talk about human behavior is interpretive. It can be transformed into the truth by argument, rhetoric, and persuasion. As we come to believe things we give them truth status. And this is "true" even when we claim we do not believe in truth. Such is the ontological nature of man.

Truth is what we call our understanding of things: when we say something we say it as though it were meant to be true. And because of this some people are driven to poetry, irony, and other ways of hiding their meaning, protecting themselves from the charge of overt truth-saying.

No interpretative sentences, ideas, or even perspectives are complicated enough to be "true." They may have an air of truth about them which encourages one to forget about complexity—but this is the seduction of simplicity well said. We convert these partial truths into true parts of the whole. We do not settle for having an idea which is itself incomplete; rather we think we have something which, to rectify, we may merely add to. But a series of partial truths never adds up to *the* truth—they simply cumulate into a more or less plausible series of partial truths.

We ourselves personally verify very few assertions which we experience. Yet we accept some assertions as true, some as false, some as doubtful, some as half true, etc. On what basis do we do so?
Generally, the context in which one comes across the assertion determines whether we will believe it or not. This context consists of parts, but the parts appear together in a more or less complete pattern, how "more or less" in part determining how willing we are to believe. The parts are such things as the person from whom the assertion comes, the point of view from which it is believed to emanate, and whether the objects we like and dislike are being put in a good or bad light. These contexts may be very rich, consisting of many clues and check points; they are also, in part, idiosyncratic.

But we all have a congeries of devices with which we sift incoming assertions, not for their "inherent" truth, but to recognize whether the context in which they are asserted is consistent with the context we have come to use for legitimizing truth claims.

And once we understand this about ourselves (and others) we can more fully appreciate how devilish this business is of believing as true what we believe. It is not because the statements are true that we believe them to be true—they are thought (believed) to be true because we accept as legitimate the basis from which they come.

Science

One can believe that all thinking is the same—that it doesn't matter what we think about, the processes of thought will be the same. But clearly this does not mean that all the things we think about are also the same. For example, we could believe that we can never really know anything, that all of our thoughts about things are merely our own constructions. But we need not conclude from this that therefore whatever we think about is the same as whatever else we think about—that, for example, physical objects and man's behavior are the same thing.

We generally talk about physical objects as though they were mostly one thing. A red ball, for example, is mostly a red ball. It is other things as well (a piece of rubber, perhaps, a group of molecules, etc.), but we have no difficulty narrowing in on its most "salient" features, at least in general we don't.

Human beings, as physical objects, are also mostly one thing: human beings. But in the case of human beings we do not expect, really, to tarry very long on physical object properties—we want to know what kind of nonphysical-object properties the physical object has. Is he or she, for example, a dangerous human being, an important human being, an insane human being, a friendly human being, etc.?

When we speak of physical objects we have an opportunity to be factual in a scientific sense. When we speak of nonphysical-object properties we make statements of a different character.

Most "facts," for example, about human beings need careful ontological inspection to determine the kind of reality in which they are presumed to lie. If someone asserts that "X is rich," presumably this means that X "has" a lot of money. First, does X have a lot of money? Second, in what sense does X have it, and third, what does this mean? We sometimes think that to say "X has a lot of money" is self-explanatory—but it is so only if we are narrow in our construction. It is true that X has a lot of money if by having a lot of money is meant X has at his disposal a lot of money (or some other, probably longer and more complicated construction). If, however, X has a lot of money is to mean that X is different in ways other than in his having a lot of money at his disposal one has clearly gone beyond the original construction.

Most of our conversations about people, however, are of just this sort—we give people meanings by not speaking factually—we like to explain while we describe—we like to communicate some significant message. And our language about humans is consequently scientifically messy. Because what we "really" want to know about people has little to do with science (in a physical-object sense). We may use science to try to legitimize what we say, but what we say, generally speaking, is not science.

Of some things we can say they are true or false in a physical-object sense of true and false. But little of what we say about human beings is of a physical-object sort. We may, therefore, either drop the use of true and false when speaking of nonphysical-object properties, or recognize that when we use true or false this way we are not using them in the physical-object sense.

The question is not whether science has been successful and whether it should, therefore, be honored. The question is in what way science is an appropriate mode of analysis of human behavior. Those who call themselves social scientists may not all be doing science just because they may make such a claim.

If one speaks of science in the analysis of human behavior one must distinguish what is studiable scientifically from what is not. First, scientists should study behavior. Second, scientists should look for regularities. What kinds of thoughts, and of what quality, are matters separate from the method just described.

There are many people who study artificial behavior of people, for example, those who design tests and study the responses. This is an analysis of behavior, but any regularities one sees are regularities of the designed situation which must not be confused with the world as it is, except as the designed situation is an addition to the world as it is.

People can do science on human behavior, but not on data that sheds much light on human behavior, for example, when human behavior is artificial. The question, then, in these cases, is not so much whether science is appropriate given what they want to know (although this may not be a trivial question), but rather whether what one studies is interesting.

The rationale for setting up and analyzing artificial situations is multifaceted, but at the core is a notion (explicit or implicit) that the test situation and some behavior in natural settings is isomorphic, or so nearly so as to allow regularities found in artificial situations to represent themselves as data for natural situations. And the question is the extent to which this assumption is valid, or, more precisely, the extent to which this assumption is thought to be valid.

I would suggest that the error we make lies in pretending that what we find in artificial situations is usable in situations other than the test situation, rather than, for example, erring in believing that science should be applied to natural situations if data is to be useful in our understanding of human behavior. For, although science is being practiced, if what is said here has merit, then we foolishly chide those who will not practice science under these conditions, and are even sillier to believe that science can only be practiced under these conditions. The question may be the appropriateness of science to what one wants to know; but it may also be the appropriateness of what one studies to an understanding of human behavior.

Being clear as to what it is we talk about is prior in importance to how we talk about "it." For example, if we study something and the something turns out to be many things (or even something else), then it is fair to say we didn't know what we were studying. At the minimum we should try to insure that this doesn't occur. For although it is possible to stumble upon something important by accident, we might benefit from knowing what it is we talk about in the first place, at least in the short run. And very frequently this is what those who practice science in human behavior neglect. One can even understand why. When things are ambiguous and difficult there is a temptation to let a routine (in this case science) provide the decisions as to how to proceed.

Understanding

There are some things that people do that we can't know they are doing. We can guess that they could do them in general, but we can never know if or when they are doing them in particular.

If we inspect the reasons people give for what they do we can distinguish three groups: doing things for oneself; doing for others; and doing for nonhuman reasons (principles, or whatnot). None of these reasons may have anything at all to do with why people do what they do, assuming one could ever answer the question of why in the first place. They may simply be viewed as part of what people do, as a part of their behavior rather than as an explanation of their behavior. People give reasons for what they do, justifications, and these reasons in turn reflect upon the person. For example, someone who says he is selfish may be seen by others (and himself) as "honest," "frank," "loutish," or some other characteristic. He is, of course, no more selfish "really" than anyone else, he simply says he is selfish.

People do things which are more or less easily seen or justified in terms of one or another of these three categories. To the extent that the associated categories are seen as valuable, a person may gain value from it (from himself and/or others). It is frequently useful to be able to justify oneself in such a way that one impresses others, that they "see" that what one does is sensible and reasonable —not necessarily good or beautiful—but that what one does makes sense, has a logic. (Unjustifications are justifications too.) And this is, in part, a matter of practice, seeing what works.

There may also be "surprises"; people sometimes shock others. For example, if a priest gives a personal reason for his activities this may be seen as incongruous, the justification may appear inappropriate. If he is able to turn this into a lesson in which he becomes admirable (which, for example, someone glib may attempt to do, and someone wise can do easily), the impression he has made will be considerably different than if he had given a straightforward answer. We learn to give reasons—and we can be clever about the reasons we give. We can attempt to manage the impressions others have of us.

In order to exist we must think we understand. These understandings force us to bump into the world as it is (since it isn't how we understand it). We then try to fix up the world to fit our understanding of it, or to improve our understanding. In either case we make more work for tomorrow since the world, as we don't know it, will still be there. The effects of this are that work piles up, and we find ourselves, as we grow older, settling for less and less. One dies appropriately when one expects nothing either from the world or his understanding.

If it is impossible to understand, then it is very tempting to make an argument that somewhere along the line one should stop and live with what understanding he has. The problem is not how, or where, or when to stop; it is how to keep going, and how to recognize that when one shares his understanding with someone else that this is a form of stopping.

Any behavior may be justified—adequate justification is whatever it takes to convince others. Any justification may be challenged—adequate challenge is whatever it takes to convince others. Some situations appear easier to justify than others. Frequently it is not possible to convince others, but it may be enough, in those circumstances, to convince others that one's own justification is legitimate, that is, an adequate, if "wrong," alternative. We lead if we convince—we hold our own if we legitimize—we lose, and earn the scorn of others, if we neither convince nor legitimize.

One cannot, ultimately, do anything about how the world is because in doing so one is simply contributing to how the world is.

Ideas and actions have very little in common. We often think that actions put ideas into practice, but that is a mistaken notion. Ideas are thoughts, and live in our consciousness. Actions are behaviors and may, ultimately, become data for our thoughts in the same independent way that thoughts may be thought of as a basis for action.

It is easy enough to justify taking action. One is, after all, a part of life. But for the same reason one can also justify not taking action.

If everyone simply sat around and had thoughts there would be little to have thoughts about except, perhaps, that people seem to sit around. And one might, under those circumstances, do something, and later have thoughts about it.

The world cannot be complicated to those who believe they can have their way with her.

Situations

Everyday Behavior

There are so many ways to be good at things that one should not be surprised to find himself in opposition to and unable to deal with others who are good at things. It is one of life's disappointments to recognize just how interesting, in principle, some others are, yearn to talk with them, but realize that bitterness and mutual contempt would be a consequence. This is one of the clearest bits of evidence I know for a world encompassing more than any individual can cope with and the necessity, as a consequence, to attempt to define a little, sensible world of one's own.

All separate, named behaviors may be seen as efforts to compensate the self. For example, asking for someone's love is a way of asking him to give up his self and thereby become more pliable (it is also true that being in love is a form of stimulation— it is exciting, after all, to risk the self). Pity is a behavior which allows one to feel superior to those whose misfortunes are threatening. And if compensation is true of such lofty behavior as love and pity surely there will be no argument concerning more base or more trivial behaviors.

People like to feel that other people believe as they do. For others not to do so is a challenge to one's ability to see things as they truly are, for if others think differently there is a chance that one's own thought may be wrong. Hence we must put others straight, call them fools, or believe them.

Even a man who disapproves his own behavior approves of his own judgment.

People will decide what we are and how good we are whether or not we wish them to do so. One has an opportunity, in his behavior preceding the time the other draws his conclusion, to affect that conclusion. But one has an opportunity to do so after as well. If someone is complimentary it is easy to respond in a manner unflattering to oneself. If someone is uncomplimentary it is similarly tempting. The difficulty, in each case, is to act better than the other's evaluation, thus increasing one's stature, even when the evaluation is high. It is this latter case that presents the greatest difficulties.

For example, let us assume that we have done something of great merit and receive a compliment. Will our response to that compliment be at least equal in quality to the quality of the act for which the compliment was made? People change the situation by their compliments. Even in the case when the act to be evaluated is in the same approximate domain, for example, if we say something interesting and receive a compliment, the chances that our response to the compliment will be better than the description of ourselves in the compliment, or more interesting than what the compliment was for, are probably small. We are being asked to play another game. One of the ways in which people like to redress an imbalance (by putting us in their debt after we have shamed them by our "excellence") is to give us praise. One need not assume that people do this intentionally—most are simply responding defensively, and naturally. It is the consequences of their actions (and ours), not the intention, which is of interest. An additional consequence of a compliment, for example, is to allow the person to illustrate how good his judgment is. But back to the point: unless we can give an interesting answer, an answer which will increase our stature, we might say "thank you," or nothing at all. The alternative is that we partially erase our stature by looking foolish in a situation where it is extremely difficult to look good.

As with compliments (praise), so too with other "good" things which people offer us: love, pity, understanding, blessings, forgiveness, sympathy. We are placed in a new situation where the kind of response which will excel is different from what we were doing. And as with good things, so too with bad. Our reactions to hate, anger, indignation, mocking, despair, puzzlement, etc., are responses to situations different from the one in which we were engaged up to that moment, are defined by someone else, and produce a greater probability of acting in a fashion unbecoming to ourselves than the situation from which we are being drawn.

What can we know about people if we discover what they find stimulating? We know, I think, how the person wants to be taken, what it is he stakes himself on, in what he is willing to be most arrogant. Searching for stimulation entails risks, and we do not risk ourselves without some safeguards (although we may sometimes err in how good the safeguards are). And this is true even of someone who indicates he wants to be known as a person willing to take risks in general.

If we are put down by someone on something in which we have little stake we are annoyed but can discount it because we have no reason to believe it should not be that way. But if we are caught in something we want to be known for then the results can be devastating. Each of us must feel we have a stake in ourselves as something. And because we do we are most vulnerable when it is pointed out to us that we are not very good at it.

We can grant to the young the proposition that they have a better way to live, that we should quit our terrible jobs and join them in doing what they want to do, only if one is miserable because of what he is doing and would be less miserable under other realizable circumstances. We can all believe that we would be happier out of our own "traps," but as a mass phenomena the proposition is rather dubious. At the minimum there seems no reason to grant its truth without thinking about it. For see what it entails: a knowledge on the part of the young not only of what would make them happy, but what would make *us* happy. It is indeed tempting to believe that we *can* be happy and that there is a secret to happiness which is easily had. No one could really fault us for believing it—or could they? Do young people know what will make us happy? Is the key to happiness finally ours? The fact that we are made to feel uncomfortable at not being happy lurks within these questions. And what a stranglehold to have on one's elders. Poor fools that we are we have always been accessible to those who would make the world right, who believe they have the answer. There is nothing new in this—but certainly no precedent for its actually happening.

If one asks a person the question "what do you mean?" he will answer whether or not he had a meaning at all. He may answer "I don't know," but many people are able to talk "meaninglessly" (in the sense we are using it here) at each nudge, and a few can do it quite facilely. Some may even make it look as though they had a meaning to begin with.

It is easier to add knowledge than to change a thought. To add knowledge we may keep what we have; to see something differently we must make a replacement. As a consquence, learning knowledge is most of what learning consists—seeing things in new ways is resisted.

Some experiences which we have had or expect to have generate within us a large amount of what we call worry, anxiety, agony, etc.—for example, a heated conversation, a coming event in which we must play a major role, an embarrassing situation. All of us, from time to time, find ourselves focusing on these things, providing ourselves with a sharp awareness and a sense of the dramatic. And sometimes we wish to escape from these dramas, these feelings, these thoughts. We have a strong wish to be "preoccupied." Let me illustrate.

It is commonly thought that whistling is a way of showing happiness. When people whistle, for example, they are treated as though in a special state of ecstasy. And, indeed, they are "excited," but not in that way.

Whistling is a way of occupying one's mind, of not thinking, of escaping. When one doesn't want to think a thought (which he doesn't even know, by the way, since thinking it is exactly what he is attempting to keep himself from doing) whistling is a behavior to accomplish just that. So too, of course, are a number of other behaviors, like chatting with someone, or "keeping busy." But the point here is that whistling is not a sign of happiness—far from it. It is an effort to avoid being unhappy, driving away possible discomforting thoughts. This may appear, to others, as cheerfulness.

Why would someone do something, or become something, which appeared self-sacrificing? Might it be because it appeared self-sacrificing?

One of the lessons we learn when living with others is how important it is to be selfish, to look out for our own interests. This is one of the ways we talk ourselves into thinking that we are giving: by comparing ourselves with the exploitations of others and using our feelings of our own comparative givingness as justification for serving ourselves.

Nature and man should not be thought of as in aesthetic competition. Natural phenomena and man's constructions are different: those who worship nature's are following a path unlike those who glory in the works of man (perhaps they worship God and his works).

A first criterion to be applied to any "thing," then, is: could it have been done by nature? (A second, related, is: could it have been done by a monkey or other nonhuman thing?)

Man is capable of thought and feeling and of framing thought and feeling in various forms (for example, writing, sculpture, music). He constructs, and may be judged on his constructions. Nature may also be said to "construct," but this should not be confused with what "construct" means for man. Those who believe man competes with nature do not appreciate the difference between God and man; men who attempt to rival nature do what something else can do better, and miss their own opportunities; those who glory in nature's rather than man's constructions have little appreciation of the wonders of man.

We terribly misjudge the value of misery: few things give us such a strong sense of "being there," of the substantialness of existence, of the fact that we are seriously in this world. Our own principles and morality are specifically designed to bring misery to ourselves—our hopes, dreams, and longings are frequently conveniently unattainable. Nothing makes us more aware of ourselves than personal tragedies, and hence we must have them. Some appear "naturally" legitimate (for example, a death in the family) — others we must more actively construe.

Some people hide their seriousness behind a mask of bubbling, pleasant, yet pointed and mildly disconcerting gentleness. And some hide their seriousness behind a mask of hardbaked, trenchant seriousness.

How does one give credit to someone for what he did not do? Are there any really great not-doers? Can some who not-do not-do better than others who not-do? If one were to measure greatness in not-doing would it be by a mixture of quantity and quality? That is, with respect to the latter, would some situations of not-doing be more praiseworthy than others?

Our minds are like old-fashioned rolltop desks, except, in the center of all the little pigeonholes, is a great big pigeonhole called "nonsense" in which we file most incoming messages. We could not keep track of the world as it comes at us if we did not have this filing system. As long as we can label most things as "ridiculous" we can devote ourselves to systematizing the little pigeonholes around it.

If one said "9:24" all day long he would be correct twice a day. And perhaps that's a reason most of us say the equivalent of "9:24" all day long. When it *is* 9:24 we are very proud, even self-righteous as, of course, we are demonstrably correct and begin to *feel* it as we realize the argument that it is 9:24 is prevailing because others see the reasonableness of our position. We take on the posture of someone who thinks it's 9:24 *because* we have said so. And when it isn't 9:24, reality feels a little uneasy around us which, of course, it does most of the time anyway since over the years we've accustomed ourselves to the consequences of our insistence that it's always 9:24. And occasionally we vary our utterances slightly, feeling somewhat giddy in doing so. And if we ever say 11:13 and are reasonably correct, we become insufferable.

What is the explanation for our undercutting the bases to which other people seem to be anchored? Does their insecurity somehow make us feel more solid?
Similarly if we see someone else genuinely fighting for a place to rest, why are we so willing to take them in? Does that, too, help us to shore up our pilings?
We see our bobbing selves in relation to how secure we infer others to be. Let them come on like islands and we expose to their view the water rushing under their platforms—let them be seasick and we seem quite willing to comfort them with our own heady airs. But if, in being sick, they strike out at our supports, we will be perfectly willing to cut them even further adrift, and glad for the excuse.

Explanation and anger have at least one thing in common: each is an effort by an individual to come to grips with complexity.

But whereas explanation is an effort to suggest that one's simplicities conform to the world, anger is an attempt to make the world conform to one's simplicities.

We very frequently feel frightened when someone tells us something which makes more sense to us than the way we would have told it. And the more we feel it inappropriate for that someone to do so (usually because we feel ourselves of higher status and the incongruity is therefore embarrassing, or when we feel ourselves of equal status to someone who is in fact higher), the more frightened we become.

We also become impatient with others who do not accept our way of looking at things as wiser than their own. And the more appropriate we feel it is that they should, the more impatient we become.

If we assume, in any given activity, that a few people are outstanding and the remainder are not, then what is going on when those who are not make comparisons between and among themselves in that particular activity? Clearly reasons are devised to support some as being better and some as being worse than others.

As long as we understand what is involved here, that we differentiate ourselves from others on at best marginal and at worse mythical criteria in order to make ourselves look good by making others look bad, then we might tolerate this nasty business as part of the human condition. But if we take such invidious comparison seriously we are hopelessly lost in intolerance and caviling.

If the variation among people is essentially zero (or, for all practical purposes might be considered so, given the distance between those who are outstanding and those who are not), what silliness to take seriously our distinctions among them.

Telling another what one thinks he would like to do about a particular problem is a form of behavior and frequently inconsistent with other behavior which follows. Would it have been different had one not told it?

There reaches a point when we find we have "decided" either to trust our instincts or not, implying something about how fundamentally sound we perceive them to be. We conclude this partially by remembering our own experiences, by finding our self-confidence adequate, and by evaluation of our abilities. These are not things which young people can readily do. They are advantages of age—part of what is a consequence of wisdom. And in time we may learn to do things without checking with others. That is an element of what it means to do a job creatively. If the performance one wants to stage is "really" for a confidant (wife, friend, subordinate, etc.) then that is an appropriate audience for some plays, by some actors, but not for others. For example, a subordinate, in the guise of giving advice, may act out the position of his superior before the superior. This is, given certain situations with superiors, an appropriate performance. But the reverse, in the same situation, is probably not appropriate.

To remain silent, to allow others to see no aggressiveness, is to leave to others the power of intimidation. This is not to gainsay that "goodness" may be a useful strategy—but not in the presence of the devil, not unless one does not care who is in charge. If devils are not to prevail they must be opposed, and in opposing one inevitably takes on devilish characteristics, assuming again that one finds important the question of who shall dominate. To do good requires, sometimes, that one do bad (when doing good consists of fighting the bad). To let the opportunity to fight evil pass is not only to miss the chance of doing good, it is also to run the risk of being so beaten by evil that one will never again be in a position to fight. Good does not win out over evil if there is no combat. Good can exist, and evil can exist, and when they come into contact either can win, but not without evil being done.

When people preach a thing they don't believe in, they believe in the preaching of something they don't believe in, for reasons which they may or may not state.

When one is having a conversation in a general way about people and someone asserts that something is a matter of fact, the chances are very large that what is asserted is not a matter of fact at all. And almost always such matters of "fact" can be known only by the person making the assertion—they are a part of his personal experience.

This very frequently "works." In order to continue the argument one now must argue with a "fact" asserted by someone which cannot be verified for purposes of the conversation, a "fact" which is probably false. People are able to trade upon our good graces in this fashion for we are left with either letting the statement stand and arguing around it or challenging the veracity of the statement and thereby the veracity of the utterer. Most people find that, except in unusual circumstances, they are not so challenged, and the conversation continues with the other bending his own argument all out of shape.

Conversation which is explicitly personal is conversation which is immature. We expect children to fill their talk with how they feel, what they want, and what they like and dislike, as though others should be interested in these things (as, indeed, a few are, at least occasionally). But we would find conversation at such a level among adults to be childish. Indeed, part of what makes an interesting adult conversation is the extent to which the parties can mask or hide their own involvement in expressing themselves. Too explicit an acknowledgment that one is simply talking about oneself could only be appreciated by those who, for one reason or another, want to listen, or who are willing to listen if they may use the other in the same way. Many adolescents listen to other adolescents tell them who they are because they can then measure themselves as well as reciprocate. Mature conversation is also, of course, personal—but not explicitly so.

Many conversations begin with one idea or assertion which then becomes modified and elaborated upon. We cannot say everything at once. Whatever we say at the beginning will, presumably, be only a small part of what can be said. In our experience some people improve upon first ideas and some make matters worse. And because to do the former is so difficult we cannot expect others to do it. If conversations are to become progressively more interesting we must be capable of doing it ourselves.

If we converse with someone who has a way of looking at things which he doesn't tell us directly but from which is derived what he does tell us, then we are speaking to someone who knows his way around conversation, who can be playful, and who, if we attempt to get the better of him, will have an enormous reserve upon which to draw.

How frequently do conversations occur in which one person simply rephrases what another person has already said. We frequently, ourselves, do not even recognize this, so anxious are we to pretend we are having a conversation. In such cases, unless we drop the pretense, it would be more interesting if one actually did talk to himself.

There are some people with whom it is not fruitful to talk. They have put together a big, partial explanation with many big, partial parts. Nor is what they are saying very good—that is, it is not terribly convincing, or perhaps even clear. The "major" topic is about, say, society, or politics, or the economy, or life. And the person does speak to some of this large topic. But to argue with him would be to discourse on separate, isolated, large topics. And one must then, himself, give a complicated picture for each of the separate topics. It is actually more fruitful to talk about the difficulty of talking and why and how it relates to the talk than to talk about the talk itself.

It is difficult to think a new thought. It is easy to contrast the thoughts one already knows with the thoughts of others, which they already know and which you may as well. And this is one reason why most conversations are dull. One has said what one will say before, one speaks with someone who has said before what he will say, and both have heard the arguments.

But even this "conversation" can be made stimulating if the relationship between the speakers makes it so. Among friends the bond of affection may make what one says funny, interesting, etc., even if it is common and trite. And similarly with non-friends: conflict is very stimulating.

If what one said were itself interesting our relationships in conversations would be less important to us.

Even if all talk is silly, we are still left with how good the silly talk is. Just because what we can say about human behavior is ultimately circular and/or essentially speculative, that does not mean that some may not be more interesting than others.

Words do have meanings—so do sentences. There are multiple ways to respond to these, each, under some circumstances, being dangerous to one's reputation. One can simply be expressive, saying things which have little to do with the content of what others say. Or one can assume an intention on the part of sayers, and respond on the basis of the presumed profit. Or one can follow the words closely and try to come to some terms with them, even if one does so playfully rather than seriously. The danger of the first is that one can be made to look a fool; of the second that one can be far afield; of the third that the content might not warrant attention. But, nevertheless, the last named way is probably safest, as long as one is not playful inappropriately.

When we seek respect only, we should not also expect to be liked; when we seek approval only, we cannot expect to be admired (though, of course, we may think that *wanting* either will *bring* both). Those who seek approval may win neither respect nor approval—and those who seek our respect may win neither approval nor respect. Perversely, we may grudgingly admire, to some extent, those who do not care for our approval, just as we sometimes condescendingly say we like those who do not earn our respect (although with the latter we are much more likely to say they are "nice" people).

Being liked (approval) and being admired (respect) are results of entirely different processes. Admired people may also be liked, and vice versa, but they will not be admired and liked for the same reason. We win respect by doing something which earns respect (sometimes even in spite of its affects on approval). We win approval by doing something which earns approval. *Seeking* approval and respect in ways which make it obvious that what one is doing is seeking approval and respect are not likely to be those things which earn them. Acts are, acts which have as a by-product approval and respect.

Those who want another's approval will not earn his respect.

We can be trounced by our own desire to be liked, for there are people who are willing to play king-of-the-hill against us, who will place more importance than we do on trying to determine a position of belief. People differ not so much in whether they are "nasty," but whom they seem willing to push to the limits of disagreement.

Systems

If we assume that in societies, all societies, hierarchies occur (both formally in terms of status and informally in terms of esteem), then we must be careful to understand their significance and consequences. At the minimum, and by definition, hierarchies mean that some people are thought of as being in different circumstances from other people, that some are more, less, and equally worthy, more, less, and equally capable, more, less, and equally likely to make a contribution than some others. The words superior, inferior, and equal are often used in this context, but they do not adequately describe what is involved. People can feel that people are different from each other in ways which promote unequal treatment without necessarily believing them to be superior or inferior. The fact of difference itself inherently implies inequality.

It leads to nonsense, then, to speak of values like freedom and justice without taking into account the circumstances of the people involved, knowledge of their status and esteem, and the degree to which they are considered more or less equal in society's hierarchies. Freedom means something different for bottoms, middles, and tops (in terms of both status and esteem); justice for a middle is not justice for a top or bottom (using these terms very loosely, almost metaphorically). And it is not a question of whether things should be this way—clearly they *are* this way. One cannot have *equal* freedom for all without equality; one cannot have *equal* justice for all without equality. Without equality one can have a measure of freedom for all, and justice for all, but not an *equal* measure. And one cannot have equality.

Systems work because they don't work perfectly.

No matter what systems do, there will always be people who add to and subtract from what the system does, each of which makes "the" system dynamic. Leaders of systems tend to want what the people in the system want (the greater the longevity of leadership the greater this is so) while at the same time comparing actual responses of the system and the people in it to a limited number of legitimations of the system. Universal counters (such as money, status, authority, and security) become focused upon in manipulations between what the system does and how the system is legitimized.

Systems, then, have system properties which interfere with how perfectly they work as the systems they are thought of as being.

Systems divide labor and establish hierarchies. Individuals develop personal power relationships for purposes of interaction.

These may or may not be congruent. It is in this sense that power and authority are different: given any interaction those in authority may not be powerful, and the powerful may not be in authority.

Power is more general than authority, more personal, more variable, and less specificable as to who has it. And it exists even in the absence of authority.

"Authority" is a term referring to positions in hierarchies.

"Power" is a term which refers to relationships among individuals.

In every human interaction there is a potential of it becoming an exercise in personal power (who shall prevail, assuming prevailing is at issue). In organized (systematic) human enterprises authority is involved. And so, too, by extension, is power. Organized activities, then, are in this sense more complicated than those in which authority is not at issue.

Authority is invested in people by virtue of their position vis-à-vis others in an organization (or collective). Power is achieved by people as a consequence of their working out a personal relationship in which they prevail in interactions with others. "Political" outcomes are the consequence of what happens in authority situations and power relationships. One can, in this sense, exercise power over people, but not authority. Authority is legitimacy to do something, and this legitimacy can obviously be a resource in power situations. It is the only resource, by definition, for authority. Authority *is* a sense of legitimacy for what one is doing.

All systems are composed of smaller systems, and those of smaller systems, etc. How necessary is it that regulations operative at one level be identical to those in other units at the same level which are presumably doing the same thing? For example, in a College of Arts and Sciences how important is it to have regulations regarding the promotions of personnel in the History Department to be the same as those of the English Department?

Actually, to ask a question this way in the first place is to start off on an unsolvable problem. One can do this if he chooses, but perhaps only if a particular answer is important to him, for intellectually there is nothing but confusion to be found there. One can make perfectly respectable cases both that units doing the same thing should have the same regulations, and that such units need not do the same things in the same ways. Neither case is "really" better than the other, but people think so, and are willing to hassle with each other about it. But who "wins" in any given situation will depend upon the particulars of the situation, not on the arguments alone. For example, the same dispute could happen in two different universities with opposite results. Hence, in every case in which there is a problem of this sort, there is no clear answer beforehand as to who shall win. And this, of course, is one of its intriguing features.

One way of attempting to avoid these hassles is to introduce regulations "at the beginning" (systems may have many such "beginnings") which are to be consistent throughout the units. Over time, however, given different past histories, units are likely to produce variations, and language being what it is, there may even be some ambiguity with respect to the procedures required by the regulations in specific cases. What is clear to some may not be clear to others. And some may attempt to create ambiguity.

When these differences occur, as they are bound to, what follows? To what extent will ambiguity and differences be tolerated? One might say, in response, that the answers one receives will have some individual as well as unit variation. That is, the "reasons" why people will take sides will be of various kinds.

There are political hassles such as this lurking everywhere. Some people find problems where others aren't even looking. Those who see problems usually see answers as well, for people rarely raise a problem for which they themselves have no solution. Others, then, may frequently be left with what appears to be only two alternatives: (1) fight the proposal for change, or (2) change one's regulations. But notice, in each case, that the response is action of some sort. If there are people in organizations who like action better than others, who like to see problems, then we are at their mercy with respect to what hassles we will be in. An alternative to this is to raise hassles oneself. And from such considerations are things like organizational tension derived.

In hierarchies superiors may attempt to maintain superiority in two ways: by making all inferiors more or less equal, and by creating hierarchical subdivisions. The former reduces the effects of bureaucracy in general and increases the relative importance of personal power (especially among the inferiors). The latter promotes the exercise and consequences of authority and establishes competition to personal power as a determiner of outcomes.

In hierarchies inferiors may attempt to gain equality by decrying the existence of hierarchy itself. If those who are superior can be made to feel ashamed for their superior position, inferiors have gone a long way in neutralizing their (the superiors') authority. With authority (more or less) neutralized or attenuated inferiors may then attempt to assert power in personal relationships. To the extent that inferiors are more willing to deal in power than superiors (and this will be the case with at least some inferior-superior relationships) the inferiors have something to gain by such a strategy.

The question of "standards" is applicable to all systems: essentially the question is how well is the system keeping up its quality in whatever it is it is doing, a question which may, in some situations, be answered quantitatively (if quantity of output, for example, is the measure of quality). To the extent that a system has an output, one can check up on standards by measuring how well the system is doing compared with other systems.

But people raise questions, as well, about how well one goes about producing the output. Standards are applied to processes as well as outcomes, and especially so if the outputs are difficult to specify precisely, and hence difficult to compare with other systems.

In such situations "peculiar" ways of doing things are flagged for review on the grounds that they are not commonly observed, and commonly observed phenomena are allowed to pass on the grounds that there is nothing odd about them. And what is going on here is obvious when pointed out, though disconcerting to those who would apply standards: no criteria at all for oddness is being applied other than that it is odd, and oddness is presumed "bad" until shown to be "good." Hence one is expected to legitimize oddness but not commonness. In fact, one common strategy to defend oddness is to assure people that it really isn't any different, it just looks different. Which, of course, is to agree with the position that what is odd is less legitimate than what is common, *without specifying what the criteria for being legitimate are other than to be odd or common.* Hence, the whole standards question, as it is normally presented, is simply circular, playing upon the ideas in all of us that to be odd is to be less legitimate.

One might, instead, stress the fact that something is indeed odd. One might then also ask the criteria one would apply to evaluate whether something odd were legitimate. And if the criteria

are difficult to specify for something odd, they are just as difficult
to specify for something common (which is exactly why one relies
on people's agreement that oddness needs legitimizing and commonness doesn't). Frequently, then, the case for standards rests simply
on this: that those who do things commonly, desire those who do
not to do things commonly as well. Because to do things differently
threatens the underlying presumption that the common way rests
on principles which legitimize it other than that it is common.

Those who are interested in standards will support bureaucratic (that is, authoritative) procedures. Those who are interested
in innovation will minimize the "standardizing" effects of hierarchy.
"Standards" become loosely translated into authority and bureaucracy—innovation into power and unpredictability.

Most of our everyday interactions are quiescent with respect to
the power relationship inherent in any interaction. Parties to an
interaction usually proceed on the basis of an unstated acceptance
of a certain power mode (equality, superior-inferior, inferior-
superior) which, when left alone, permits an interaction unthreat-
ened by power considerations. And in "new" interactions, as with
strangers, a certain amount of preliminary information exchange
and coyness unearths the basis for an acceptance of a relationship
of a cetrain kind. Any interaction may be awkward and encourage
self-consciousness (as when one is the inferior in an infrequent
inferior-superior interaction), but it takes place as both parties
"expect." (Sometimes, for example, we may be surprised when an
interaction is not as awkward as we thought it would be, such as
coming to speedy relationship terms with a stranger.) It is not that
power is not involved in these interactions—it is that people accept
the power relationship and treat it as an arguable given.

But it is always possible that one or another of the participants
may desire a change in the heretofore accepted relationship, or may
not be willing to accept the expectations of the other with respect
to the relationship, or may inadvertently threaten the other, or himself feel threatened by the other. In these situations the existence
of power as part of the interaction quickly becomes apparent, with
one consequence that the interaction becomes more complex (and
more stimulating). Each participant now finds himself with a double load: himself as an individual, perhaps advocating a position
or expressing his self, and as a party to a now obvious power relationship. One is not only aware of himself, but has an awareness of

his relationship to the other, the other's relationship to him, an awareness that the other may be having the same problems, and that these matters are no longer part of the interactional givens. Those who have strategies for disturbed as well as undisturbed power relationships have a greater repertoire of self-defense—just as those who are capable (and willing) to challenge (and thereby make uneasy) existing power givens are often considered offensive.

Those who are committed are not unwilling to use power. If the young are more committed than the older then one would expect the use of power to be a more likely practice of the young. Besides, older people can often use authority rather than power, and so, in some ways, lose incentives to use power.

One characteristic of a willingness to use power in personal relationships is one's willingness to tolerate not being liked. If, given two people, one is more willing to be disliked by the other, the person less willing to be disliked will have a power disadvantage.

Whenever we disapprove something there are *always* two issues involved: the grounds upon which we disapprove (are there "good" grounds for disapproval?) ; and the effects of the act of disapproval (is disapproval itself appropriate?). Sometimes, for example, we may "legitimately" disagree with someone, but we may wish simply to express that disagreement, or to encourage the other to change his mind, not prevent the person from doing what he is doing.

The best protection of our own freedom may lie in the protection of the freedom of others.

It is useful to encourage others (and oneself) to state objections in terms of general rules. If one encourages *ad hoc* objections then mysteries may be proliferated. If people are asked to give reasons, at least one can come to grips with those reasons, to "argue" with them, point out the usefulness of stating one's reasons in terms of general rules, and then see whether the person "really" wants to accept those general rules.

Presumably, if one objects, there are criteria involved for objection. But in many instances people will object without being able to specify why, or if they do specify why one might want to argue with the reasons. Frequently, the "real" basis of their objection is simply that they would *prefer* the world one way as opposed to another—if they had their druthers the world would look like this ("this" being either as it is or as it isn't) . And if one encourages people to object to and disallow the activities of others on grounds of "I wish the world were 'such-and-so'" (a world which would exclude the thing being proposed) it will encourage a general restriction on the activities of people. The reasons for stating objections in general rules is simply this: if people are made to formulate their objections in general terms the objection may include things which the objector would not want to include, or have consequences which the objector would not favor. If criteria are made explicit one can inspect the reasonableness of the criteria and attempt to assess the consequences of a general rule formulated in that particular way.

Those who have much to offer will let those who wish to bestow mutually advantageous benefits come to them; those who have little to offer must work with diligence in making themselves candidates. Most public flurries of activity, then, are sustained by those who have little to offer, following their most promising strategy.

The most tempting mistake in the world is to think of oneself as one who has much to offer.

Ambivalence

There comes a time in one's life when things settle down, when the swirl and business of getting on ceases its wildly progressive activity and we have a chance to see ourselves almost still, creating an opportunity for reflection in which we can extrapolate our life into the future. This, when one does not like the result, can be a devastating experience and will lead, inevitably, to a change of life of some sort.

All of us, from time to time, come against the following problem: we want desperately to believe in something while at the same time realizing that such a belief would be in the nature of a superstition, that if we believed we would be believing in a myth. We also seem to half realize that in these moments of doubt we reveal that we believe in beliefs which when we doubt them appear to us as myths and superstitions. Our myth at these times is that our presumed myths are all there is to beliefs, and that they are explicit and knowable (in the sense that we think they are what we think they are). Doubt is the other side of faith—they go together like good and bad. Doubt pushes us to what we believe in when we question the faith we think we used to believe in.

And from this point we can go in one of two directions. We

can either reject the previous faith, suffer pain (in the form of emptiness), and attempt to erect a faith in its place (which branch itself has several possible branches), or we can return to our original faith, realizing it as imperfect and thereby embracing it somewhat more distantly than before. Most of us are reluctant to push ourselves in the first direction—and in that lies the basis for much cynicism and a sense of detachment from one's own life.

We all have double vision, and can use each eye singly as well. We see, and we see ourselves seeing. And sometimes we only see ourselves seeing, even though we aren't seeing at the moment; and sometimes we see at the moment and only later see ourselves as we think we were seeing.

When in double vision we experience a strange, but quite normal sense of distance, as though we were and we weren't doing what we are doing. As we are doing two things and only think of ourselves as really doing one this sense of "strangeness-to-oneself" should not be unexpected—the inner eye, when operating in conjunction with the other, is thought of as an illicit and even abnormal interference.

When we only see ourselves we experience a murkiness we would just as soon clear up, and so try to do so. Contemplation is like constructing an edifice in the fog: one knows it's there even though one can see only hazy bits of it. It is a somewhat unreal experience, always conjuring up what one knows it must be like.

And when we see only, we are so highly committed to action that our sense of engagement, of attachment, of being at one with the outside world (which, interestingly, is usually produced by being at twos with it) overwhelms our inner eye.

Since we alternate among these three modes of vision, life takes on a number of peculiar properties, peculiar not only because we have different visions of the world, but also because we think they must all be part of the same thing. Much of our mental life is spent integrating a naturally disintegrative set of experiences.

We "have" many things in the sense that in making sense of what we do we attribute to ourselves and others properties which produce what we do. One of the things we may be said to have in this sense is generalized anxiety, a state of ambivalence with respect to the world around us, wanting to be connected to it but realizing that connecting ourselves would commit us to something slightly unworthy of us. People work out this generalized anxiety in many ways, one of which is to work for the creation of bureaucratic-like structures to do some particular thing which becomes that which the generalized anxiety focuses itself and one's other resources upon, at least for a time. It becomes one of life's projects which keeps us busy and connected—connected in the sense of committing ourselves to the betterment of the world which only incidentally connects us to working within the world as it is, a connection which is therefore justified by not being a commitment to the world as it is. We may then feel worthy. It would be fair to say that when we do this we feel little sense of what we do personally and by ourselves as being of value, of intrinsic importance. We externalize our generalized anxiety to give meaning to ourselves as we work it off. And at other times we turn inward and want to construct an internal structure to sift the generalized anxiety for nuggets of meaning. We become immensely aware of our own value, of what we have to offer, and we wish to let others do what they want to do, knowing that our generosity is prompted by a feeling of superiority, and want others to leave us alone while at the same time showing us respect. One of the features of generalized anxiety is that it is not solvable for either of these options, and we find ourselves frustrated and bouncing back and forth between them.

All of us develop some notion of poor quality in our intellectual preoccupations, and the exercise of poor quality by others is frightfully threatening to us—as if our very justification as processors was being called into question by the existence of inferior products (and producers) in the market. Vacuousness in the things one identifies with, when produced by others, brings out the specter of emptiness in ourselves, as if people will now find us out as we have reluctantly, and not explicitly, found ourselves out.

It is partially by recognizing emptiness in others, however, that we establish what we ourselves do as important, so that our own products are shown to have some substance. So we counter our emptiness for ourselves as processors with significance for what we do as compared with others, an enterprise that leaves us strongly ambivalent and disquieted.

Whenever something significant is said or happens there develops an explosion of meaning brought on by a doubling procedure: not only has something significant occurred, but the fact that something significant has occurred is itself significant. And an interesting feature of this is that we think about and attempt to act upon both.

When one wishes to understand the world (or be successful in it) a command of complication is essential. One cannot catch up the nature of significant occurrences (nor, for that matter, act effectively in them) without acknowledging this duality and thereby coming to some conclusions with respect to both features.

The state of becoming is itself a state of being.

We all demand to be treated as respected objects while knowing, really, that we are in a state of becoming, a precarious state of becoming, and that becomers cannot be the objects they would like to be treated as. Social intercourse is stimulating partly for this reason: can we carry off our objectness without being seen through? And interestingly, although we see through ourselves, we seldom think of others as in the same situation as we ourselves. We treat others as objects—in fact it is fairly clear that we have no choice in the matter, for in dealing with people as becoming they become, to us, becomers.

It is a part of intimacy to allow others to hear one speak of oneself as becoming (for a becomer is a speech person, not an action person) and it is an act of betrayal to take advantage of this confidence and use it against the other, rebuking or chiding them for not being a "finished" object. Intimates, however, partly to illustrate that they have a special right, sometimes exploit this confidence, a feature of intimacy which brings our wanting to be thought of as a respected object to a cruel conclusion.

We have no choice but to treat others as objects.

When we know we shall experience a future different from our routine (and are thereby less certain than usual of what it will consist), we express the accompanying anxiety in ways which increase our sense of ourselves and reduce our attention and connection to the unknown future. All of our levels of consciousness become more highly activated—to the purpose of filling the sense of void the self experiences surrounded as it is by an enlarged emptiness. We then experience a sense of oscillation as we attempt to bring the relation of self to ambience back to routine proportions, succeed somewhat in short spurts, and fall back again.

Pretense

Pretense is acting as though one is not aware of what he is doing when one is. This is often contrasted with "natural" behavior, acting as though one is not aware of what he is doing when he isn't.

We do what we do. And we think about what we do. We may even think about our thinking about what we do. Sometimes we find that we have been so involved in what we have been doing that we have not been thinking about ourselves doing it. We do so only later. When people feel that they or others are acting in this fashion such behavior may be referred to as natural. It may look, however, as pretentious as behavior which one refers to as really pretentious (as defined above). We ourselves may know when our own behavior has, in the past, been associated with awareness or not, but clearly others cannot. Also, since we all think about our behavior and anticipate (when possible and feasible) future behavior, and are behaving and thinking relatively continuously, does it make any difference whether one acts pretentiously or naturally? If one is aware of his behavior is his behavior any different than if he weren't? There is, and can be, no answer to this question, since we slip in and out of these things all the time. We may feel there is or should be a difference, but is there?

Acting pretentiously is a way we keep tabs on ourselves, and all of us do so. Pretense is not something that can be analyzed at a particular time. Since only the person himself could ever know when he was not aware of himself, then he could not give an "on the spot" testimony, only later. And when he does so later he is then aware of his natural behavior and therefore, after the fact, is in pretense. This is not exactly the Heisenberg principle of indeterminancy, but it has a similar consequence.

Pretense is a natural consequence of man's capacity to be aware of himself. We might more appropriately ask other questions about pretense, what it means, for example, to despair about one's behavior, or rejoice in it, rather than pretend that natural and pretentious behavior can be fruitfully contrasted.

People who dress or act unusually, particularly if they follow other than the most common trend, may be thought of as especially pretentious. Examples are men who adopt a Mexican look (including mustache), or women who adopt one or another nationality costume. It may be safely assumed that people know what they look like—indeed, they have undoubtedly made something of a study of themselves. But then we who conform to another style or who dress idiosyncratically have also thought about ourselves and what we look like. It is possible we do not feel as excited as those who dress unusually, but clearly it requires more than the concept of pretense to account for those who appear pretentious because they stage themselves unusually.

We all seek stimulation from time to time, and some adopt styles which will occasion comment. It is an easy way of bringing attention to oneself, anyone could do it, and it requires no work or skill. Is it any wonder, then, that some opt for unusual costumes? Others may seek such attention by more "marginal" activities, such as a slight variation in the expected mode, or by buying a Cadillac, or by watering the lawn without a shirt. There are many ways to try to make one's life exciting. And one interesting feature is that it often works: that is, we do become excited over other people's efforts to give themselves excitement by wearing or doing something which is thought by them to bring attention to themselves by exciting us.

A pretense, as the word is frequently used, means an attempt to be something one really isn't. In this sense people whose pretenses bother us are people who seem to be trying to make it by pretense alone. For example, if a very attractive middle-class white girl dresses like an Indian we may be quite impressed. But if a rather plain middle-class white girl does so we will more likely think of her as trying to be what she isn't. It is difficult to do something well, and this includes pretenses.

When we are in strange of uncomfortable surroundings we pretend, we stage a performance, we become actors. It is only when we are accustomed to situations that we can behave "truly."

This is one of the reasons why intimacy is a pretense in all situations where the parties are not truly intimate. The rules of intimacy are inappropriate to strangers who are likely to feel distant from each other. Pretending one is intimate when one is not simply adds to the sense of strangeness.

Once we have become comfortable with acting as though something makes a difference even when we know it doesn't we have a view of ourselves and others which protects us from being down to most people, and which allows us to be up on some. Knowing how to be serious and how to be playful is a form of control. When others are serious we can be seriously playful.

Artificiality has a certain charm, especially as one grows older. After all, only God can make a tree.

How much of our talk depends upon our belief that our words are "real." We can only talk about things interpretively if we, at the minimum, pretend our words are real, and actually the pretense is in one sense impossible. One can pretend, but can one pretend about the words one uses to talk about one's pretense?

If we know that even a pretense is a pretense it undoubtedly mellows us inside although it could result in ferocious outside effects. If one knows he speaks precariously he can become debilitated —but he can also use his speech for effect, he can control his contribution at the level at which most are out of control.

Sometimes we know we have something even though we don't know what that something is—we act and feel as though we are telling someone even though all we have is the feeling that we have something. It's the obverse of the feeling we have when we know we have nothing.

Cynicism

Cynicism has a progressive history in individuals. It starts the first time one sees through someone's actions or explanations. A child may feel he is being put on, that someone is misleading him, lying to him, not telling him everything, and that something still remains lurking underneath, that all of what is involved is not on the surface. As the child grows older he becomes increasingly aware of things hidden, of inadequate explanations, of half-truths and outright lies. And, of course, the child itself participates in this— he himself also masks his activities, thoughts, and feelings.

As a child develops his own perspective on things he also learns to view some people as simply misled—they are not so much lying as wrong—they are simply incapable of understanding the way the child (now part adult) sees and understands things. And we are, of course, taught to be cynical of some things. Little children may be made aware not to accept rides with strangers, national enemies are seen as liars and deceivers, advertisers are after your money, etc. Once a child begins to learn to be cynical of some people, a measure of seeming to be in control becomes possible. Mothers and fathers, friends, and especially enemies are sometimes seen through and their base motives exposed.

As a child grows he develops a commitment to his explanation and becomes somewhat alienated from that which he uses his explanation to see through. Early cynicism is normally combined with the hopes and enthusiasms of youth. Not only can a young adult expose the selfishness and baseness of others, he also believes his world is not like that, and that the worlds of others need not be like that either. In order to give themselves importance they give to themselves ideal motives and then expose us all.

But as the simple cynic grows older he gains experience. He meets failure, becomes frustrated, has his dreams thwarted, and takes on a more complicated world, including responsibilities which drive him to the very selfish, economic, personal motives he has condemned so ardently. And he begins to become cynical of his own cynicism—to see through his own see-throughs—and become confused. He may even, with others his own age or older, begin to express his doubts. And he may look upon those younger than himself as somewhat naïve.

But even in confusion and despair one must continue to protect himself. And so one becomes aware of the rhetorical tricks, arguments, and demagogy that one practiced but never thought about. One becomes aware of these devices for what they are and for what they can do. The world has become too complicated for simple cynicism—truth is less clear and what one has to do to win more obvious. And those who are in the heat of simple cynicism, who see their underlying explanations as true, who possess hopes and dreams for the world, find those who have become cynical of cynicism as flippant, non-serious, dishonest, and/or irrelevant.

People who have reached a particular level of cynicism will not be able to see those who have reached a higher one as those who have reached a higher level see themselves. Levels of cynicism have associated intellectual feeling-tones—one must experience these tones to know them in the sense of understanding them as those who have experienced them understand them. One can read about them in books, or be exposed to talk about them, and not "know" in the sense just described. And not to know in this sense is to be in potential conflict and misunderstanding. Those at lower levels of cynicism will see those at higher in terms of categories consistent with the lower levels, for example, categories perhaps like "intelligent-stupid," "selfish-generous," "good-evil." "Highers" will be inclined to "understand," and to be didactic, which, by and large, will simply make "lowers" angry. Highers are condescending to lowers because lowers can't see the point of view of the highers. "Lowers" are arrogant with "highers" because they cannot see the view of the highers. And all of this makes for turmoil.

To believe that "things are not what they seem," to believe that one knows what they really are, and to believe in the truth and goodness of what one is doing is the height of *primary* cynicism.

But one can become cynical of cynicism. To believe that "things are what they are," that nothing can be done, that no hopes are possible of fulfillment, is the height of *secondary* cynicism.

One then, perhaps, may enter tertiary cynicism and believe that although nothing makes any difference we must live and try to prevail, even though our words are fabricated. Tertiary cynics often attain a sort of wisdom and a capacity to make their way in the world. They have two jumps on the young, one on many adults, and few have a bigger jump on them.

The intellectual predicament of a third-order cynic is precisely this: he feels he can never take himself seriously, nor others—yet he also knows he does, will, and must. His sense of importance is derived from his being able to assert this as knowledge; his fear, constant and terrible, is that he will take this knowledge seriously, and lapse into a confirmed (almost enthusiastically embraced), blistery, and acid mental paralysis. Whenever we know something we find it difficult to act *past* what we know.

Intellectual Development

People are quite accustomed to discussing mental development, mostly in terms of intelligence. Test results of various sorts, or performances in kinds of activities come to "stand for" some imagined mental capacity. In everyday language some people are thought of as "smarter," some as "dumber." And we also develop such concepts as "mental capacity" and with it "under" and "over achieving." All this is a dreadful manner of speaking and has and will lead us nowhere.

But clearly there are people who partake more frequently in what might be called intellectual things. We all use our minds—but some of us focus on some things, some on others. Intellectual activity, which will be defined here as continuing efforts to understand one's world, is a kind of mental activity which might fruitfully be discussed in terms of more or less discrete stages, and on the following dimension.

Some people do not recognize paradoxes. These are usually the young though many of us sip at this particular fountain of youth all our lives. Some recognize paradoxes but think them unimportant (some of these *make* paradoxes unimportant by learning "solutions" to them). Some live with paradox, recognize it as a constant companion, and become, more or less, contentedly confused. And some use the existence of paradoxes to attain great heights, by playing with paradoxes, becoming involved in their intricacies, and rising above them and the rest of mankind, intellectually.

When we analyze human behavior we will analyze differently if we are self-conscious that we are analyzing than if we simply analyze unaware that the analysis is an analysis being done by us. Those who do not feel this sense of distance from themselves as analyzers are likely to be interesting only as objects of someone else's analysis. Those who do, have a chance to say something of universal interest.

Sometimes we find others insulting our intelligence, a situation we could interpret as giving themselves reason for thinking of themselves as of superior intelligence. When *we* think of *ourselves* as of superior intelligence (which we may inadvertently fall into from time to time) we might ask whether our own actions could be similarly interpretable.

It is possible, of course, to have something of greater worth to say about a particular problem than someone else, although the chances may be slim—but even in this case there will be *some* others for whom it is not true. If we are in the same league as Dostoevsky, Plato, Hume, and T. S. Eliot, we certainly shouldn't expect others to be. It may be that the people with whom we quarrel intellectually indicates the level of discourse with which we feel competitive.

If we assume that no one will ever "really" know the answers to human behavior then we can allow ourselves to be much more impressed by the cleverness of answers which some people give. If, on the other hand, we think there is *an* answer which we may some-day discover, then we are likely to be much more tolerant of pedestrian activities in some areas of inquiry and intolerant of brilliant activities in others.

When we judge another's "theory" we usually do so on the basis of how close we apprehend its being to "the truth": we accept those theories which are perceived by us to be "essentially" true, and reject those we think are false; we marshal arguments and evidence in favor of the perspectives we judge correct, and against the perspectives we feel are wrong.

But think how it might be to look at theories as neither true nor false but more or less interesting, brilliant, elaborate, comprehensive, and sensible. We would then find some theories more attractive than others, not because some are necessarily truer—rather because they partake more or less of these other criteria. One of the major advantages of this is that we would be able to reject mediocrity (and worse) pretty quickly—at a great saving of one's intellectual life, though perhaps a bit hard on one's intellectual safety. After all most interesting, brilliant, elaborate, comprehensive, and sensible theories are threatening, since we must admit an incapacity to provide one ourselves. One can agree easily enough that *one* of them is truth, and labor in *that* vineyard. But if the vineyard is itself intellectual brilliance then one "finds" there (by attribution) mostly sour grapes. If we allow someone to be a genius (and hence a superhuman) then it is important to protect ourselves by pointing to the nonsense which some other attributed geniuses contribute. It is somewhat easier to grant the category "genius" if we can reject some of those who are judged by others to be in the category. That way although we do have to grant the category we maintain control over who is allowed in. Related to this is the idea that we can more easily tolerate genius if we can call what they do "true."

The question should not be whether one is right or wrong, but how well one can say whatever it is he wishes to say—now intellectually powerful one can make his position—in what intellectual league one aspires to play. Right and wrong, truth and falsehood, are poor ways to judge intellectual gaming, since it is a good deal easier to fit someone's notion of correctness than of intellectual brilliance. Thinking we have "the truth" will, in the face of intellectual combat, turn out to be an unviable defense.

The more complicated one makes his understanding of men, regardless of content, the more useful will be the understanding, the greater the individual's ability to deal with the world as it comes at him, the more interesting the person will be, the better he will be able to protect his position, and the more persuasive he will be in showing others what the world is like. What we do, when we increase our understanding, is to increase our elaboration of what the world consists in terms of our ability to think about it. All positions force a complicated world into certain channels, and the more simplistic the understanding the more this is true.

Raveling a complication can be a lifetime activity. One can have respect for some fellow ravelers, depending, essentially, on how complete an understanding one is given (and this is why the category "genius" usually requires an enormous commitment and a large corpus of work). (One can also feel patronizingly toward some young, "promising" ravelers or toward those who left a temptingly small product, due, perhaps, to an early death.)

And one can have more or less passionate disdain for those whose level of complication is embarrassingly low, who are lacking proficiency, and who therefore threaten the dignity of the enterprise itself (and, by extension, oneself as a participant).

But one will simply treat as inferior, as lesser folk entirely, those who think that assertions can have intellectual merit on some basis other than raveling. For these will be followers who don't understand what their commitment has committed them to.

One can have ideas. And within these ideas one can move horizontally or vertically. And when one moves vertically he can move up or down. In the context of this metaphor how we move in our understanding of things affects the kinds of complications we confront.

In moving horizontally one can have "additional" ideas, ideas which relate to the previous ones "at the same level," ideas which are cumulative. This is one way in which one can become more complicated. Frequently in our thinking, when we add ideas, we add them in this manner.

In moving vertically, but downward, one can increase complication by adding "evidence" for one's ideas, examples, "facts" which are meant to show the validity of one's ideas. What becomes complicated, when this occurs, is not the ideas but the implications about the relationships between the "data" and the idea. Other ideas (often criticism, for example) may be suggested and one could move laterally. Often, however, one will simply add another idea which itself becomes an "island" to be discussed as the previous island was being discussed—in a more or less self-contained way until another island is suggested.

When one moves vertically upward one has ideas about one's ideas; and one can have ideas about one's ideas about one's ideas. And this is not "just" a word game (although it is, among other things, a word game). The complications involved here include such things as paradoxes (an assertion which seems peculiar because

it could be interpreted as being about itself as well as about the
"intended" object) and other difficulties which we may find discomforting.

Moving vertically upward or downward, of course, also "adds"
ideas (as in horizontal movement), and thereby increases complexity, but in a basically noncumulative way. In moving downward one is likely to find separate clusters of single ideas; in moving
upward one is likely to find ideas which have "peculiar" relationships with each other, many of which are sometimes interpreted as
self-destructive.

The nature of one's intellectual experience is affected fundamentally by the extent of one's repertoire on these dimensions.

There is a false distinction made between intellectual activity
and doing. Intellectualization is a form of doing, and what one does
and how well one does it are certainly partly a function of intellect.
It turns out that most intellectualizing is thought of as not worth
doing. But then neither is most doing.

The same great book is written over and over again: the questions, the doubts, the thinking, the task, these are all the same; it
is the answers which we find different.

Those who steal the thoughts of others are hardly reproducing
those thoughts, and it is this, and not the repetition, which makes
plagiarism a waste.

There are two thoughts (which one also feels on the occasions
one has one or the other of them) which distinguish people intellectually (frequently, but not always, by age): 1. if one can see his
own life as a failure; and 2. if one can see that life itself can be
viewed as a failure.

Philosophy, or any sort of intellectual creativity, is important
only to those for whom the obviously important has lost its attraction (or never got hold). One must first pass over worrying about
"getting on," about making one's own world materially and spir-
itually better. Concerned with marginal problems a mind will see
importance only in the intensely personal and will eschew the general, vacuous, and intellectual. One cannot create beauty when one
wants to trivialize—one must want to devour one's creation and
become a thing that is now beautiful.

To intellectualize is to engage in meaning-giving. An "intellectual," then, in the context of social reality, is someone who spends

a good deal of his time giving meaning to things. Someone we call an "interesting" intellectual is able to give meaning to things in ways which stimulate our own ontological natures.

To be creative, intellectually, is to construct one's own meaning. Most of us are satisfied with the meanings provided by others.

When one is being intellectual he is concerned with the interpretation of something, rather than with fact alone. Most human activity and products are intellectually thin. Those which are "fat" frequently are categorized as profound or sophisticated. Intellectual sophistication, although a difficult concept to define and to keep separate from what one finds intellectually creative or interesting, is the extent to which one is able to surround one's world (and others') in complicated meaning.

One can test his own intellectual abilities in the following three ways (in order of difficulty):

1. Can one provide interesting, profound, and creative (these, too, are in order of difficulty) contexts for the trivial utterances of others?

2. Can one himself utter interesting, profound, and creative utterances?

3. Can one provide at least equally interesting, profound, and creative contexts for the interesting, profound, and creative intellectualizations of others?

All of us, then, are intellectual to some extent. That is, we all give explicit meaning to things and events (and ourselves). But for some, giving meaning intellectually becomes a way of making meaningful their whole lives. And these are more properly called "intellectuals," a few of whom do their work interestingly, creatively, and profoundly.

In understanding it is never possible to be too complicated.

Epilogue

There's a difference between a "solution" to a puzzle and to a problem. A puzzle has *an* answer—all of the pieces go together in one way. There are, of course, a multitude of ways of putting them together, but with only one result. Some things in life are like puzzles—for example, how much do the following numbers add up to: 44, 2, 18, 117, 0, and 23? There are also problems. Problems are those things which disturb us, for which we want answers, and for which there are none.

Having no answers there are also many answers, including no answer, many answers, and, interestingly enough, one answer. (In this formulation the meaning of "answer" has changed, which is part of the point.) And there are things in life which are like problems.

We notice, sometimes, that some people treat puzzles like problems; there are people who do not know some puzzles when they see them. We are also likely to notice, perhaps more frequently, that some people treat problems like puzzles and argue about the correct solution to *the* puzzle when *the* puzzle is a problem. Or, someone treats a problem like a problem, someone else shows an answer as though it were a puzzle, and the other person believes the original problem is now a solved puzzle. And there are a few cases where puzzles are so difficult that they take on the character of problems. And there are many who think that some problems are so easy they take on the character of puzzles.

When we have a puzzle we can argue about the character of the answer, but the argument assumes there is an answer. When we have a problem we can argue about the character of the answer too, but it might be important for the nature of our understanding of what goes on in arriving at an answer to realize the difference between this and arguments about answers to puzzles. Also, in both puzzles and problems we can argue about strategies of arriving at answers, but again the contexts are different. When we argue for a solution to a problem we might try to keep in mind that there are no solutions like there are to puzzles. The nature of argument, however, may not promote this. Puzzles drive out problems, which is another way to say that there is a tendency to argue as though problems were puzzles. But those who so argue with the knowledge that they are really arguing about a problem will have an edge on those who do so "mistakenly."

Puzzles have answers (a single answer) —problems have solutions (one of a number of possible ways of dealing with a phenomenon). It is at least as important to be aware of whether one wants to treat what one is talking about as a puzzle or a problem as it is to find an answer or a solution. For clearly whether something *is* a problem or a puzzle is determined by how we wish to look at it. For example, in 2 + 2 = 4, 4 looks like an answer to a puzzle. But it could be treated as a solution to a problem depending upon what we mean by 2 + 2. For example, 2 gallons of sugar and 2 gallons of water do not equal four gallons of sugar water. We must make some assumptions to make something a puzzle. We must "absolutize" something. So whether we have a puzzle or not depends upon our willingness to make assumptions.

If puzzles can be turned into problems by relaxing assumptions, then, conversely, problems can be turned into puzzles by tightening them. And clearly we have, ourselves, control over what we are going to assume. Hence we can make anything a problem or a puzzle, depending upon our purposes. For example, rhetorically it is often useful to change what someone else thinks is a problem into a puzzle, and vice versa. This is, indeed, the way in which many arguments run. And again if we are aware of this, not only can we do it ourselves if we want to, we can spot it in others as well.

We give answers to problems and puzzles, but in doing so we show what we are "really" up to. Our answers, being efforts to settle matters, show us as restless and anxious to put questions to rest.

BOOK

2

About Hugo Potts

1
The Office

Professor Hugo Potts sat pensively in his office, hands to lips. Actually, at the moment, he was thinking about what he was doing at that very moment, sitting there, hands to lips. And then he did what he had come to do frequently of late. He thought that if he did it, so too must others. And he thought, yes, that's right, he had frequently seen people put their hands to their lips, especially men, beardless and mustacheless men. Those having facial hair seem to play with it, but those without can be seen to rub their lips, or rest the side or tips of their fingers on them.

Hugo Potts sat musing. He often sat thus, hands to lips, half-thinking, half-fantasizing, half-resting. He was never sure why he did this, and he was especially puzzled as to whether or not it was *productive*. He liked to think it might be, but then he liked to think that all of his "mind-wandering" was constructive. Potts was, you see, a writer, a creative writer, a putter-down of thoughts which he fancied he thought of himself (and which indeed he did, for if he had a thought which he knew to be someone else's he would cast it from his mind, and certainly not write it down). He didn't like to think that just sitting there might be wasting time, that it wasn't in some way related to his work. He preferred to view these reverie periods as being *necessary* to his creative moments when he would actually write down a thought he knew he had never read nor heard anywhere before. And this—this creativity—was such a joyous experience (in a quiet sort of joyous way, as in a longish mood of reverence culminating in exhilarated exhaustion) that he knew he couldn't do it all the time. And so he must sit, and think, and muse, and let his mind wander. And although he suspected that great writers with great genius didn't sit around and muse like that, he actually didn't know if they did or not. And if he were resting—

then he was resting, and there's an end to it. But he hoped it was more like *germinating*.

There was a knock on Pott's door. He welcomed the knock, and immediately came to. What could ensue as a consequence of opening the door might give Potts something to think about—some *real* material from which to fashion a thought. Potts, by the way, almost always kept his office door closed. This was not because he did not like to see people—in fact he did. It was simply a way of sealing himself off as an encouragement to do more than witness the bustle of activity outside his office: secretaries across the hall, students rushing to class or looking for a professor. These chance glances were not very good material for thought. Nor were short hellos and nods. Potts liked to do three things: write, think, and have *significant* conversations ("significant" meaning producing thought). And so he closed his door to the furtive and brief, and waited for the sustained and meaningful. A knock on the door was an opportunity, and he always found it exciting.

"Come in." Potts had to shout, as the door and walls were thick and knockers not likely to hear. "Come in, come in," Potts shouted again. The door opened and a girl entered, stopped, and asked, "Professor Potts?"

"Yes, come in," Potts said mildly, "have a seat" as he motioned to the chair next to his desk, pushing back his own chair as he did so. Potts smiled at the girl. "What may I do for you?" Potts always asked this, or alternatively, if he felt jocular, "How may I serve you?" (an allusion to a Kurt Vonnegut, Jr. novel, *God Bless You, Mr. Rosewater*). He did try to make students feel at ease, but he had a sneaking suspicion that in fact he was not very successful at it. Oh well, no matter. We do the best we can. And besides, what difference could it possibly make?

The girl sat down, directly in front of Potts now as he had pushed his chair out away from his desk, and crossed her legs, adjusting her skirt as she did so. Potts was a sucker for legs. Actually, Potts was rather bothered by this habit of his—looking at the legs, breasts, and faces of girls and women. He liked to think of himself, Potts did, as someone immune to such things. And, in a way, he was. That is, he had never done anything about it. He did still feel the desire to look, though, and although he talked himself into believing it to be a harmless pastime he was vexed that he couldn't give it up. He sometimes thought that it was simply the price one pays for being a man—nature's way of insuring species survival. Just as nature induces women to provoke such attention. "I'd like to take an independent study with you this term," the girl said, sweetly. She looked directly into his eyes. Potts accepted her stare, then looked toward the door.

"What did you have in mind doing?" he asked, again mildly, returning his eyes to her and glancing all over the girl, as she looked down at her feet. He wished she were very bright, and very witty, but he didn't count on it. He always wished for brightness—it gave him an excuse to carry on an interaction—even to take the initiative. No other incentives would do. If the person weren't bright he or she would just have to initiate for herself.

"I thought maybe something on symbols," the girl replied. She looked hopefully at Potts. She had nice breasts, too, strongly suggested in the shirt she was wearing.

"Anything in particular?" he asked further. At this point it could go either way.

"Well, I'm not really sure." The student was now a bit perplexed. Potts had a dreadful feeling that this might not get anywhere.

"What interests you about symbols?" Potts ventured. He was really going out of his way for her, although he might have done the same for anyone. He wanted so much for her to have some ideas of her own. But then he wished that for everyone, too.

The girl didn't quite know how to begin. "Well . . . I suppose . . . how symbols are such a part of man's existence—how he is what he is because of them. I can't really say it easily. It's something I would like to look into."

Not bad, thought Potts. He'd heard worse. Not good, of course. I mean, not brilliant, but not bad either.

"Can you give me an idea you have about symbols?" Potts asked, almost embarrassed. He didn't expect very many people to have ideas, and he knew he was running a risk of putting the girl on a spot. Nevertheless he did want to see what this might lead to, so he risked a complete break: that is, a realization by the student that she had no thoughts whatever, and would never have.

"I'm interested in the way symbols are used by people to provide meaning . . . to make sense of things for people."

By God, she had almost hit the jackpot. And to think of all the things she could have said, from "I haven't thought about it much" to "I'm interested in symbols as a form of communication." UGH. But she didn't. She wants to know about how symbols provide meaning. This was absolutely grand, and just a mite threatening. Perhaps that was why he felt so exhilarated. He must test her further.

"Do symbols ever not provide meaning?" Potts asked quickly, realizing halfway through that the question was not yet appropriate for her. He actually felt somewhat relieved. But why should he? What had he to feel threatened about? How old was she? Nineteen? Twenty? It was certainly sufficient that she was as far along as she was. After all, how far along had he been at her age?

"What do you mean?" she asked, looking a bit frightened and visibly tensing. Potts had done it again. He had asked something that didn't make sense to someone who thought it probably did but not to her. She had no defense for this. She literally didn't know what to say. And she was frightened.

Potts went on now, but trying to smooth it over as he went. "Well, the question of symbols as meaning-providers might be looked at from a number of different perspectives. And one question to ask, one among many, is whether symbols can also not give meaning. And I ask this to get at the question of whether one is willing to say something like the following: 'Meaningless symbols are also meaningful.' Because if that's sensible to you, if you're comfortable with that, then we're in one world. If you're not we're in another."

From the look on her face, a bit pained, actually, Potts saw they were "in another."

"But," Potts added quickly, "the important point is that you do have some direction for this thing. I'm just delighted. It sounds like it could be a very interesting project." He smiled delightedly. She took some time doing so, but she expanded a bit herself. Slowly, ever so slowly, she was relaxing again.

"Would you be willing to write a paper? It's standard practice with me. I demand some sort of intellectual product at the end, or during, for that matter. Normally something written, but under some circumstances I would take a painting or sculpture. It depends, a bit, on what you want to say and how you think you'd like to say it. And the paper, by the way, need not be a regular term paper. It could be poetry, drama, fiction—whatever you like." Potts enjoyed giving this little speech. It had taken him a while to come to so liberal a position concerning what he would accept as evidence for a grade and he was proud of the breadth of his demands. Most students found such discretion difficult to handle, and this student was no exception.

"Well . . . ah . . . It's . . . Yes . . . I could do a paper," she finally got out.

"Yes, well why don't you think about it a bit. See what you think might be suitable for you and the topic. I just want you to know, by saying all this, that anything, any *style,* will be suitable for me. I don't require just a straightforward term paper. Yoy may certainly do one if you choose. But it's your choice, not mine. All I really ask for is some sort of intellectual product, some *thing* that shows what you've been thinking about."

As Potts said this it occurred to him that he hadn't thought of her face, her breasts, or her legs for some time. He did now. He figuratively gorged himself in fantasy.

"Why don't you think about this a while, see if it's what you want to do, and then come back and let me know. You might also let me know in more detail what you would like to do. I'd prefer that the ideas be your own. In fact I insist on it. I will give you some of my own, though not explicitly, and I will give you other people's, and I will comment on yours. I'll also help you as much as I can with things you might like to read. All right?"

As Potts said this he felt that the interview should be over. He liked to cut things off quickly. No prolonged good-byes, no dragging things out, no idle chitchat, if possible. With some students, if they didn't catch his intentions in his voice he would sometimes stand up. They, of course, would have to do the same. At least no one had not done so. The student, fortunately, did take the hint.

"I have a card. Do you sign it now?" She handed him a registration card for the independent study she wanted which Potts, if he were agreeable, would then sign, and she would take to the Registrar's Office.

"Yes, I can sign it now. Are you sure it's what you want to do?"

"Oh, yes," she said.

"Let's see, your name is Leslie Larkin, right?" Potts asked, reading her name from the card. "Here, let me copy it down so I don't forget." He signed the card, opened a drawer of his desk, and took out a sheet of paper. Standing he stooped over and wrote "Leslie Larkin, something about symbols and meaning" on the sheet of paper.

"Fine," he said. "Think about what you want to do, then, and come back and we'll talk some more. Okay?" He was smiling profusely, ushering Leslie Larkin to the door.

"That will be fine. Thank you, Professor Potts." She disappeared out the door.

Potts watched her walk down the hall. She had a fine body. About five feet five inches, slim, long light brown hair, a lovely pair of legs, a nice behind. Yes, it would be fun. More things to think about, maybe, and some lovely breasts, legs, and a face to fantasy about. He looked forward to having her come back.

Potts glanced at the clock which jutted out perpendicular to the wall just down the hall from his office. Eleven forty-five. Almost time for lunch. He looked at his secretary, Alice Beechum, across the hall. He caught her eye and smiled. He then stepped back into his office, closed the door, and slowly walked over to his desk.

2

A Meeting

As Professor Hugo Potts entered the Champlain Room (so named after a rather famous former chairman of the Department of Anthropology which preceded the Department of Sociology in Eastman Hall—there was an abortive attempt to rename the room when the sociologists took over the building completely from the anthropologists, but Champlain had been such a major figure, and had contributed so heavily to sociology as well as anthropology that the room name was retained) he caught the eyes of several of his colleagues, greeted them by nodding and beaming brightly, and, in one case, to Martha Hyatt, bowing low and sweeping his arm in front of him, and made his way over to an empty place at the far end of the table, between Howard Greenberg, a new young assistant professor from Illinois whom Potts had not as yet met, and Myron Fleigelman, a full professor who has been at Regents State University since receiving his Ph.D. from Michigan twenty-four years ago. As he sat down he turned to Fleigelman and said, "Well, Myron, nice to see you. How was your summer?"

"Not much, really, though I did manage to get a lot of work done. We stayed here all summer. I was on an NSF grant and spent a good deal of time with my small group experiments."

"How was the weather?" Potts asked, not wanting to get off on the subject of Fleigelman's research findings in his small group experiments—none of that stuff was worth a damn anyway and one had, when talking to a colleague about his work, to pretend that what was talked about was important. To be flippant was not appreciated when it centered around what a person considered his contribution to knowledge. At least that was the case with many professors. These people had to think that what they were doing was somehow significant—and most of them genuinely believed it.

One's identity, as a professor, was almost entirely rapped up in the narrow little research project on which one spent a good deal of his time.

"Hot," answered Fleigelman, "and humid."

Good old Fleigelman, mused Potts, he always looked at the gloomy side.

"Sounds terrific," replied Potts. "I wish I had been around." Any attempt at humor was lost on Fleigelman, but Potts wasn't deterred. As it turns out Potts also had a summer research grant, but he hadn't stayed in Ramsey. Instead he took himself and his family to England and treated them to the opportunities and advantages of London and the English countryside, with Switzerland as a side trip and added delight, the Maraschino cherry on top of the sundae. Pott's research had little to do with England—he certainly didn't have to go there for his work. But he and his family loved England and went there at any opportunity.

"And how was England?" asked Fleigelman. "Lots of tourists?"

"Yes. It was quite dreadful," replied Potts, speaking ironically, but obviously so only by the smile with which he spoke. "The theatres, which we went to two or three times a week, were crowded; the streets, which we walked and admired frequently, were full of pushy Americans; the museums and parks, some of the best and most beautiful in the world, were well attended; and the countryside, a green paradise, was accessible only by car, bus, train, bicycle, or foot. It really was quite terrible." It became clear, even to Fleigelman, that he was being put on. Potts smiled when he finished. Fleigelman couldn't manage one.

"You should stay home and enjoy the wonders of America instead of messing up our balance of payments abroad."

"Yes, I suppose I really should. Maybe next year," said Potts, still smiling.

There are lots of people like Fleigelman, thought Potts. Tight, narrow, lacking humor and perspective. Too bad. But then I suppose I look that way to some people myself. Potts only half believed this. He didn't want to think it about himself, but he knew it was true. Indeed, he scolded himself now whenever he thought of people in whole categories. Fleigelman isn't tight and narrow, lacking humor and perspective. Potts himself had seen Fleigelman on several occasions with what were obviously close friends in what could only be described as open, friendly, good-natured, and laughing conviviality. It was slowly coming to Potts that people are not all of a piece—that how Fleigelman, for example, appears to him,

Potts, is not how Fleigelman appears to someone else. And, how he, Potts, appears to himself when he's with Fleigelman is not how he appears to himself when he, Potts, is tight and narrow, lacking humor and perspective. We have relationships with people. And for unknown reasons we work out different parts of ourselves with different people.

Potts turned to his right. Two young men were having an uneven conversation. He caught the eye of James Barker, two seats away. "Hello, Jim. How are you?

Both men now turned his way, glad of a chance to focus on something besides their own awkward discussion.

"Greetings, Hugo," said Barker. "It's nice to see you."

"How do you do," said Potts to the man sitting next to him, "I'm Hugo Potts."

"Oh, I—I . . . My name is Howard Gr—Greenberg," said Greenberg, stuttering slightly. It made Potts quite nervous to talk to a stutterer. He hoped it didn't show.

"Howard?" Potts repeated. He wasn't very good at names and he would sometimes repeat them.

"Yes."

"Nice to meet you," Potts went on. "When did you arrive?" Potts recalled Greenberg's name, and the decision to hire him. He was now trying to remember something about him from his file. Potts had been out of town when Greenberg visited for his interview, but everyone, apparently, had been quite favorably impressed with his enthusiasm and abilities. He was surprised to hear the speech impediment, but he now recalled one of the letters saying something about it, how it was noticeable but didn't seem to interfere with his teaching, something like that.

"About th—three weeks ago" replied Greenberg.

"Are you all settled now?" inquired Potts.

"Yes, we're living in Archway. We moved in 1— 1—last week."

"Good. You'll like it there, I think. Lots of interesting young faculty in Archway." Potts was indeed maturing. He was handling the problem of chitchat quite conventionally now. There was a time when he was desperately uncomfortable with this sort of thing. But now, for some reason, he took pleasure in passing odd moments amiably, trying to put others at their ease. Since he learned how very difficult it was to say anything significant he seemed to develop a good deal more tolerance for the art of passing time in conversation.

"You live in Archway, don't you Jim?" Potts looked at Barker.

"Yes I do. Although now that we have a baby we'll have to move out soon. We're hunting around now for a house."

There was a time, Potts remembered, when assistant professors didn't hunt for houses. One didn't hunt for a house until one had tenure. But all that was changing now.

During the chatter Harold Crimson, the department chairman, had arrived and seated himself at the head of the table, at the opposite end from Potts. Crimson was forty-seven, looked younger, and was now about to call this, the first faculty meeting of the new academic year, to order.

"Maybe we should begin. Most everyone seems to be here. We do manage to get bigger every year. We shall all look forward to the day when we're too big for this room." People around the table took this last remark quite privately. Some chuckled, some nodded at others, and some merely continued doing what they were doing, looking around at people, biding their time. It was an ambiguous remark, as befits a leader. There is something there for everyone, if they find it. And if they don't like what they find it can always be denied that "it" was there in the first place. Potts smiled. He enjoyed subtlety, and he always learned something from Crimson.

"There are some here who will always be too big for the room," John Edelson broke in. This brought a general round of self-conscious chuckling, except from Potts. Potts himself enjoyed thinking of one-liners, and appreciated good ones. But, as anyone proud of something, he also deplored obviousness and crudity. This, on occasion, made him say things which were obvious and crude.

"And some of us who will never be," Potts added, setting some to snickering but making a few somewhat uncomfortable.

"I see the summer vacation hasn't dulled any wits," continued Crimson, comfortably. "It's always nice to know we can start the new year as fresh as the old." This again brought general amusement. Potts, slightly flushed, looked up at Crimson and smiled. Each was very fond of the other. "Perhaps it would be helpful if I introduced the new members. Let me just go 'round the table. I'll try not to awaken anyone's *true* identity." Again a cryptic remark. And again multiple reactions. Crimson did keep people on their toes.

"On my left is Nigel Daniels, a lecturer at King's College, Cambridge. Professor Daniels will be with us until Christmas. It's a great treat for us to have such a distinguished visitor." Crimson looked directly at Daniels.

"It's a great pleasure, indeed, to be here. I shall look forward to it," said Daniels. The accent brought a general sense of well-being and lightness to the room. One feels, in the presence of an English don, a sense of participation, a sense of involvement, a sense that something worthwhile is going on. It's difficult to put one's finger on this reaction, but it's there nevertheless. The English are very charismatic to Americans, and engender either a fondness or a disliking, but in any case an immediate reaction. The English set a tone, define the situation, provide an immediate context for things. Most Americans find this useful—those who like to set their own contexts are likely to chaff somewhat.

"Next to Professor Daniels is John Edelson, a stalwart around here."

Edelson nodded his head and grinned, looking at his hands and a bit put off by an introduction which left him so little to work with. There was a peculiar movement which followed, a kind of hesitant moment. Edelson might have made a quip, but he didn't. It threw everyone off a bit, as unfulfilled half-expectations are likely to do.

"And next to Professor Edelson is Mark Traber," continued Crimson, a little more swiftly now. No one expected a comment from Traber, and none was forthcoming. Traber looked down at the table.

"And then Peter Rothman, new to us from Harvard." Rothman was an associate professor, and hence had tenure. Harvard had a practice of promoting very few of its assistant professors. Therefore, to let one go was no mark of incapacity on the person's part. Rothman was indeed a fine catch. "Many of you will remember Professor Rothman from his visit last February, I believe."

Rothman nodded at Crimson and said yes, softly.

"And next to Professor Rothman is Martha Hyatt. Professor Hyatt will be with us only half-time, as you know. We share her, reluctantly but understandably with the Department of Philosophy."

Martha Hyatt smiled, and glanced around the table. She was one of the most distinguished women in America—a noted philosopher and author.

"Sitting next to Professor Hyatt is Rhoda Maxwell. Professor Maxwell has been with the Institute for Human Behavior for three years since receiving her degree from Columbia. We all welcome her most warmly."

All eyes, except for a few, were on *Miss* Rhoda Maxwell during the whole of Crimson's introduction. She was indeed very pretty. And if her recommendations are to be believed, very bright. Why she was still unmarried must have passed through the minds of most of the men around the table. At first appearance she did seem to lack something, some quality which would make one think of her more as a woman. In fact she seemed not to *care* that she was a woman. It's not that she hid it. She simply didn't use it. The *idea* of Professor Miss Maxwell was clearly more intriguing than the *appearance* of Rhoda Maxwell.

"Next to Professor Maxwell is James Barker. Nice to see you again, Jim." Most of the people there who had been away for the summer Crimson had managed to see and welcome back. This was not the case, apparently, with James Barker.

"And then we have another new addition, Howard Greenberg, who comes to us from the University of Chicago. Professor Greenberg is the last of our new members to be introduced, I believe, so I'll go quickly around.

"Hugo Potts," said Crimson, nodding in Pott's direction.

"Nice to see you all," said Potts. "Welcome to haven." A multiple play on words—Potts was very fond of doing this.

"Professor Potts is a most intrepid member of our little group," replied Crimson. There were smiles and chuckles. Some laughing at Potts, some in simple merriment. Potts himself joined in.

"Myron Fleigelman," continued Crimson. Fleigelman nodded.

"Erasmus Brown." The only Negro on the staff.

"Christopher Hanks, who was away the end of last year.

"Luis Manola.

"Henry Porter, one of whose major responsibilities it is to assist me in recruiting this able staff."

"Hear, hear," said John Edelson, enthusiastically. There was general laughter.

"Where?" replied Potts. Several members looked in Edelson's direction. This was the second time Potts had countered Edelson. Edelson, without looking at Potts, sank back into his chair.

"And I'm Harold Crimson, your servant and general facilitator, and this, ladies and gentlemen, will be the last year I will be able to serve in this august position as chairman."

This news was received variously. Some gave quizzical looks at each other. Only a few, the senior four, Potts, Fleigelman, Porter, and Hyatt, did nothing with their faces at all. Each had been informed, privately, of Crimson's decision. Each had made efforts to prevent Crimson's stepping down. As a final effort they had even gone into Crimson's office together, at the behest of Potts, to try to prevail. Crimson's decision was made, and he stuck to it. Now the department as a whole was learning of it for the first time.

"I have learned a good deal in these past few years as chairman," volunteered Crimson, picking up the slack made by the absence of protestations from the senior men—the junior faculty did not feel bold enough to speak first, and the senior men, unbeknownest to the junior, had already had their say, "but feel it is now time to return to other matters." There was still only general face-moving and exchanges of expression among the junior faculty. No one had yet uttered a public word. "I, of course, intend to remain here at Regents State, but I shall take up my studies again, even though, to you, from the state they were in before I took on the responsibility of chairman, it might look better that I leave bad enough alone." Crimson smiled. A few of the company chuckled.

There is a game, it seems, which academic administrators play. So central to one's life is one's research project that administrators can never admit that they are ever far from returning to it. In truth, of course, most administrators become administrators because they come to realize more or less explicitly to themselves, that what they are doing is nonsense and what they will be able to do in the future will warrant no better epitaph. We pay a great price for this pretense of importance which covers the work of scholars—most are not capable of performing at an adequate level and so quickly realize their inferiority to those who play the game of publish or perish more skillfully, while at the same time preserving their own dignity with a slight shift of emphasis to the importance of teaching, or pleading lack of time, or trumpeting the faults of quick publication. While others, who think they are making it, suddenly realize, after ten or so years of pursuing a research career, that they finally, really have nothing of very much interest to say, even if their career line has been a successful one.

And so even Crimson was not immune from the administrator's game, although he recognized it sufficiently at least to avoid saying it straightforwardly. Modesty, whether false or otherwise, is, in academia, meant to be irony.

Crimson's announcement had indeed left a rather difficult situation. Not that he couldn't be replaced. Life has a way of going on and we have a way of making the best, or worst of it, as is our wont.

But simply socially. The junior men were presented with an announcement, an announcement which was obviously final, and no one was saying anything. Crimson himself finally spoke again.

"It might be appropriate, then, to discuss how we might fill the position of chairman for next and subsequent years. The agenda, I realize, does not explicitly call for such discussion, as I wanted to make my announcement to you before making it public. But there is, just to cover us legislatively," Crimson smiled at this point, "on the agenda the first item called 'Announcements by the Chairman,' and the second called 'General Problems of Organization.' I believe we can safely assume that this topic is applicable."

Crimson was filling the void nicely. The company was beginning to warm up again, to realize that the world goes on even when interruptions take place.

"I think the reason we are so quiet, Harold, is that we literally have nothing to say. This comes as a great surprise, at least to me, and I think to most of us." Edelson offered this in way of an explanation and an insight. He was fond of making his insights public, especially if he could, at the same time, offer an explanation which was meant to include everyone. As is usual with such insights, which are in effect justifications, only those who are in need of this particular justification will believe it.

"I can appreciate that," said Crimson quickly, "and I am sorry to have to announce it in this way. It was a very difficult decision to make but, I'm sure *you* will appreciate, an inevitable one. One doesn't stay chairman forever." The effect of the decision was finally taking root. Crimson had now nailed it down.

"I take it we must now elect a new chairman?" asked Edelson, more in the form of a statement, but with a slight questioning pronouncement.

"Let's not hurry things along too quickly," observed Porter. "Harold will be serving out the year."

"How do we proceed, then?" This from Barker. It was a question on the minds of most of the junior faculty. There was, for the junior faculty, a sense of a void, a pit which must be filled.

Crimson looked quickly around the table. "The rules of the university state that department chairmen are appointed by the dean of the college, with the recommendation of the departmental faculty. That has, in the past, meant a vote of the faculty."

"And what happens if the dean does not take the recommendation of the faculty?" asked Christopher Hanks. Why is it that young people do not see that such a question is of interest only if it happens? Do they need to create problems just to solve them?

"Perhaps we should wait for that to happen and not get into it now. Legally, of course, it is the dean who appoints. Presumably this means he could appoint anyone he chose, regardless of the department's recommendation. I don't know, however, the circumstances under which this might happen." Martha Hyatt had seen the problem and sealed it beautifully.

"Some of us are bothered, I think, by what we do next." Edelson, again.

"The last time this occurred, I believe, we established a search committee to help us with our task, and to provide us with a nominee." Porter was providing another clue.

"How does the committee get chosen?" asked Barker.

"I think it would be most useful if we asked our present chairman to choose a committee for just such a purpose." Another clue from Porter.

"It would certainly be helpful if the committee were small. No more than five members I shouldn't think. And representative, as much as possible, of the department." Henry Porter was letting it all out, now. It was beginning not to be a void any longer, but simply another job to be done. The room over the past few minutes had considerably relaxed.

"Would you be willing to suggest such a committee?" asked Potts, a bit impatiently. He looked directly at Crimson.

"Of course. Let me think about it and suggest a few names. I'll then circulate something to you" (meaning the whole department) "for your reactions."

The matter was almost ended now. A procedure would be established, a committee formed, a nominee suggested, voted upon, recommended to the dean, and duly appointed. This was more or less clear to everyone, now. What wasn't clear was who the person would be: people began, at that moment, to speculate. The senior faculty had had time to give it thought already. It seemed certain that Porter would be recommended. For the senior faculty, then, there hadn't even been a problem. The discussion which had just taken place had been, at least for some, didactic. There was a sense of presenting by some who could already foresee the outcome to others who had not previously even known there was a problem.

The remainder of the meeting was taken up with the kind of trivia which one can use to justify what else he does. Except for the chairman's announcement, which offered much fertile scope for contemplation, we could go away from the meeting believing what we believe about all meetings after they are over (and even, in most cases, before they begin), that they are a waste of time. This is actually the most useful function of meetings, viz., to give meaning and significance to the time one does not spend in them. But then none of us really know this, and so we go on complaining about the time wasted in meetings while at the same time glad to spend time there, to be forcibly occupied in a way which we can begrudge later. If meetings didn't "happen" they would have to be called. Occasionally, of course, one did attend a meeting at which something "happened," a circumstance which lent legitimacy to all meetings although irrelevant to their purposes. And such was the meeting we have just witnessed.

3
Teaching

Hugo Potts walked into his 3:00 class one minute before 3:00. He was puffing a bit from the walk. It annoyed him that he should puff so, he didn't seem to be out of condition. Potts thought he would take to old age very reluctantly.

As he quickly walked down the side aisle toward the front of the room he nodded and smiled at the several students who happened to be looking his way when he came in and who were caught in his gaze. Some quickly looked away, as though not properly introduced. A few caught his eye and smiled back. Potts recognized several faces from courses taught in previous years. This always puzzled him somewhat, although he wasn't unpleased to see repeaters. What in the world were they coming back *for*, he sometimes thought. Potts, you see, didn't really think he had very much to say to students, at least very much that they would understand. It wasn't that what he said was so profound, although he liked to think so sometimes. It was more that most of his students were simply at too young an age to come to grips with some of the ideas Potts liked to talk about. In fact Potts sometimes felt a bit *immoral* in raising issues which he might agonize over but which he knew there was no good reason for such young people to bother with. But, he reasoned, the earlier they became exposed to such things the less of a shock it will be to them later on, or so he liked to think. And better they think about it than not.

Potts carried with him a folder which contained two sheets of things he might say this, the first day of class in this course, "The Earnestness of Being Important." Potts got a kick out of the title, even now. Its origin was twofold: first, Potts appreciated plays on words, he liked Oscar Wilde's pun, and he enjoyed the opportunity to play some more upon it; and second, Potts, in his own writing and thinking, was attempting to get at the problem of why. Just the other day, for example, he added the following to his growing list of poems.

Solutionizing

There is only one question,
and it can be
Asked in a thousand
ways.
"Why?" "Where do we come
from?" "What does
It all mean?" And just
as surely there
Is no "real" answer,
only more or less
Beautiful, moral, and
interesting presentations.
Is it a paradox that the
question of life
Is answerable only by such
solutions as these?
Is it indeed worthy of
the question
That truth is irrelevant
to its solution?

If you knew Hugo Potts, and were at all interested in what makes him "tick," you would know that a poem such as this is a key to his thoughts, to his way of looking at things. But few people know Potts, even that he writes "poetry" (that is, what Potts calls these word arrangements). And if they did they would not think it central, but peripheral to Potts.

He reached the front of the room. The classroom was a physical science lecture-demonstration hall, seating about one hundred and fifty people. There was a table at the front on which Potts placed his folder. With his back to the class he pulled out his two sheets of paper and glanced at them.

Pott's method of teaching was probably somewhat unusual

(though given the comparatively few number of things one can do in front of a class not *too* unusual). He prepared, in the formal sense of prepare, for his classes very little. Sometimes before his class, an hour before then, he would jot down some topics and ideas that he thought it might be useful to talk about. Often these "notes" would service two, three, or even four classes, or until he tired of them. Occasionally, the notes themselves would be incorporated into his own writings. Certainly the ideas were likely to be. What made this format most unusual was that the ideas were themselves formulated by Potts out of his own head. What he would do is take a central topic from the book currently being read, what Potts thought the book was about, and think about it himself, writing down, changing, and elaborating upon his ideas as he went along. Potts would then save these notes for the next time he taught the same course, or perhaps a different course but using the same book, but he would invariably throw these notes away and think afresh, devising new notes.

His style, in class, was to forget the notes if he could and simply talk with the students. He would encourage them to start the discussion, usually by asking whether anyone had any questions or comments. Frequently someone would, and off he (they) would go. He would use his notes only if topics were not freely suggested in this more open, extemporaneous manner. Potts was of the opinion that the classroom was a poor place to do almost anything. What he tried to do, but undoubtedly failed, was to provide the students, and himself, with an interesting *intellectual* experience, to show, by example (and this, of course, is what made the whole thing so difficult) how one could think through and construct some ideas and thoughts about whatever topic was at hand, how this was both possible and fun. It was not a place, by and large, for giving large amounts of "information," and it was not a place to give polished presentations. At least Potts did not think so, nor do so. It is probably true that most teachers opt for either of these alternatives or, more probably, a combinaion of the two. And it is also true that most teachers, in doing so, use someone else's polish.

The key to Potts's teaching, indeed the key to his thinking and writing as well, was that he did not believe in truth in the sense of ever knowing why, really, people do what they do (the poem hints at this, for example). He was not bound, therefore, by books and materials which he had a stake in thinking correct. True, Potts himself had a way of looking at things, a perspective, a point of view, which he had developed himself, laboriously, and with a good deal of anguish and despair (although he didn't feel he really had much choice in the matter—he merely did what he did). But he didn't even believe that what he said was really true—simply a way of looking at things which, more or less, might help people think they understand, or better yet, which they might find interesting. He could, therefore, say things, and assign things, because he found them stimulating, not because they were right (or wrong).

It is amazing, parenthetically, how little shared Potts's opinion about truth is. Almost everyone in universities and colleges believes in truth and the pursuit of it. In some cases it seems entirely appropriate to do so, as in the physical and biological sciences, for example, or in engineering and medicine, in which physical objects and their structures, processes, and movements are the topics of study. But for those who study man, undertaken by the Humanities, Social Sciences, and Fine Arts, there was no good reason, it seemed to Potts, for believing in the truth of one's assertions in the same way as in the sciences. Why we do what we do was, to Potts, a mystery, an unsolvable mystery, and to believe that the answer one had (and we all are doomed to having one) was *the* answer was sheer nonsense.

Potts, in some ways, envied the sciences this almost absolutist position. He could remember, at a meeting of the University-wide Personnel Committee of which he was a member (which reviewed new appointees to the various departments) remarking to a physicist and medical doctor, when they were discussing the merits of an appointee to the Medical School who had discovered a particular enzyme secreted by the kidneys: "Can you imagine actually discovering something that exists?" They looked at him, puzzled, and did not really take the remark seriously. Interestingly, Potts did half joke when he said it. But Potts was genuinely intrigued by this possibility. So accustomed had he become to his own ideas about truth in human behavior that he could now marvel at the idea of discovering a "thing" that was really there but which no one else had yet found. He knew he would never have such an experience, and he lamented a little at the loss of something he knew he could never have, but he was hopeful over the prospects of invention and creation to which he now knew his studies to be heir.

"This is Sociology 187" Potts began, turning toward the students, leaning back against the front of the table, and avoiding their eyes, as he always did until he felt more comfortable with them,

"The Earnestness of Being Important." There were a few smiles from the class, and indeed Potts still smiled inwardly. "And my name is Hugo Potts." At this Potts stopped and looked around. "No one in the wrong room, apparently," he observed. Then, as an afterthought, "Perhaps we are all in the wrong room." He said this with a smile.

The room was not filled to capacity, but it did look crowded from where Potts stood. He did not use teaching assistants for grading, given the somewhat idiosyncratic nature of his assignments (or so he liked to think of them—that only he could really read the assignment equitably), so it did cross his mind that, although he liked large classes (the more students the more likely there would be some good ones), the more he was able to discourage early in the term, the fewer papers he would be compelled to read. Potts, however, was always flattered by having large numbers of students in his classes. He really didn't want to discourage very many.

"Let's put a few preliminaries out of the way before we begin." Then adding, in a light tone, "If we ever do." Potts often commented on his own sentences. It apparently was a form of talking to himself which some people, especially his wife, found most irritating. It was a sign of his *self-containment,* a trait we all despise in those with whom we wish to share.

"The course will consist of two meetings a week, Monday and Wednesday, at this hour. We will not meet on Friday." He paused, almost expecting applause and getting it, in a way. Simulated glee, a performance put on for the benefit of one's friends, Potts himself, or perhaps even one's own self. At least it seemed so to Potts, sometimes. But he was quite aware of the difficulties of distinguishing "simulated" from "real," and finally decided that something was "simulated," in the sense in which he was using the term, when it annoyed him that others performed as he expected, almost as though it was *because* he expected it. He didn't really like this kind of power over people. It made him feel very cynical. "With the stipulation that you spend the time reading, thinking, and/or writing something interesting. Also, I will be in my office during this period, as well as most times, for any of you who want to see me. My office, by the way, is in Eastman Hall, Number 429. If I'm not there my secretary, Alice Beechum, is across the hall in 430.

"On Mondays we will talk about topics which I will bring up having to do with the books, or the general problems of how people give themselves significance. And also, topics which you might like to talk about. This will all become clearer as we go along . . . presumably, anyway."

Potts probably wouldn't have been thought of as a very good teacher by most people, although, like most teachers, he liked to think that he was an excellent teacher. But he really didn't try to teach people things in the usual sense of teaching, like information or knowledge. He didn't even really care if they learned anything. In fact he thought they probably wouldn't. Most of them would pass, of course, but none of them would be able to say very much about what went on in Potts's class. Part of the problem was that Potts had nothing he thought they *ought* to know. He knew it would be useful to try to awaken their interest in things, and he settled for that. But there seemed so little to show for it at the end.

"On Wednesdays," Potts continued, "we will have what I call Wisdom Day." Potts did not smile here, partially because he knew the students would buzz a little (which they did) and he did not want to be seen in so obvious a play for attention—or at least to give it explicit recognition. "Every Monday I would like you to turn in what you consider to be a piece of wisdom. Wisdom, as we all know, can come from anywhere, and you should be alert to it in the books we will read, outside reading you do or have done, class (which seems highly unlikely—still, you can never tell), your own thinking, or wherever. If you would write it down on a piece of paper and hand it in. Okay?"

There was a pause, and Potts took the opportunity to look over the class. He especially liked to look for familiar faces. A girl in the third row raised her hand.

"Yes?" asked Potts.

"I don't understand exactly. Do we make up the wisdom ourselves, or just write it down from somewhere?" She seemed genuinely puzzled, and if she were puzzled it was a good sign that others were too. This was not, however, unexpected.

Potts liked to put himself in perspective. In some ways he was, perhaps, put in his place better by himself than by others—at least more accurately. But perhaps even more he liked to suggest to his students that they put themselves in perspective, that they see themselvs in perspective, that they see themselves as older heads might see them. Potts replied.

"The likelihood that any of us here, you, me, or anyone, has anything of real interest to say is quite small." There were a few noticeable titters, and even some broad smiles, especially, for some reason, from the male students. "I'd be delighted if you turned in your own wisdom. And I certainly encourage you to do so. But it's probably a little more difficult than you think it is. More likely you will, in the course of your reading, and not necessarily for this course only, come across something you think is wise. When you do, write it down, verbatim, and hand it in. But either way is fine with me. The former is most to be admired—the latter a miserable, but necessary substitute." Potts smiled at the girl as he finished. Poor thing, she really didn't know what to think. Without a trace of arrogance Potts also thought that she probably never would, either. A nice girl, like most.

He continued to glance around the room. He would be happy when the "information" questions closed and more interesting matters were brought up.

A boy toward the back on Potts's left raised his hand and asked, "What do you mean by wisdom?"

Well, there it was, finally out, and pretty quickly, too, Potts thought.

"That's an interesting question," suggested Potts. But he didn't continue. He looked out at the class and smiled. When they seemed to feel appropriately nervous, as though, somehow, it was up to them to come up with the answer, Potts continued. "I wonder if it's possible to do the assignment without knowing the answer to that?" Again Potts stopped.

"I should tell you something about my style of teaching, by the way"—changing the topic of conversation in such a way as to leave the important question hanging by bringing up another topic that would be of sufficient interest that it would be unlikely anyone would not wish him to continue. He wanted students to think about what wisdom is, and if they started by thinking it wouldn't be answered in class, well, that was a start.

"I really have very little to say which you might call 'information.' So I'm not going to give you very much knowledge. The reasons for this are somewhat complex, some of which we might talk about sometime, but put simply, I don't *have* very much information. Or at least I don't have much that you don't already have.

"I have, then, nothing I feel you must know. My conversation will consist of comments, observations, analyses, wisecracks, flippant remarks, etc. Since I don't know much I don't feel as though I have to talk, or even that what I am saying is particularly important. I'm prepared to talk for the whole class time, however. Not knowing anything has never stopped me before." This brought thunderous laughter. The end of a speech which Potts delivered quite seriously. It turns out that Potts is like a lot of people (although he would be disappointed, genuinely crestfallen to be told this, probably in part because he knows it's true). What was serious to him he had to deliver in a way which would not bind him to its seriousness, just in case it was trivial. And what was, he knew, peculiar, he had to deliver in a serious way, because he had the feeling that it might possibly be profound. This is, in truth, the style for someone who has not quite got his bearings.

"So," continued Potts, "please feel free to interrupt, ask questions, give answers, protest, or whatever. This is your class, as well as mine, and I want to talk about things which we both want to talk about, which all of us, if possible, find interesting.

"And while we're on the subject, let me say something else." Potts was clearly warming up. He never liked the idea of going to class *before* class, and he wasn't particularly fond of the starting-up exercises. But ten minutes into it and he was usually going strong, having a very good time, and would rather be there than anywhere. This was probably partly stage fright, like an actor or an athlete who becomes anxious before a performance or an event but who, once the performance has begun, *does* remember his lines, *does* manage to run as fast as usual, does manage to spell correctly all the words he knows. But partly, too, it was a consequence of Potts's having nothing to occupy the time with other than his brief notes and wit and relying, instead, on what happens in the class itself. This is not a particularly easy style of teaching, and it is certainly difficult to do well. Like sending an actor out on the stage and telling him to make it up as he goes along—or sending an athlete out onto the field without telling him which event he's in or when it is to begin. But we can see how it might cause some anxiety. Knowing that the class period is fifty minutes and that he does not have even five minutes of prepared notes should produce anxiety. But Potts preferred it that way. He enjoyed, above all, saying something he had never said before—having a new, interesting idea. When this happened he would actually stop and take a note himself of what he had just said, for further elaboration later. He also often wrote a whole morning (which is when he did most of his writing) on the implications of classroom material raised as much as a week earlier. Potts was quite fortunate in this regard. He could find interesting the interaction itself, regardless of what the content was. So, he could in fact be having a dull conversation and yet have an interesting idea about what was happening in the course of the dull conversation between the conversants.

Potts also enjoyed hearing others say interesting things and he wanted to give them the opportunity to do so. Potts continued.

"It's very difficult to have an 'interesting' class. It's very difficult to *say* anything interesting at any time. What I want to avoid, in this class, is for you to have the opportunity to go away from here saying 'How boring!' or 'What a dull class' or 'I'm not finding this very interesting.' If it is dull, boring, or uninteresting I want you to know it is your fault as well as mine. *We* didn't have anything interesting to say—not just me, but we."

Most of the students were listening very intently, except for the usual few who seemed to have better things to do. Potts found that reactions in a class would always be heterogeneous. There were some who would seem to hang on every word, others who listened, or seemed to listen, but who wouldn't look at you, and a few others would seem to doze, or read, or engage in reverie. And of the ones who were most intent, some, a very few, would smirk, and screw their faces, and show other signs of disapproval. Potts found himself fascinated by these people. They seemed to exert a strange power over him. First they made him feel quite uncomfortable, as though what he was saying was a lot of drivel, but they also seemed to direct his actions, he seemed to perform for them, the disapprovers, much more than for the head-nodders in agreement, even though they were equally as intent. Potts had never spoken to anyone about this, but he felt it must be a common experience.

"So your participation is more than welcome. It is very unlikely that I will have fifty minutes of pearls every day. It would be nice if I had five minutes. In fact, before we started each day, I would settle for five minutes and call off the rest of the class. But maybe together we will have more. Let's see," Potts began to calculate out loud. "If I have five minutes that leaves forty-five minutes. And there are approximately one hundred and forty students, so that's . . . no, let's make it one hundred and thirty-five students. Each of you is responsible, then, for a third of a minute, on the average. Twenty seconds. Can any of you not come up with twenty seconds of devastating goodies, twice a week?" The class was very amused by this. There was much laughing and chortling. No one, at the end, raised his hand. "Excellent. Perhaps, then, we will be able to get through class after all."

Potts looked around again. He was happy to see people laughing. He was, at heart, a comedian. That is, he would much rather make people laugh than to make them cry. Perhaps that was what bothered him about the ones who screwed up their faces.

A student in the back raised his hand. "Have you ever told us what 'wisdom' is?" he asked. A number of people laughed, including Potts. Potts noticed that the span of attention of most students, probably most audiences for that matter, except very specialized ones, is very short. One cannot really keep one sustained argument going over the course of fifty minutes. Or, at least, not obviously so. So, he was perfectly willing to jump around. And his students obviously were.

"I don't think so," answered Potts, quite noncommittally. He looked directly at the student. He felt playful, he didn't know what would happen next, and he found it all quite stimulating. He let a rather longish pause develop.

"Are you?" asked the student slightly embarrassed that his first question had not brought more of a response. This brought a number of chuckles from the class.

"Not if I can help it," replied Potts.

"Why not?" said a girl in front, quite quickly and somewhat indignantly. She did not like the playful style Potts was now assuming. And, indeed, it was somewhat puzzling to most of the students.

"Why should I?" replied Potts.

"You're the teacher, aren't you?" she uttered, almost defiantly.

"Am I?" asked Potts, tensing a bit himself. Since he himself wasn't sure where all this was going he would worry, too, when attacks of this sort came, as they did every once in a while.

There was general silence in the classroom. Almost everyone sniffed danger and was keen on finding out what would happen next. The girl in front was very uneasy. She had launched her attack, but had not been able to get Potts to own up to her expectations of what a teacher should be. She had, in fact, challenged Potts to do differently than he was doing. She had committed herself, emotionally, to this line and she was *in medias res,* so to speak, but without any notion of what to do next. She was, however, quite angry now.

"Aren't I allowed to learn, too?" asked Potts, becoming serious himself and trying to encourage her to make the transition from anger to a less explosive state. "When I come to a classroom I come to learn. I'm actually very disappointed if I don't learn something. Why do you think I carry on in this ridiculous manner?" asked Potts, referring to his general conduct of the class. And with these words, an explicit acknowledgment of what the girl was herself unwilling to say, snapped the tension immediately. Even she had to smile a little, but she shook still with nervous energy. "Why do you think I want you people to talk? Precisely to learn something if someone has something interesting to say. As I've already mentioned, I'm not going to give you any information—I'm not going to actually *teach* you anything. If you learn anything, it will be because you yourself thought about something. We shall try to have interesting conversation. That's not easy. I want to operate that way because I'm anxious to hear what you might have to say, and I'm also, I hope I can say this without having it sound the way it probably sounds, interested in what I might have to say. If I come in prepared to talk about something, then I already know what I'm going to say, and that's not very interesting, at least not for me. I don't think, however, that we should have any false expectations about what percentage of what we will say will be interesting. My guess is it will be very small, probably close to zero." Potts hoped very much that this was a gross underestimate—he hoped—but he wasn't sure whether it was true or not. "If we have that kind of expectation then we'll be better off. At least we won't have any illusions about what this is all about."

When Potts had finished he looked out over the class, and then directly at the girl. Everyone sat in silence. Potts liked to teach that way, to pick out someone to talk to and then widen the discussion into a kind of general lecture, and then refocus on the single person as though he had been speaking to him or her all the time.

She had calmed herself considerably. All trace of hostility, actually, was gone. They looked at each other—nothing passed between them. Potts, at least, had neutralized her anger, and he felt a sense of accomplishment.

"Any other questions? Or comments?" Potts hoped for some crushingly brilliant thought to emerge every time he asked this question. Actually it was, for him, mainly a way of resting, of catching his breath, and of offering the floor to someone else who would, in his fantasy, occupy it for the remainder of the period, and even beyond, with fascinating discourse. As usual, however, the mundane emerged and he came crashing back to his task. A student raised her hand and asked, "Will there be a midterm?"

"Oh, I'm sorry, we haven't talked about that yet, have we?" Potts didn't like to talk about the details of examinations, assignments, and the like. He found this part of academic life, the bureaucratic and paper-shuffling part, most dreary. His ideal of a university would be a place where "teachers" would sit in their offices, doing their own work, and "students" would come and talk about whatever they decided to talk about. The student would be free to come and go in the university as he chose—that is, there would be free entrance and free exit. The university would not credential anyone: it would not give degrees, it would not give grades, it would not certify anyone as anything. It would simply be a place where people who thought they needed to know something (and that "something" could be, for the young especially, as broad as everything) could go to learn about that something. When the student felt he knew enough, or when others outside the university were satisfied with what the students knew, he could leave. It would be agencies outside the university who would determine when someone was qualified to do something. The university would have nothing to do with that.

But Potts knew that this was just fantasy, a fantasy which gave him a thought from which to base his conversation about education in general, but a fantasy pure and simple. The university did have a bureaucratic structure; there was not free entrance, a student had to be in the top ten percent of his high school class to enter Regents State University, a percentage which was approximately the same as in other major state universities. Students with averages below that could go to state colleges, junior colleges, or private colleges and universities, if they satisfied the requirements (and if they had the money). Nor, of course, was exit from the university free, at least exit in good standing was not. The university was a credentialing agent for all manner of enterprises in society, from giving degrees in medicine, engineering, and chemistry to certifying the qualifications of school teachers, to producing undergraduate historians, English majors, and social scientists who would man the nation's business positions. And to justify receipt of such credentials obstacles had to be overcome in the form of course requirements and examinations.

"We won't have a midterm and we won't have a final. In fact, we won't have any examination at all." This was greeted with enthusiasm from most quarters of the classroom, not because, like Potts, they felt such things were of no use to those who were interested in subjects for their own sakes, but because they were interested in no subjects at all, at least not for study. College students, like others their age, are primarily drifters—thoughtless and careless, with only their personal (mostly sexual) interests to exploit.

"I do, however, require four short papers . . . one on each of the books we shall read . . . no more than five pages each." This was greeted by a few groans. Some were testing the limits of this free expression. They hadn't even come close.

Potts turned and took out one of the sheets from his folder. "We will read the following books, and in this order." He was speaking matter-of-factly now, without enthusiasm, "The first is Konrad Lorenz, *On Aggression*." Potts paused. There was a general shuffling while the students opened their notebooks, borrowed pieces of paper, snapped their ballpoint pens, and generally got into positions to take notes.

"Konrad Lorenz, *On Aggression*," Potts repeated. "All the books, by the way, are in the bookstores. Three of them, all except Watzlawick, are in paperback.

"Watzlawick et al., *Pragmatics of Human Communication*." Potts pronounced, because he recalled the introduction had said the name was pronounced this way, the two *w*'s in Watzlawick as *v*'s. He spelled the name for the students.

"The third book is Eric Hoffer, *The True Believer*. Some of these books, by the way, many of you have undoubtedly heard of and some of you may already have read." Then Potts said again, "Hoffer, *True Believer*.

"Kurt Vonnegut, Jr., *Cat's Cradle*. Vonnegut, V-O-N-N-E-G-U-T," Potts spelled it out. "*Cat's Cradle*."

"Excuse me," a student started to say, "could you . . ."

But Potts cut it short. "I'll read the names again." He did so, and gave them the due dates for the four papers. He explained that late papers would not be accepted (although he always did accept them, usually docking the student a grade if he had no good excuse) because the class was so large. He also said that their final grade would be an average of their grades on the papers.

Someone asked what the papers should be about.

"Anything you'd like them to be about," answered Potts, "with one stipulation, and that is that they have something to do with the book you are reading at the time." Potts again looked around. The period was drawing to a close and he was glad of it. Teaching was very tiring—having constantly to be on one's toes. Potts usually felt after class the same way he felt after an airplane ride—exhausted. He never felt as though he were working, but he must have been expending enormous nervous energy. But now he had run down. He had, again, successfully negotiated a fifty-minute period in which he had had nothing to say at the start. And, it seemed to him, it went fairly well, at least for a first meeting. He hadn't really learned anything, but then he hadn't tried to cover any topics, either. He felt his handling of the girl's anger had gone well. He had avoided an embarrassing situation, and he felt he might have stimulated her into a genuine learning experience. But who knows. These little confrontations in class—he was certainly getting better at setting them up and getting through them—but all the same he wondered what exactly he had accomplished. Was it really necessary to make the classroom so dramatic?

The students again seemed quite perplexed about the writing assignment. Most students are used to having fairly clearly specified assignments. Potts's assignments were usually not clear at all, and for a purpose.

"What I want is probably the most difficult thing in the world to do," Potts began by way of explanation. "I want you to write me a good, thoughtful paper about some idea or ideas that are either in the book you are reading or that come to you as you read the book. Now, you obviously don't know what those ideas are, yet, because you probably haven't read the book yet. But, as you read the first book, think about what you are reading. What is being said? Is it interesting? If such-and-such is true then doesn't such-and-such follow? Now that fits in with this idea I read in that book, or with the conversation I was having with X just the other day. When you think you might also jot down your ideas so you can come back to them. Many you will want to throw away. But some, maybe only one or two, you will want to keep. Think about them some more. Talk to people about them. Try to come to some conclusion, or even some interesting questions. The important point is that you *think*. And that, of course, is where most of you will fail miserably. Most of us write much too fast. We say the first thing that comes to our minds. And if we haven't given the subject any prior thought the very first thing is likely to be silly or trivial."

There was a bit of twitter in the class. He knew he had struck home. Laughter is a sign of people trying to o' comfortable situation.

"I don't care in what form you write it. You usually write, in straightforward prose, or you (drama, poetry . . . anything you please. As long than five pages, it has something to do with the book, ιι ιυ — ful, and it is good." Potts smiled, and so did most of the class.

"My guess is, by the way, that very few of you will write a good paper." There were some twitters. "It's hard to write a good paper—just like it is hard to have an interesting conversation. But then I don't really expect you all to be a Dostoevsky or a Nietzsche. But one's level of aspiration, and what one finds he can do, is not clear at your age. And you have that going for you. No one really knows if you have anything interesting to say unless you try."

There was now a shuffle of papers. Potts glanced at the clock. It was twelve minutes to four. The class would be over at ten of four.

"Always, at this hour, a mysterious breeze sweeps through this hall and makes all the papers rattle." Potts looked out at them once more. "I guess that's all. See you on Wednesday."

The voice level increased precipitously as the students made ready to leave. Potts watched them as he put his papers back into his file. Several students came toward him, holding cards. They wanted to know if it was too late to sign up for the course. Potts said no, and signed their cards.

Potts walked out just behind the last student, a rather attractive girl in a short skirt. Her name was Lucia Ambrose (Potts had just signed her card admitting her into the course). She seemed very young. This surprised Potts. She was too young. He realized, then, that he would never have anything in common with students of this age—and with that something seemed to have gone out of his life. He enjoyed the freshness of young people but he disliked their silliness. What on earth could he ever talk to them about?

Was this what it was like to grow old? How nice. To be able to look at a pretty girl without desire. How very nice. Potts turned toward the door that would take him back to his office.

4
Writing

Potts put down his pen and sighed. He had managed to write his four pages, the minimum he aimed for on the days he wrote. It was odd but whatever it was that he might have to say seemed to come in four-page spurts. He was not able, as he had heard about other writers, to spend hours writing. He worked in short periods, about forty-five minutes at a time, and could manage two, three, or even, sometimes, four such writing periods a day.

Potts thought he might read over what he had just written but decided against it since it was revised copy and instead gathered it together, added it to his folder, and put it away in his carrying case. His desk was clean once again. He then got up, went over to the door of his office and opened it, glanced at the clock, and, smiling at his secretary first, began to walk down the hall to the lounge where the mailboxes were kept. He decided against taking his half-full-of-cold-coffee coffee cup on the grounds that he had had more than enough already. Too much coffee gave Potts a sour stomach, and it also seemed to hop him up a bit. Potts felt he needed neither.

Potts tried to write, if he had no other pressing business, and he always tried not to schedule appointments, classes, or other activities during the morning, every morning. He wasn't sure whether he liked to write or not—"like" isn't quite the word to describe what Potts was to his writing and what his writing was to him. He suffered when he wrote, he sometimes felt very deeply, and often he thought very deeply. But Potts would write, he knew, even if he knew what he wrote wasn't very good, although he would have always thought that if he kept at it perhaps he would finally be able to say something profound, something interesting. Potts had become a writer—and he could have thought of nothing else to occupy his time if writing were somehow taken away from him. We all face the problem of filling time in a way which makes a large part of our life somewhat routine, and Potts had chosen writing as his way. He did read some, and he liked to talk, but neither of these, even together, would have filled his writing time adequately. In fact he only read and talked as respites in his writing. He would feel he could have long conversations with people, for example, or teach a class, or read a book, only after he had done his morning's writing.

And Potts was afraid. He was frightened that what he wrote, and, perhaps even more importantly, what he would write in the future, was not and would not be any good. He was afraid, deathly afraid, of being mediocre, or worse. And that fright, strangely, became a reason for writing—to see if what he had to say *was* worth saying, to prove the fears groundless, to emerge, finally, as a significant person of letters.

Most men, by the time they arrive at Potts's age (thirty-seven) have gone through and are probably still experiencing (once it starts it must be irreversible, but maybe not) the terribly ambivalent feelings of realizing that what one does is trivial, that one's "contribution" to life is hardly a contribution at all, and that one is simply a liver of a life, a life not unlike the lives of other, fellow human beings. Potts somehow felt that this must be different for women, or perhaps he only hoped it was, but it seemed true to him in observing women, and especially his own wife. Somehow women were still (and more) connected to a *stream* of life, an existent thing of life, a biological function of having and rearing children. Perhaps women experienced what men experience after children grow up.

But men, in going off to work, come to realize that the work they are doing is of no consequence. It brings in a living, it provides for a home and divertissements, but it has no *intrinsic* value. And this, reasoned Potts, is a terrible thing to conclude about what one is about. It is the male despair, probably begins to occur in most men at about thirty (with a large variance, Potts guessed), and for most probably goes on even to death. Potts himself was enmeshed deeply in this web of self-awakening, since the age of thirty-two.

Before thirty-two Potts had been quite successful at being a sociologist. I say "quite" because his status in his profession deserves some elaboration and may have a bearing on his particular *realization,* though realizations in general happen in most circumstances.

Potts, at the time he was most professional, was probably not among the very, very top of his profession, even for his age group. He was considered by some to be mediocre, and by others to be good, but no one, except perhaps an eccentric few, considered him to be the very best, or even among the top three or four sociologists his age. In Potts's case it seemed to be this realization of not being quite good enough and, what is crucial in self-awakening, a realization that he probably never would be really first-rate, which drove Potts to begin to try to understand his predicament when he did.

Potts knew there was a trade off between what might be loosely called "talent" (an ability to do something others aren't able to do) and hard work. As it turned out Potts discovered not only that in most academic pursuits one did not need to be especially talented to succeed fairly well, but that he was not especially talented. In research and scholarship it is not so much an inability to do something which separates the non-scholar from the scholar, but the unwillingness to do so, the lack of drive. One could, with drive, combine hard work and talent could be bypassed. And so Potts prospered—or at least this was how he finally characterized himself. Potts discovered, slowly, as admitting anything of this nature to oneself must perforce be done slowly, that the academic profession of sociology, as in any academic profession, was filled with rather talentless, willing workers aspiring to and achieving a moderately successful career. The differences which one encountered were due as much to differences in perseverance as to talent. That is, if Potts thought of himself as not quite first-rate it was not because he was less talented, but because he was somewhat less willing, and probably also somewhat less well trained to begin with. To gain stature in the profession one needed to work hard, learn a literature (the more, obviously, the better, so that this as well as everything else is related to perseverance) , learn the techniques of a discipline, and do research applying techniques and expanding upon the literature, making a place for oneself as one goes along. One could also write books and articles critical of others, conceptualizing problems, and summarizing literatures. All of these help to bring one's name before others, and all can be achieved through diligence.

Potts had done the work. He had written two books and seventeen articles in the space of eight years since achieving his Ph.D. This was not outstanding—many had done more—but it was a considerable record. (Potts had, as a result of this effort, been promoted to a full professorship at the age of thirty-three. Again some had gone faster, but not many.)

Consider, then, how it might feel to conclude that not only did this not take talent, but that if one kept at it it would not get any better. That, through hard work, one could have a comfortable career, and when finished one could safely conclude that nothing of importance had happened. These are the particular circumstances in which Potts, at the age of thirty-two, began to become self-aware —better yet, began to become aware of his self-awareness—and entered the process I have called *realization*.

Why realization occurs is, I think, an enigma. Not that one cannot give explanations for it. Nor is it ever clear *what* it is, whether all people go through it, how fast or slow it is, when it starts, etc. In Pott's case there was a steady deterioration of his attitudes over a year and a half toward what it was he was doing. This seemed, to Potts, to be rapid enough. Had it been much more rapid the consequences might have taken a bad turn. This year and a half, as far as Potts could tell, was a period of genuine disintegration—that is, Potts quite literally fell apart. He lost his center, his purpose, and he had nothing with which to replace it. The despair mounted and became, at some point in his life then, overwhelming. He became morose, terribly inward, obviously preoccupied. He began to question everything in his life related to his work and what he was doing. And for the first time in his life he thought of all the things he wouldn't be, couldn't possibly be, had no chance of being. He realized, also for the first time, that perhaps as much as half his life was now over, done with, finished and that he had only as much again left to him, perhaps a bit more if he were lucky. He realized, too, how out of shape, physical shape, he was getting and he made a determined effort to exercise. In doing this he discovered that he would never, ever, be a boy of eighteen again, have the physical condition which he once had, enjoy the ability to do almost anything he wanted because his body would do it if he asked it to. All of these things came together at once and acted as a great weight which came crashing down upon him, making him smaller and smaller.

And he clearly and systematically rejected the discipline of sociology as his activity. He came close, even, to rejecting all of academic life as well, realizing, for the first time, the kinds of people he was among, the kind of person he himself had become. Narrow, thoughtless accumulators of books and what they called knowledge, pursuing a career in a most restricted and in most cases trivial specialty which hardly justified the term intellectual. This last came especially hard since Potts would, above all else, now like to be considered to have lived his life intellectually. He found himself to have become, quite frankly, a narrow bigot with almost nothing to say to anyone except, perhaps, a few "facts," a few bits of knowledge he had acquired as a consequence of long hours spent in pursuit of his now unholy grail.

During the next year and a half Potts began, slowly, tentatively, and furtively, to put himself back together again. It was, in many ways, very, very exciting. He began by reading new, exciting books. He forgot how he came across them. In some cases he asked people what the most intellectually exciting books they had ever read were; in other cases he browsed bookstores and libraries and ran across a large number of books which, sometimes, suggested other books; he recalled the several really good books he remembered reading and went back to search them for other books which those authors used. In this way he put together a reading list, what he called his star list. These were books which Potts would call brilliant—at least for the time being. No one else need think of them that way, it was only important that Potts think so. I will reproduce his list here for you so you can get some idea of what he read and what he considered brilliant. There was, of course, a much larger list of books which Potts read and rejected—these are only the ones he put on his star list.

Star List

Thurman Arnold, *The Folklore of Capitalism*
Daniel J. Boorstin, *The Image*
David T. Bazelon, *The Paper Economy*
John K. Galbraith, *The New Industrial State*
Erving Goffman, *The Presentation of Self in Everyday Life*
Murray Edelman, *The Symbolic Uses of Politics*
Ken Kesey, *One Flew Over the Cuckoo's Nest*
Konrad Lorenz, *On Aggression*
Thomas S. Kuhn, *The Structure of Scientific Revolutions*
Kenneth Burke, *Permanence and Change*
Ludwig Wittgenstein, *Philosophical Investigations*
Walter Kaufmann, *Existentialism From Dostoevsky to Sartre*
Paul Watzlawick, Janel Beavin, and Don Jackson, *Pragmatics of Human Communication*

Johan Huizinga, *Homo Ludens*
Peter L. Berger, *The Precarious Vision*
R. D. Laing, *The Divided Self*
Eric Hoffer, *The True Believer*
Isaiah Berlin, *The Hedgehog and the Fox*
Kurt Vonnegut, Jr., *Cat's Cradle*
Samuel Butler, *Erewhon*
Jean Paul Sartre, *Saint Genet*
George Bernard Shaw, *Man and Superman*

Potts would seldom discuss these books with anyone. He was finding out the joys of an internal, highly personal intellectual experience. He was even, occasionally, euphoric.

And, about a year into this new reading course Potts began to write. It came hard at first, because he didn't know what to write or how to write it. But he did know that whatever he wrote he wanted to be his own. One of the first things he did was keep a notebook of quotes from the books he was reading which he found particularly interesting. Not that he agreed with them—in fact he would rather not. They only had to be interesting, stimulating of thought. And Potts would think a good deal about the ideas raised by the quotes and by his ideas about them. He tried to figure out, for the first time he thought, what his intellectual position on things was. What, for example, was truth? What was reality? What did it mean to explain something? Why do people do what they do? How can he talk most fruitfully about what people are?

Slowly, ever so slowly, Potts would think about these things. And slowly, ever so slowly, his notebook would begin to have more and more of Potts, less and less of other people.

Finally, and for no apparent reason, Potts stopped reading. All he wanted to do now was to *create,* yes create, his own way of looking at things, his own perspective, his own ideas. And he wrote, and wrote, and wrote. For two years Potts wrote. At the end of the first year of writing he went over what he had written, found that some of it was usable, and put together a manuscript consisting of poems, a play, some philosophy, and a dialogue. And then he plunged back and wrote some more. He was having, without doubt, the grandest intellectual experience of his life. He was actually thinking for himself—he knew the ideas he was having were his own, his very own. He didn't even care *(almost)* how good they were; they were his, he knew they were his, and that, he persuaded himself at the time, or half persuaded himself anyway, was what mattered.

During this writing period Potts did a great deal of experimenting. He tried fiction, drama, poetry, dialogue, prose, anything but what he had been used to doing, trained to do, that is, writing sociological research papers. His dialogue, for example, the first thing he completed successfully (for he had many false starts), was a discourse between two parts of the same person—although somewhat hidden, it was between Potts as he saw himself becoming if he had remained unaware, and Potts as he might have been had be been aware earlier. But most of the time, regardless of how he wrote, his writing contained Potts's ideas about things, what he thought about creativity, how he felt about science and social science, and what it meant to be awakened. He became reflective on his own reflections. He even devised four new psychological concepts to handle what he considered to be the levels of consciousness problems, i.e., how we can be conscious of ourselves being conscious of ourselves, etc.

And at last Potts *seemed* to be finished. He finished a "second" manuscript and then found, with only slight editing, that the first and the second belonged together forming one larger philosophical-literary work. No one, except Potts's secretary, had read it, not even Potts's wife. She had suffered so through Potts's despair that she felt she really couldn't read what was a product of that period. Even he had not read the work through completely since he finished it and rearranged some of the chapters. It was, he thought, possibly an interesting book—certainly it was a curious book. Looking back over the three years since he had begun he would not have thought he could have succeeded so well in achieving a break with his past. He was vastly pleased, and somewhat frightened. But now it was time to think of having it published. Now was the time of trial. He had put the manuscript away since it was typed in "final" form. That was six months ago now. Potts was, it seemed, delaying.

As Potts walked to the lounge he ran into Fleigelman just coming back to his office. Potts guessed, since he was carrying a cup of coffee, somewhat precariously, in his hand, that he had just come from the lounge.

"Mail in yet?" asked Potts.

"Yes, but it isn't sorted, as usual," replied Fleigelman.

"Well, you can't have everything," said Potts. "You can't have Regents State and personal mail service too."

Potts didn't linger. He didn't particularly enjoy conversations with Fleigelman, especially long ones involving some issue or other. Fleigelman had no theory at all about people, and simply assumed that if they behaved in ways which were contrary to how he thought they ought to behave that they were simply being perverse and would have to be told better. But that wasn't the only reason Potts hurried on. He frequently simply greeted people with a hello, a flippant remark or two, and then left. It was as though standing still would somehow commit him to having a conversation. And what would happen if he did that, he did stand still open for a conversation, and the other person passed him by, or he couldn't carry off a conversation? To avoid such a contingency he would stop and talk only if the other person made the first move to make the arrangement more permanent than a brief hello. And it had to be a definite move—not a hint, or a signal which required a response from him before a deeper commitment were made, etc. Such games were not for him. It must be a definite commitment on the part of the other, so that he, not Potts, would have to bear the responsibility of failure, and Potts would not be in the position of being slighted. Potts hadn't really thought about this much. He wasn't even aware of it. He only knew he didn't feel comfortable in these greetings and he needed to hurry on.

Potts smiled at Fleigelman, who merely scowled and continued into his room. Potts continued on to the lounge. When he reached the main departmental office, through which he must pass before coming to the lounge he said, very exaggeratedly, and with a broad smile, "Good morning, Sally."

Sally beamed back. "Good morning," she said, partially mimicking his sweeping gesture. They grinned at each other as he walked past, as though they had just been thrown together in a charade and asked to work something out.

A bit further on he said hello, quite shyly, to Flora. And then he entered the lounge. There were two students, undergraduates by the looks of them, seated on one of the new, modern, lounges, and a graduate student whom Potts knew slightly (he had taken a class with Potts) seated on one of the chairs around a large oval coffee table reading a journal. He looked up as Potts came in. The undergraduates were interested in each other, sniffing away.

"Hello, Hugo," he said.

"Good morning, Steve," Potts replied. When Potts was a graduate student no one ever called professors by their first names.

But times change. Almost every graduate student, and even some undergraduates, some of whom Potts hardly knew, called Potts "Hugo." He wasn't sure he would ever get used to it and he wondered how some of the men older than he stood it.

"Working hard, are you?" asked Potts, in a slightly English way.

"No," said Steve, "just sitting around waiting for Carlyle. Have you seen him?"

"No, I'm afraid he didn't tell me when he'd be in. I must remember to have him keep me up on his schedule." Carlyle was a graduate student and Potts, also saying this playfully, meant it sardonically. He was reacting, he supposed, to being called "Hugo." The sarcasm, if not the point, was caught by Steve Haverman. He quickly looked back to his journal.

Potts walked over to the mail sacks on the counter. Someone had dumped the mail from the sacks and it was scattered in jumbled piles all over the counter. It seemed to beg to be put safely away in the mailboxes hanging on the wall, and it was painful for Potts to see the mail pleading so.

Potts wasn't expecting anything in particular, but he did, frequently during each day, come to the lounge hoping for a letter of importance. He was always excited with this mysterious prospect, as though he were expecting some unknown but huge reward which, in his reverie, usually was in the nature of some fantastic job offer at a very large salary, an offer which would be *explicit* and *immediate* recognition of his superior talents. Of such dreams, apparently, are paths and shoe leather worn.

He quickly looked through the first-class mail, paying special attention to the airmail letters. For some reason, perhaps because if they were sent airmail they must be in some hurry, perhaps because the airmail letters were obviously of more pagentry and pomp, appropriate to the significance of the expected event.

There was a letter, not an airmail, with a strange name and address, sent from New Haven. He knew immediately that this was not it, so he merely clung to it as he reached anew. But he found nothing else and so, after quickly riffling through it once more to make sure he didn't miss anything (like glancing back at his desk before leaving his office, an indication that what one was about to do couldn't be very important because somehow one left what *was* important behind), satisfying himself that he hadn't and if *the* letter were to come that day he would simply have to wait a little longer. Potts took his letter off to a chair, much like a dog would take off an especially tasty bone the better to savor it alone, opened his letter, and read.

"Dear Professor Potts:" the letter began,

> I am a graduate student in sociology at Yale and Professor Wexford [well at least someone was being called by his last name—Potts wondered whether the author of this letter called Wexford "Chuck"], my thesis advisor, suggested I write to you to inquire about the data you have on . . . .

Nuts. Another request for something he didn't give a damn about. Six years ago, in several of his articles, he reported some findings of a survey he conducted relating to the problem of cynicism. Since then he received five or six requests a year for the data from that study. Each time it required having someone (his graduate research assistant in the days when he had one) to duplicate his punch cards and manual. Several years ago, in a flourish, he had had ten copies of the material made, as a kind of stockpile against future requests, but the last of them was shipped off last year. So now he would have to think of something. He no longer had a research assistant (what he was now doing was obviously quite personal and could not be shared with anyone like a research assistant—he had given up *training* graduate students several years ago) , so he would have to do it himself if it were to be done at all. Either that or ask Fleigelman or someone to have his assistant do it. He would have to think about it.

Potts walked back to his office, stopping by the men's room on the way. When he got to his office he quickly went in, quietly closed the door, and dropped into his chair at his desk. He could almost feel it coming.

Potts was thinking now of the end of yesterday's class, his thoughts of how he and his students were divided into separate worlds, and how he wanted, desperately, to say something timely about this. He had been thinking about the problem for a good long time, the "commitment" of the young, the "awareness" of the old. Potts took out his pen, pulled the yellow, lined pad over to him, and began to write. The first draft took about twenty-five minutes. He then read it through, making additions in the margins and changes above the lines. And finally he copied it over, making yet another set of additions and changes, less frequent however.

When he had finished he wondered what he would do with it.

Oh well, he thought, he would find some place for it. He stuck it in a folder and put it away in the filing drawer of his desk.

Potts got up, opened the door, and looked out. He was tired, but he felt very good. Getting in that extra hour's worth had really put a head on the morning. He decided to eat at the student Commons, as he frequently did. On his way he glanced at the doors of his colleagues, half hoping to find someone to talk to. He was beginning to feel expansive. But apparently everyone had gone. Either that or like him they worked with their doors closed. More likely the latter.

Potts ate lunch alone, musing, hoping, as he did, that he was germinating, developing new ideas for some future writing session.

5

Marion

When Potts turned the key and opened the front door he could have recognized, had he been aware of it, that he had become tense. It was due, clearly, to what he had come to find inside over the years, and he was simply reacting in anticipation. We come to know how things will be without really thinking about them, and we develop responses which provide what can be interpreted as an accommodation toward our expectations. The house, he could tell as he stepped in, was in shambles. Potts had this difficulty (among others) with his wife for the whole of their marriage. He apparently was cursed with a bad reaction to disorder. He did not know why and, like many things about which we feel passionately, didn't care why. To him it was a sign of being out of control, that he was not master of the situation, that one's surroundings had not been conquered, and these things frightened him. It was, or so it seemed, as simple as that.

Potts's wife, Marion, clearly did not share this feeling. Picking up the house *is* maintenance, and maintenance, especially that kind which rapidly undoes itself and which seems to have no other rationale than for its own sake, is wasting one's time. Potts himself, intellectually at least, was sympathetic with Marion's attitude. Potts recognized that his desire for order was oppressive—he found it so himself. But to know these things about oneself is one thing, to dispel them is quite something else. So he suffered inwardly every day, even feeling a sense of disgust with himself that knowledge of his suffering being self-induced would inevitably bring, raising the matter publicly only when he and Marion pushed each other into fits of seething anger.

Marion Potts was probably in the upstairs guest room, reading or resting. Potts deduced this from the sound of the television upstairs (indicating the children were watching the late-afternoon cartoons) and the absence of anyone downstairs as he tramped back into the kitchen to confirm his impression. He glanced at the shelf where the mail was sometimes placed, didn't see any, looked around and noticed a few things by the radio. He went over, flipped through the few pieces, threw away some insurance circulars and a request for funds from the Cornell Alumni Association, and read over the bills, electricity and an Enco credit card. He turned and his eyes lit upon his wife's handbag nearby. He went over and took out the checkbook, sat down at the kitchen table, and wrote out the two checks.

When he had finished he put the checkbook back in Marion's handbag, threw away the envelopes and receipts from the bills he had just paid, sat down again, and let things roam through his mind. He felt uneasy now, he could feel it himself, and he found it strange. Potts liked the *idea* of coming home, of having a family to come home to, of having someplace to go with people which, as far as he knew, he loved (in the sense in which one can say he loves his family). His awareness that he felt strange was bothering him—somehow it was incongruous that he should feel so. He wanted not to. But he also seemed to want to be swept up in someone else's activities, to have things done for him, to be made the center of attention without having to earn it. And, of course, although he didn't realize it then, that's exactly what the other members of his family wanted. At the end of the day we are all willing to be amused, entertained, made much over, while remaining passive. Just before dinner is a peculiar time of day. Everyone is tired, hungry, out of sorts, and likely to be in an accepting but not a giving spirit. And so families confront each other every night, hoping one amongst them will give direction to the group, and glad of any small achievement in that direction.

Potts got up from the table, carried some cups and bowls left over from breakfast to the sink, turned on the water, and began to wash the dishes. His doing so gave him a sense of purpose but didn't reduce his nervousness any. He heard his wife coming down the stairs and, for some reason he didn't want to think about, he felt trapped.

"Don't you want to see us?" she asked.

Potts felt a burning under the skin. He now realized he should have gone directly upstairs and somehow (but how!) involved the family in some project. And at the same time he knew that that would have been simply a minimum—that Marion, especially, wanted to be startled, shaken out of the routine she found herself in. And Potts knew he had no such news that would do the trick. Was that why he hadn't gone upstairs immediately? Lacking news that will startle, one has to work hard at involving the family in something. And husbands who come home without startling news sense this lack in themselves, the task before them, and develop what at best might be referred to as ambivalence about coming home at all.

"Hello," said Potts, trying to sound committed, trying to be cherry, but sounding only halfway so, as though to protect himself from what he felt the situation he was in was and having no way, really, of breaking out of it. "Did you have a good day?" This question was meant to be formal—a polite response to which would have been to say something noncommittal, in a pleasant way, to show oneself a friend. And he wished that she had had a magnificent day, that she would bubble and carry on about her activities very excitedly, so he could listen, so he would not feel responsible, so he could exist inside the private world he felt himself in without having to give anything to the outside—and he knew that no such thing was going to happen, that Marion was going to tell him, implicitly at least, that he was somehow responsible for the state she was in and that it was up to him to do something about it.

And then she said it, the thing which all families who can afford it come to when they have nothing else, and she said it only because Potts had not said it first.

"Let's eat out," said Marion. "I don't feel like making dinner."

"All right," agreed Potts, glad of a chance to capitulate, to show his good faith, still half hoping she had somewhere in mind but sensing she didn't and realizing that he would have to pretend that what they were about to do was a big thing to make something of. "Where would you like to go?" This was said with a good deal of false enthusiasm, borne of a desire to be enthusiastic, but at the same time was the wrong thing to say. He realized it as soon at it was out. He was supposed to take charge, to suggest some great surprise, to make her happy, not have a desultory conversation about a stopgap dinner.

"I don't care," she answered sharply. "Anywhere. I just want to get out of the house." She made no move to help him with the dishes, nor to tidy up the kitchen. She just stood there, waiting, then sat at the table and started to read whatever was there, left from this morning. Potts wanted her to pitch in, to work with him, to get a *rhythm* in the house, a rhythm they could both be part of. Potts was, of course, in a rhythm of sorts. This scene played itself similarly almost every night, with obvious but minor variations. But the feeling tone of the rhythm was all wrong.

"I'll just be a couple of minutes," he said as he continued to rinse off the dishes and stack them in the dishwasher.

"Do you have to do that?" she asked. Potts felt it getting warm in the room. He hoped it was from the hot water in the sink. "Can't we just go?"

"I'll just be a minute," Potts answered, wanting to finish. It was such a trivial problem, he was really ashamed of himself. What difference could it possibly make whether the kitchen was clean or dirty, whether the dishes were done or not? Yet he had to clean up. He tried other things. He tried, for example, letting the dishes pile up. But it never worked. His tolerance for a dirty kitchen was simply very low and he would eventually do the cleaning up anyway, only then it would be much harder, with encrusted bits of food, which he would have to scrape off. This business of tolerance fascinated him. He who had the lowest tolerance would have to do the work. This was, in fact, one definition of power over other people: having such high tolerance on everything that others are moved to action before you are. Most people living together develop trade offs. On some things one person has the lowest tolerance, on other things another person. Potts, for example, was a good deal more tolerant of general deterioration than was Marion. If something in the house needed attention or repair it was often Marion who had to do something about it.

"Why can't you just leave it alone—I'll do it later," she said. Potts knew she wouldn't. That he himself would simply do it later if he stopped now, and he felt like doing it now.

"I want to do it now." Potts stopped there. Anything else he would say would simply contribute to a further deterioration of relations. Or maybe that really isn't true. What he would say would simply exemplify the state of deteriorated relations which existed between them. "How are the children?" he asked, hoping to change the subject.

"They've been awful," said Marion. "Having them together is dreadful. They're constantly teasing each other and it's driving me batty. I want to get away."

"Well, as soon as I've finished here we'll go. We all need to go out." Potts knew it would be one of those nights. They would both be on edge, they wouldn't be able to talk about anything, there would be no chance of smiling or laughing, of feeling good, as though Marion was preventing them from even being civil to each other, Marion probably believing that matters had slipped so far that it would be a compromise with her principles to allow civility. Marion was wound up, and she needed to let herself go. And the person she needed to let herself go at was Potts. The evening, then, would be like that—no fun, no pleasantries, winding down by emptying one's discontent.

Potts believed he had brought all of this on himself, that he was essentially at fault. It is the kind of experience we all feel when others make us feel guilty—we feel responsible for how bad they are feeling. He was convinced that somehow all that was happening and had happened between him and Marion was his doing, that the failure lay with himself. He was, somehow, simply unable to satisfy her, to make her happy. A simple view of things, perhaps, but when one is squirming and feeling guilty one has no time for sophistication. Perhaps later, someday, Potts would sort it all out. He might, then, be able to see it more clearly. But not now. Not now.

"Could you get the children ready?" he asked, in that patronizing tone we use when we are trying to be sweet and kind to someone who is not. He was trying to encourage Marion to participate, to become less hostile, to be friendly, even though he knew she wouldn't be because she couldn't be—she was locked into something and had to play it out.

"I don't feel like it," she said. Neither said anything further, and Potts continued clearing up.

"I'll go up and see what's going on," volunteered Potts when he had finished. He looked around, admiring his work. The floor could use a sweeping, a washing for that matter, but at least the table and sink were cleared of dishes and debris, the counter was wiped clean of crumbs and spots, and he could, if he wanted, sit down at the kitchen table without feeling discomfort.

Potts climbed the stairs. He found his two children in front of the television in his and Marion's bedroom. They had, as usual, built themselves nests of blankets, books, pillows, dolls, stuffed animals, and toys. It all looked very cozy and lived in. Potts could remember, when he was a boy, getting everything down from the shelves, bookcases, and closet in his bedroom and surrounding himself, like an island, with his possessions on the rug in the middle of his room. He also remembered that without being told he had put everything back and restored the room to its original condition, as though nothing had happened and before anyone but himself saw what he had done. And that was the only recollection Potts had of nesting. It seemed like such a natural, and satisfying thing to do.

"Hello, girls," Potts offered. There was a "Hello, daddy" from Karen, the elder (seven), who put on a little performance of enthusiasm without taking her eyes from the television. The younger one, Lisa, made a point of staring directly at the screen. He went over and gave each a peck on the head.

"What are you watching?"

"*Gilligan's Island,*" Karen said.

"*Gilligan's Island,*" said Lisa.

"Oh," said Potts, glancing at the clock and seeing it was ten of six, "is it good?"

"Yes," said Karen.

"Yes, it is," said Lisa.

"You know what, Daddy," said Lisa, suddenly very animated, "Karen hit me."

"She did?"

"Yes."

"We shouldn't hit one another."

"Well, she did."

"Well, she took my blanket," said Karen.

"Yes, but you mustn't hit people. We're going out to eat."

"Goody," said Karen.

"Goody," said Lisa.

"We'll go right after this program's over." Potts sat down on the edge of the bed. He didn't want to go back downstairs—Marion was there—and besides he would just have to come back upstairs to hustle the kids again. And he didn't want to turn off the program before it was finished. He tried to watch the program, but he was very tense. After a minute or so Marion appeared.

"Aren't we going?"

"Yes, in about five minutes," he said, turning to look again at the clock. "The program is almost over."

"Let's go," Marion said. "They've been watching television long enough."

"We want to see the end," said Karen, pleading but without looking up.

"You've watched enough, now," said Marion, and she came over and switched off the set.

Potts simply sat there, on the bed, not knowing what to do. The children looked at him. "Okay," he said, getting up, "let's get our shoes and socks on, we're going out to eat."

"Can't we see the end of *Gilligan's Island?*" whined Karen, sensing that she might have an advantage.

"No, not now," he said (with no enthusiasm). "We've got to get dressed now. It's getting late and we're all hungry. Where are your shoes?" Potts began looking under the blankets and in the nests. The children didn't seem to want to help. "Let's find your shoes."

The children were protesting, Marion was standing, and Potts was beginning to get angry. He began to put shoes and socks on Lisa. "Put your shoes on, Karen," said Potts, a little testily. Marion went into the bathroom.

"Okay," when he had finished with Lisa, and Karen was in the middle of putting on her socks. "Let's go wash our faces."

In the bathroom they ignored Marion, who was rubbing some cream on her face. "Let's just get cleaned up, now," said Potts to the girls, as they started to chatter, "and not bother Mommy."

"I'm all right," snapped Marion. "I just want to get out of the house."

"Yes, well, all right," said Potts. He hated these eruptions with Marion, and he especially disliked them in front of the children. He felt like chucking it all and going out by himself, or taking the children and leaving Marion to her own devices. But at the same time he knew he wouldn't, that somehow he was locked in too.

"Sometimes," said Marion, "I feel like going away by myself, away from the house. I just want to be alone."

"You can, you know," offered Potts, trying to be helpful. "You can get a baby-sitter . . ."

"Not in the afternoon I can't. I have to pick up Lisa at school, then pick up Karen, then have a snack, then—oh, hell, my whole day is gone."

The only time Potts believed in the "letting-off-steam" theory was when Marion was letting it all out. He knew it would get worse. They would probably have a fight about something before the night was over.

"Okay, let's go." Potts said this to the children, but he meant it as an announcement to Marion: see, Marion, I'm taking charge; see, Marion, we're going now; see, Marion, just follow me and everything will be all right. Potts was feeling a little better now. The only difficulty was that he hadn't figured out yet where they were going to eat. And he sensed he had that all before him. None of the alternatives at the prices he wanted to pay would be all right with Marion. And he hadn't the whatever-it-is to suggest a place which was expensive.

As they all piled into the car Potts asked a reasonable, but unwanted question, "Well, where would you like to eat?" He liked to think that he was paying deference to Marion's preference. But he was still hoping, unknown to himself at the time, that Marion would somehow transform herself into a happy person because she could now suggest a restaurant.

"How should I know?" she asked, petulantly, exasperated and still fiery. "But I don't want to eat at *The Place*" (an inexpensive, but good as those things go, hamburger restaurant).

On hearing the name the children sang together, "Yes, *The Place, The Place.*" Potts was somewhat indifferent to most food. There is really, really good food, and then most other food. And if it isn't in the first category then where it places in the second is simply argumentative. Marion, on the other hand, had a much finer palate. She liked really good food probably even more than Potts did. But she also could tell the difference between food about which Potts was indifferent.

"Well," he said, "we could go to a fish and chips place, or that Mexican restaurant near the Eco Mart." Both these alternatives were, he knew, in the mood Marion was in, unacceptable. And the children wanted to go to *The Place*.

"'I know," said Potts, brightening. "How about Harold's?" He was genuinely pleased with himself. This was a modest, but more expensive family restaurant a short drive to the next town. They had heard about it from a friend, tried it once before, and found it a welcome change. It also gave everyone a chance to have a short car ride, and to let their minds loose.

"Fine," said Marion. She apparently approved.

Lisa began to cry. "I want a hamburger," she said.

"Look," said Potts, "they have hamburgers at Harold's."

"I want to go to *The Place*," she persisted.

"We aren't going there. We're going somewhere else instead," said Potts, and started the car.

Karen, bless her soul, consoled Lisa. In a few minutes they were both giggling.

Potts turned to Marion, "Well, how was your day?"

Comment

Potts had never been able to think about his relationship with Marion other than from his own point of view or from guilt. But as he was developing his ideas for his manuscript, he began to have some thoughts about husband-wife relationships in general, thoughts which seemed very useful in understanding what was happening between himself and Marion. He decided to present these ideas in the following, somewhat unusual format.

Love Letters to Lucretia, Many Years Ago, and a Contemporary Diary

January 18

I don't think I can suffer much more of her. Let me see: what *is* the feeling like? Like I am being pressed up against a wall by some invisible machine, controlled by her, pushed further and further so that, not physically of course, I am being forced out of shape. And there is no bodily feeling, at least not of pain—just a general alarm and despair—frightened at what could happen to me, and not wanting to do much about it. The strange thing is I seem not to mind, in an inexplicable sort of way. I feel a sense of myself, that something is happening to me, something I feel I might not have if it weren't for her, or that I would feel only through loneliness, which would be worse. I guess I don't really take the problem seriously—more like a pastime, an avocation. It gives me something to think about, an opportunity to pity myself, to bathe myself in my own reflection, to coddle myself. We can ask for little more in life, I suppose. Perhaps that's why we feel this way (at least I assume that if I have such stirrings that others do too—it gives a universality to the whole process and permits intellectualizing about it).

Off and on I do wish it would stop, and for the same reason we all feel when we're sad and would like to be happy. Why is it we long for happiness? We never really want it to last long. But it's so exhilarating during that moment it occurs, even though it requires so much management to sustain. When we're sad we forget how much we must stage happiness, and when we are happy we become exhausted in directionlessness. How shallow happiness makes us! How much more profound is sadness.

January 19

Why do I settle for a settled life? Why do any of us? It's clear that some don't—at least from time to time. Divorce is frequent enough these days. People trying to change life styles by changing partners. When we're in ruts we never think that we might be rutty people, or that life might consist of ruts, and that one rut which we alternate in is to search for ways to get out of the rut we're in.

I suppose the answer lies in that it isn't yet bad enough. The whole thing is more or less predictable—and not yet a disaster. There's sufficient excitement, lodged in safety, out of which to make a life. Something will have to change for the worse. It seems it wouldn't take much, but people's inner resources can sometimes be enormous.

But this business of settling in—a bit terrifying that. One feels himself harnessed to something, but isn't sure what. I'm pulling, I'm expending energy (I go to bed quite tired these days). I feel myself a part of a moving enterprise—I must be pulling *something*. But I don't know what it is. And I know I never will. And I pull anything, I search for what it is, and I stay settled so I'll have an excuse to pull what I already know the weight of, and so I'll not be different from others and won't have any embarrassing questions to answer like "Heh, are you pulling anything behind there?" When everyone is doing the same thing only crackpots and misfits ask what everyone is doing. That's one of the compensations.

January 20

She did it again today. I woke up early, thinking about a problem, and she came down to breakfast armed for a confrontation. In hindsight it appears symbolic: a struggle to an emotional climax, not unlike the actual thing. But it wasn't the actual thing. A little easier this time, though. She's gaining in resolve about what is involved and what she has to do about it. You can almost see her calculating the chances of doing better next time, what about the children? how much money would there be? It's become a dreadfully practical problem to her. But then most problems to her are practical. That seems to be one of our differences. I prefer to think distantly, as though what happens to me is merely data for thought. Things, to me, "are" intellectual. But for her things are happening which are *personal* and they are to be talked about personally.

Anyway, I am now threatened again with the disintegration of whatever it is that I seem to feel more or less comfortable with. I seem to tolerate it better than she—not because I get more out of it but because I need less. She has no outside gratifications and mine are many. Hence her reliance on me is many times greater than mine on her. And that gives me power, and makes me a tyrant. She wants to take that power away from me. And who can blame her? I'm not sure I even want it, although I don't want to be tyrannized over either. I want her satisfaction from the outside to increase. And that, of course, is a line of greatest difficulty and I have no business demanding it.

January 21

Women expect more from marriage than men. And this is as it should be—after all their commitment and activity are greater. And this, in itself, is a general way of expressing many specific, individual, particularized marital difficulties. Whenever one has two people, one of whom expects more of the relationship than the other, there is dissatisfaction and the possibility for conflict. Women can handle this excess anxiety in many, many ways, but a very frequent mode (frequent both in the sense of used by many women and used often by any particular woman) is to express dissatisfaction in the relationship more or less directly to the husband in the form of complaints. And the husband will have an equally wide range of responses to these communications, a frequent manner being to patronize, to "understand," to express sympathy in an impatient way—that is to say, to show his indifference. So we have an omnipresent marital feature: wifely dissatisfaction and husbandly standoffishness. What varies is the precise forms these may take. These relationships are also punctuated by emotional explosions: the wife simply erupting an accumulation of anxiety and the husband showing his irritation at being put upon. The husband is seen as cold and unfeeling (as indeed he sees himself) ; the wife is put down as overwrought with domestic details.

Dear Lucretia,

I am amazed at my own exhilaration. I feel positively buoyant, as though treading air in an inner tube. When I feel this way it really is impossible to get any (other) work done (for indeed exhilaration is quite exhausting!). Do you suppose the fact that I am getting my work done after all is evidence that I don't know what I'm talking about, or worse yet, that I'm deluding myself? No. I reject that. It is simply evidence of my exhilaration. I feel as though I can't do anything even though I do. And to think I owe this all to you!

Last night you were a marvel. I think sometimes of growing old, of becoming flabby, of having varicose veins, and it just doesn't seem as though it will really happen. To have what we have with such passion—do you think it will last?

Your fly-by-night

January 22

People seem to have different ways of pacing themselves through life, different tactics, in a way, of dealing with time and how they spend their hours in relation to it. Now that I look back over my life with her it seems that we were, and still are, pacing ourselves in somewhat antithetical ways. She is a night person, and I enjoy the day; she needs ten hours sleep, and I need eight; she lives in the present, and enjoys making long-range plans so her future present can be made more enjoyable, and I live in the future, for posterity, as it were, and find hateful discussing future moves; she enjoys manipulating her environment to suit her pace, and my pace determines that I wait for my environment to come to me. There are such difficult, utterly different modes of living—how could we ever have expected to spend our lives together? I guess we didn't give it much thought. Yet we are together, and have been for twenty-three years. One can only conclude that contrast has some virtues, or at least some fascinations. Or perhaps we simply share a common desire to destroy one another. She wants to change my life, and I hers. But no, that is not quite right. "Want" is too much a word of conscious intent and this process I am thinking of is more subtle than that. It's almost as though each of us has a mission, a long-term mission, to show the other how much superior our own way of living really is, as though, by contrast, we can each reassure ourselves of our own virtuous living. And the other is also part of this didacticism we have taken onto ourselves. Have we, finally, even grown tired of this? Or in working against each other are we simply continually replacing old gains with new? Do we, in fact, have something solid which binds us together, evidence of which is that we still show enough interest to continue the fight? Interesting question, that.

Dear Lucretia,

Is it possible that we've known each other for three months? Why, it seems only the other day when we met. One thing I notice about time (regardless of what others will tell you), it sure does go by quickly. That must be how we've come to know each other so well. When you spend so long with a person you can't help but learn all about her. Yet I sometimes think there might yet be some surprises in store for me—that you might not be the girl I think you are, *really*. Wouldn't that be interesting? Wouldn't it be funny if we got married and it turned out that neither of us knew the other at all? Well, luckily that won't happen to us. At least I don't see how it could.

I love you, dear Lucretia, you know that, don't you? I can think of nothing I'd rather do than die in your arms.

Yours, with passion

January 25

Is it possible for two people to live together as one person? Why do romantic novels, movies, stories, etc., have such wide currency? Certainly not because what they portray has widespread basis in existence. But, it must be, just the opposite. The notion that people can live together for others is an idea which most of us find in harmony with our own interests, for we can impose this standard on our partners while at the same time pretending that, for our part, we already fulfill the requirements. It is, then, one of those myths which people find useful to believe—we all would like others to be subservient to our needs and wants (though not necessarily all the time). And most of us can remember a period of love when we felt that way toward another. Love is a feeling of loss of self, of putting one's self at the whim of someone else knowing it will not be treated whimsically. And love's major effects come directly from this: it is clearly dangerous (and therefore terribly stimulating) to put one's self in the control of another who could, as a consequence of this control, hurt one deeply. But we are not, by nature, kind only. We do also like to hurt people, to correct them, to set them straight. Love from another can, over a long period, be irritating. There are other things to be done which are more or less inconsistent with a love relationship. Love is not all we want to do or to have done to us. Love, therefore, is inherently a short-run phenomenon which works best when there are no other responsibilities which the partners share.

We err, then, significantly, when we expect a love relationship to last, or to be intense with our own partner. It can wax a bit from time to time (though sporadically and certainly not with the same kind of selflessness) with one's mate. But it's major place in a married person's life will be with someone with whom one does not share responsibility.

Dear Lucretia,

Our love will last forever, I am sure of it. In fact it is difficult for me to imagine myself out of love with you. What could that possibly be like? Oh, what a glorious future we shall have together. Isn't that great?!

I think I know why other people's love doesn't last: it is not as self-sacrificing as ours. I would give you anything, do anything for you. In fact, I somewhat insist on doing so. You shall be my mistress and I your servant, and if you don't allow this to me I shall wither and die, I just know it. I am yours—I exist to serve you. Just tell me what to do.

Yours, in miserable happiness

January 26

I would miss her if she left me. All of my feelings would become engaged in this after-it-happens way. I do find comfortable the arrangements of a home, children, and wife. But I don't insure myself against loss by a pretense of enthusiasm. I do not put on a front of appreciation. I *feel* appreciation, and I do think I show it in the "natural" expression of myself, but I don't think I can *devise* an expression of it other than how it is expressed already. People are clearly susceptible to the antics of a person who puts on a show. People are willing to believe if it is easy to do so, and it is often easy to do so if it is in one's interests to believe. A performance, even a lackadaisical performance, can be worth a good deal. *It at least shows one cares enough to pretend.* And it can make up for the lack of normal courtesies and behavior having to do with one's "fair-share" of the family enterprise. Marriage is no exception to this. If a wife convinces a husband that she cares enough to listen to his troubles, that she is willing to pretend she believes in his fabricated world and takes it seriously, that the husband can act "authentically" and she will not raise doubts about it, she will not point out to him how silly he is being to get so excited about such matters, this pretense can carry many burdens. It makes the wife out to be a stranger to herself, and she may have to get used to herself as having an inauthentic side, but it is a "happy home" strategy. And similarly for the husband. He can pretend that the world of the wife is of interest to him and that he wants to be consulted about all its problems. And again the husband needs only to show he cares enough not to embarrass his wife, not to point out to her the stupidity of her taking seriously the world she lives in. Clearly this is a strategy which would be satisfying to most wives. We all would like to be reinforced, shored up, made to feel that what we are doing isn't the trivia it obviously is, and that it has wide-ranging importance it obviously hasn't.

Most husbands and wives more or less recognize this problem. And like most things most of us are hazily aware of it but aren't able to do much about it. We pretend somewhat, as we are able to push ourselves to do so, realizing our inadequacy in pretense but prevented from going further by our knowledge that it is, after all, a pretense.

So, I would miss her if she left me. But I can't bring myself to act in a way which I know would guarantee her not doing so.

People have a very difficult time doing what they don't believe in if they feel ambivalent about what the stakes are.

Dear Lucretia,

I feel so much myself when I'm with you, as though when I'm not with you I live a life untrue to the real person I am. You make me realize that my life consists of merely acting out standard relationships with others, never really saying what I feel, never really being myself. And when we're together I am somehow magically and beautifully transformed: I become genuine. It makes me very self-conscious of myself when I'm not with you. I am constantly monitoring myself, seeing myself as somehow phony, and rather exhilarated in discovering myself in pretense. All I really want to do is get back to you where I can crawl out of my conventional self again and parade my true self in front of myself (and you) as the person I feel myself really to be but only when I'm with you. It's almost as though I become so involved in you that life as giving truly takes on meaning. And when I'm not with you selflessness appears hollow and unreal. I am supicious when away from you, and trusting when with you—conniving and like everyone else when out of your spell, and virtuous and special when in your sphere of influence. How can I live two such separate lives? How can I go on without you?

Yours in some frenzy

January 27

Sexual relationships with one's spouse are essentially at an animalistic level. That is, the mystique surrounding one's partnership has lost its romantic nature—the ambience is one of mutual adjustment, definitely bureaucratic in tone, and one responds in this atmosphere to physical urges without much transporting of oneself into another world (as one might have felt once and as one would like to expect it to be). Sex, like breakfast, becomes a routine within a set of other routines; and it also becomes a source of contention (again not unlike other matters). Discussions between the partners will often center around frequency and competence, but more likely the former (in sex, as in other things, one has a difficult time distinguishing between the qualitative effects of quantity, and quality as something distinct from quantity). This kind of talk has its equivalents in other parts of the bureaucracy, however. Complaints can equally often be heard about the frequency and competence of such things as houses being kept clean, yards maintained, children taken care of, garages rearranged, clothes repaired, odd jobs performed, etc. Sexual ecstasy is one item among many on which people have quarrels, debates, fallings-out, etc. One has a sense of how things could possibly be better and measures what one has against this constantly shiftly and always ahead-of-oneself "standard," except occasionally when something really good happens and one feels quite content, a state of mind which, on any particular item, lasts only for short periods. Not that most people don't essentially accept their lot—but along with basic acceptance is also a basic level of dissatisfaction. And so it is with sex. And so it will be always with one's spouse. Sex itself does not satisfy general anxiety—it is only a temporary diversion from the rest of life's problems. Yet it may be focused upon by either or both parties as *the* problem which *produces* generalized anxiety.

And so we have sex when we have sexual urges (and not because we wish somehow to possess our loved one) and always feel a little awkward in doing so since it isn't as ecstatic as it seems it ought to be, and it isn't the answer we would like to think of it as possibly being. We want from life what we can't have and we frequently see this gap in terms of our partners. And so it will always be, even when one knows it.

Dear Lucretia,

I desire you so much. When we are intimate with each other it's as though I am transported to the highest reaches of ecstasy. I want to be part of you, and I want you to be part of me. This sense of oneness, it separates me, and us, from the rest of the world and gives us (me) an overall feeling of well-being, as though nothing else matters, or ever will. If only for this reason alone I want to spend the rest of my days with you for I will always know, when I need a shelter from life's problems, that I will always be able to find it in you. I feel so free, so liberated, so otherworldly. This paradise we have is what life is all about and I thank whomever there is to thank that we have it together. Possession may be nine-tenths of the law, but it is one-hundred percent of ecstasy.

                                        Yours piningly

January 28

We both seem to understand that we have it as good as we can, and that we have come to a fairly stable position. But she wants more. The question is, can she get it? And further, can she get some of what she wants without losing sufficiently of what she already has, to make the trade unprofitable? We do find we don't have enough of some things. But when we go for more, other things change as well. By accumulating more we could then have less overall. But would one ever know this in advance? The answer: one can't. So, one works on instincts, on what one can stand, on how much one can take, on an *overall* dimension, not on particular ones. And this is what makes actions on the basis of particular dissatisfactions ring false. If one leaves, one leaves an overall situation one "knows" for one one doesn't know. And this means, essentially, that what one does know is worse than what one can only guess at. And who's to say that over the long haul a change might not be better anyway? Short, infrequent happiness may be partly the stuff of a meaningful life. There are no arguments with believing for or against anything. There are some which are more or less interesting, familiar, bizarre, etc. And there are arguments which one thinks one believes. But how can one know, even if things get worse, that in a sense different from how we look at it now it won't look better. We change the way we look at things after we change things, so our perceptions and comments are not really comparable. How then can she make up her mind? She won't, really, she'll just work into it or she won't—life will go that way, or not.

February 2

We are doomed to this monotonic relationship, to a slightly hostile stability, to an occasionally angry outburst and an even less frequent pleasant, comforting feeling. At the moment I feel benevolent, but I know that's only temporary, that something will happen to bring me back to a lower level of acceptance of her. I want to feel strongly and positively, but I sense how much work that would be, bouncing back and forth between wanting and despising. We seem to despise what we want as we realize, too deeply for awareness, that we can't have what we want and know we will continue to want it anyway. I seem not to have the kind of emotional energy it takes to sustain great changes in a relationship over and over again. We all seem to want our daily, regular lives to be more routine, more constant.

We work these things out and it seems like endless nonsense to try to justify the product. We have what we have, and when we won't any longer we won't. And it seems like it should end there. But knowing this and living through what we know are not the same thing.

Dear Lucretia,

You make me so angry sometimes. Why did you have to do what you did last night? Everything was going along so perfectly. No, I guess that's not quite right. I did have a feeling of peculiarness before it happened—I just didn't know what it would be. I want to live in harmony with you forever. There's this sense of bliss I feel when I'm with you and I don't want anything to spoil that. But every once in a while something like this comes along and just devastates me. What would happen if something like this occurs when we're married? Could it possibly? I don't ever want to think about it. It must be because we have to leave each other every night (or almost every night anyway!). If we could only always be together. Then things like this wouldn't happen.

Yours in confusion

February 3

There is something going on which seems very subtle. We want to do something with each other, to each other, use each other, in ways I don't understand. Or maybe we simply want to use ourselves in relation to the other. But I can't grasp what we want from each other—what it is we are after. All I can think of is that we may not be after anything in particular—that a relationship of husband and wife is part of working out one's entire life, and in running through a life we develop anxiety (energy) which becomes involved in other people's anxieties. We become frightened (stimulated), and we seek to establish our own importance. And we carry on this duality with our spouses as well as others (and ourselves). When our anxieties mingle with our spouses' our intimacies are such that we are less confined by formal courtesies. We are less polite with our spouses—we have fewer formalities which check our expression. So anger and moodiness are more frequently expressed, something which creates the same kind of human difficulties it would create with others if we so expressed ourselves with them. And that's exactly why etiquette is so important—and why our relationships with our spouses are frequently nasty.

February 8

There are many people, especially young people, who seem not to appreciate the intricacies of intimacy. At best it is a relationship about which, among those with whom we are truly intimate, we feel ambivalent. With intimates we may act "truly," as ourselves—but that means many things if we see ourselves as being multifaceted and having unattractive as well as attractive features. When we drop formality, that is, if we refuse to treat people courteously even if we don't like them at the time, we gain and lose. How many of us show respect of our marriage partners? How many of us are at least as courteous with them as we are with strangers, colleagues, friends, etc.? Being polite is not a "bad" thing—and absence of courtesy, even though real, is not unequivocally advantageous. We are mean and gruff to those whom we have as intimates. We are also loving and kind. But one goes with the other.

Dear Lucretia,

I have never felt so intimate with anyone before. We seem to blend together. And I'm so joyous when we're together: intimacy is certainly a special thing, a lover's thing. Others, even my parents, are as strangers to me. I'm so fortunate to know you. Being in love with you is like being in love with love.

Witlessly

February 11

What is most stimulating is a variation from a routine. Marriage is, inevitably, a routine. Those who claim it isn't have simply built the claim that it isn't into their routine. Hence excitement, even sexual excitement, does not come as a result of one's marriage partners. In marital sex one acts in a fundamentally biological rather than a psychologically excited way. And in social relations with one's spouse there is little novelty or variation. Most of what could be done has been done; more and more of one's likely repertoire has been attempted and either continued as a part of the routine or discontinued for want of further interest.

Marriage, then, is not based on excitement and those who feel it should be or who want it to be are missing its value. Marriage (meaning, in a broader sense, the home) is the fixed point against which we encounter variation. It is the absolute, the given, from which we then determine whether whatever else we do is exciting. It's fundamentally stylized and safe. The emotions we experience there are known emotions. They do not raise the specter of the world being at odds with our usual experience of it. One always knows (or at least more often than in most situations) that things will not change perceptibly. And this is an essential thing for part of our life to be—but we don't credit our spouses for their contribution to making our lives boring so that we have a way of trying to generate excitement as well. We do not properly evaluate dullness and boredom; hence we do not properly evaluate marriage.

Dearest Lucretia,

Our life together will be so exciting—I can hardly stand to think about it! I become excited just thinking about how excited I will be! By comparison the rest of my life is a dull routine, simply steps I go through because they happen to be part of the path I am on. But our life—that's so different. It's incredible to realize what one has to look forward to. It's even more incredible to contemplate not living that way now when I see how I live at the moment. Let's get married soon. Life is drab without you—I am going through the motions of a life which I want to leave behind me.

Yours in expectation

6

Voices

HUGO POTTS:

Let us to thinking, then, you and I, and let us imagine as we go, self-consciously, punctuating our thoughts with thoughts about our thoughts, and thoughts about those if we can, our purpose being to understand, to think we know, at least a little, and certainly more than those with whom we disagree. For we can do no more, nor less, being human.

We should ask along the way, wherefore man, and why? For why else write this? Beauty is beyond my grasp, goodness a sham, truth for scientists, so whimsy (and philosophy) is left for the likes of me, and you if you'll come. Let us start, then, in the middle, for what choice have we who know neither beginning nor end but who occupy . . . what? Somewhere, sometime, knowing not of what went before, or after, but guessing.

LEWIS A. TELLURIAN, JR.:

There are, it seems, two quite different ways to say things in writing. In one, if conclusions are to be drawn the reader must draw them; in the other, the conclusions are already drawn and presented for the reader. The first involves an attempt to create a situation which either resembles or symbolizes what one sees and feels—the second asserts directly the point or points one thinks are involved. The former is the way of the artist, the latter the method of the scientist (using these terms rather loosely). And there are many styles encompassing various mixtures of the two.

PHILLIP MARKINGS:

One of the reasons why novels may be thought of as more (or

less) satisfactory vehicles of thought is that in them ideas need not be presented by the author directly, as though they are true ideas about the world—ideas which are presented directly and explicitly may be thought of as "just" the ideas of one of the characters, or as contextual asides. Assertions in novels, then, need not mean what they say they mean, and no statement need be thought of as being "true." What is critical in a novel is how we are engaged by the experience of reading it.

But what is at issue in more "straightforward" styles of exposition is that what is said is somehow thought of as having to be true (or false), that individual ideas, as expressed in sentences and paragraphs, are themselves to be taken as capable of standing alone. We never think that novels are wrong—that what is said in them is wrong. But we do think that expository books are wrong (or right).

Expositions about novels suffer the same difficulties as assertion-making generally.

DURAN SEEKER:

Novelists and playwrights write at a more fundamentally descriptive level than does a philosopher, attempting to present "original" behavior as it might look if the author's (implied) way of looking at things were how the world is. The philosopher wants to describe his way of looking at the world, given what he takes to be nature's presentation of the original data. One might look at the difference as though the novelist and playwright deduce a set of activities from a point of view, whereas the philosopher re-creates reality in the form of ideas. In one sense the novelist and playwright go one step beyond the philosopher since, like the philosopher, to arrive at their ideas they must induce them and then, from these ideas, devise a reality. The philosopher stops short of this last step, becoming stuck in the ideas themselves, and concentrating reality-devising at that level.

PETER POPE:

Poetry has the quality of not having been thought, exactly, but produced on the basis of "inspiration," of bursts and flashes. Clearly this quality may be mixed with descriptive, dramatic, or philosophical styles, but a poet, essentially, deals with peculiar juxtapositions, odd ways to put things, strange and mysterious images, etc. There is a sense in which ideas and poetry do not go together—that a poet writes poetry not to present a logical and rational argument (in the obvious meanings of these words) but to communicate on a different dimension entirely. For example, poetry is a much "looser" form than drama or novels—one can jump about, leave things half-done, say things one doesn't entirely understand oneself. A poet would probably be no more capable of giving "meaning" to his poems than others. In this sense poetry has much in common with music. Most music does not "say" anything (with the usual exceptions, of course—some music is written specifically to appear to be novelistic, dramatic, or poetic). Music, however, is a different kind of medium—one does not simply translate music into sentences about the music. Similarly with much poetry. It is a separate medium, to be appreciated for what it is, and which is not at its best when talked about. It is difficult to capture the "meaning" of poetry in a language (prose) which is not designed to produce its effects and which was probably not "chosen" as the medium to use by the author for just that reason.

CRETE SEWELL:

One of the major components of being interesting is the capacity to respond honestly, to articulate one's feelings, reactions, and thoughts. We are all given responses—society teaches us what to feel and how to respond—it provides us with standard forms (even standardly unconventional forms). Honesty is a capacity to avoid society's answers; to be able to respond honestly is almost guaranteed to be at variance with other people's expectations. This is not to be confused with learned unconventional behavior—honesty, it turns out, is not only a component of being interesting, but also of being creative.

LEWIS A. TELLURIAN, JR.:

For what purpose are we here? For none you say? Yes, I quite agree. And so we ask why we are here to give ourselves a purpose. It seems so simple, yet of such duration to live, for some do so want to do something, to excel, to say something which people whom others admire will admire, in the pretense that it matters. The ambitions of a lifetime, to empty oneself of all one has thought by twisting it in a way which will bring wisdom to others.

CRETE SEWELL:

There is a matter which consumes us, all who are human, the awareness that we are aware. Ethics flow from visions of ourselves seen as though from the whole of humanity but possessed of one small part. Our inhumanity is only that which is not convenient, seen from one who is bothered and also bothers but who thinks not of the latter, or if he does, not in the same grand way as the first, the last being merely exception while the former a violation of a rule. In being ethical we commit ourselves to the grandest sin of all, if paradox be not lost in such a world. And the lesson in this is clear, equivocal: we are trapped in our own small part of the whole to condemn other small parts for the sake of increasing our size, so we may rival the whole, thinking quality better than quantity. Think on it —when you disparage do you not deny an implication in humanity? Do you not cast off from you a part which you find evil? And by what reason do you so? Are you inconvenienced then? Is it a bother? Of such stuff are priestly sentiments, even beautifully disgorged, conjured. Welcome then to life as you see others, if you can so welcome a wormy hook. And since we have not it in us to do so, we all play baleful hosts of thorny circumstance, pricking the passing scene as it suits us while thinking that in doing so we fertilize and till our own budding fortunes in the thready eyes of goodness. Can you accept this? Can you even think it? Then now you know that one can understand yet not do anything about it.

HUGO POTTS:

We bustle about, exuding ourselves into the cavities of our worlds, filling them with us. But we can't squeeze out fast enough. We have gigantics of time and so little substance to occupy our allotted room. So we keep forcing it, hoping at the end to have filled a life-space.

MARION POTTS:

The wedges of time leap up at me and lick at my mind, teasingly. I feel annoyed (have I not a right?), she, undoubtedly, playful. I am not part of time—no other like her is there—but in time, affected by her, and puzzled still. She is God's ultimate cruelty, hurtled at me by chunks, even though fashioned from ever invisible parts, passing by only, one notices, from her villianies, her erosions, her endless lapping and searching. That for someone, something, it should not be so is man's final argument. Out of such despair is fabricated beauty, truth, and goodness and their twins, sin, deceit, and ugliness against whom we rage all of our descending lives, the outrage we tender for trials at futile escape.

PETER POPE:

The turn of the day, reddened clarity after so much transparency. We see too far at dusk—our lives enlarge like shadows upon the shifting sands—the depths of restlessness are felt more strongly then, life once again becomes a mystery and we die a little, never knowing why. Age seems to flow away, even as our heads are flooded—we, the noisemakers, who finally learn to scream sensibly, can no longer feel the will to scream—not, at least, when skies picturize our unknown fears, and we are swallowed, swallowed by the night.

MARION POTTS:

We cannot take the world, not the whole world, not the way we really want to take it, for in trying we lose the part we left behind to take that which we did. We will always have the thought of how it might have been. Greed for life is insatiable: even the gluttons look back and see all the fine things they have missed, how it could have been better, how what they had, though good, was only a little bit. We try to gain more through secret (and not so secret) admirations, those we would also be who live full lives in different ways. And this is but symptom of the disease—that being is being only a part of something (we think) —something large and great (we feel—it just has to be) but which we know is really nothing at all, added up. Which makes our half-filled lives an even deeper mystery. How can we want a bigger part of something which may not make any difference anyway, once over. Time past makes us feel good and bad, while time future has all the anticipations of pregnancy.

JEAN SEEKER:

I am waiting for it to happen, I am waiting to be called. Won't

you come and carry me away? Why must I do for myself? I
can't you know. I can't do. Won't you come and carry me away?

PHILLIP MARKINGS:

Born, made it through life without serious accident—died.

Born, life cut short by an unfortunate circumstance and thereby
died.

DURAN SEEKER:

Childhood provides one with two fundamental arrays: data for
the construction of one's history ("past"), and a source for the
development of dramatic experiences. One spends the remainder of his life ordering and reordering these arrays in such a
way as to give one's current life situation a sense of fitness, of
being reasonable under the circumstances, and, at the same
time, of being fantastic, surprising, and done in spite of.

HUGO POTTS:

I stand before my justifiers, as we all dream of doing—they
hold a child of mine, in flesh, and all my manuscripts. These
judges sternly ask, as though it were natural to do so, which
I would prefer to keep, and which commit to flame. What a
bottomless image, feelings all afright, my love and my work. It
is not even a choice. We realize how we come to pass the time,
and what is lasting even though it dies too, eventually.

CRETE SEWELL:

The dawn has come—yet there is not dawn. The sun set of an
evening; but there is no sunset. Stars slowly fill an empty sky—
cumulus clouds come rolling by.

Phenomena abound which are but corners (often rounded) of
time, place, and particular men (who stand for all men if in
that time and place). Our observations are but consequences
of regularities seen from a few of their consequences.

MARGARET FLEECE:

What are the consequences of looking at oneself as on a different level from other people?

MARION POTTS:

> Passing time. Things seem to be happening. I want to feel. I
> want it to last, to stop so I don't have to worry about it's being
> over with nothing having happened, that it was without obvi-
> ous, full, anxiety-relieving, blessed, so-that's-it meaning. I am
> holding myself together. I'm not sure what to do. I want to be
> king of the world. Forever.

> Man's philosophical problem: living life in the interstices, the
> empty spaces, always bumping into various of the letters, some-
> times words. We are willing enough to die—frightful human
> honesty. And we want to live more fully than anyone else. We
> are less than we want.

LEWIS A. TELLURIAN, JR.:

> We live in a world of many peoples, all the same. And so a
> life of paradox to be lived. When we think it not so we are
> hustlers after others' souls, to satisfy our lust for carping. We
> cannot have different, not at the cave. More might live con-
> veniently, but what is that to our humanities, insatiably, liv-
> ingly finding fault. Misery is ably the consequence of paradox
> found, and happiness of temporary single-mindedness. Let the
> complexities come, for they will find this way: to drown the
> pleasures of insight, to weigh down the airy spirit. Accept,
> then, and you may, at least, expire in the wisdom that it could
> not have been different, that it all is. And if infused by this,
> can joy be stifled?

JEAN SEEKER:

> I think I know now what it feels like to lose an opportunity, a
> possible happiness, or at least a changed experience, that would
> have been costless, or nearly so, to test the possibility of. It's
> gone now. And this particular one won't come again, it will not
> be mine, I will never know what it would have been. If a day
> is to be lived for what it will bring, then that day was one-
> quarter full. If a day is what it teaches us then I am wiser for
> it, and glum. Wisdom is a lonely possession and not at all like
> what I might have had. I will go to my grave wiser, but this
> piece of knowledge I could have done without for I would
> never have known if I knew it not. But to know it now is to

have done without something I will always have wanted. It was possibly mine and I let go. What makes us so?

HUGO POTTS:

Sitting at my desk thinking what to write, winding up sitting at my desk writing of sitting at my desk thinking what to write.

MARGARET FLEECE:

A colleague (junior) comes into my office (what now?) smiles, unfeigning feigned pleasantness (miraculous our plasticity). What do I think of the Mark situation (where do I begin? how does one bridge fifteen years of experience?) ? I feign unfeigned pleasantness (that is one of the differences) and we have a discussion: didactic. (Forty-five minutes I'll never see again.)

PHILLIP MARKINGS:

I have an appointment in three-and-one-half hours. What will happen between now and then? Will I be here, I wonder? Will my father die? Reaching out for a jar of pickles my daughter bumped her head. In the middle of the street was a sack of ten dollar bills with a note attached saying "take me." I have seven new and profound thoughts which I write exquisitely. I do the things I left over from yesterday. It's gone.

HUGO POTTS:

The little people come to listen, perhaps to giggle, and some, they say, to learn, to think. I drag myself to the podium and utter ponderous truths, and chitchat, perhaps laugh. It seems it should be a good time, and is, I s'pose, if you like to talk to the little people who come to listen, perhaps to giggle, and some, they say, to learn, to think.

JEAN SEEKER:

In nature time goes from right to left. How do I know such a thing, you might ask (although you need not, of course). When I stand still on a summer night, I feel it on my left cheek first.

PETER POPE:

The sun has gone in, I must go now. When I feel warm, and flushed by the glare I can sit for some time and interpret your sort, and mine. But the sun has gone in, and I must go now. Why I don't know, except the sun has gone in.

DURAN SEEKER:

With the exception of the state of love, which has several peculiar features, one of which is a high degree of instability, we like and do not like people at the same time. We do not recognize this ambivalence for what it is and come to transfer our feelings onto separate, distinct people, our friends and enemies, those we say we like, and those we say we dislike. But few of us have "real" enemies in the same way we think we have "real" friends. What we do have are people with whom we get along and like and dislike, and people with whom we don't get along and to whom we transfer our *sense of* dislike. But, of course, we don't really transfer this ambivalence we feel for our friends —only our conscious sense of it. And so we are cruel to our friends, we act out our dislike in ways which we have no strong concept of since we are likely to deny we have any dislike to begin with.

PETER POPE:

It would be so convenient, wouldn't it, if I loved you. Since we live together, I mean. What that must be like. I do admire you (how patronizing that sounds—it isn't meant to) —your way of life, your projects. It seems a sensible way to live . . . active, exploring, on the move. Not for me, of course, but an interesting life. It's funny, isn't it. I can see circumstances in which you would be happy, even joyous. If he were rich, outgoing, successful, and demanding of the best. Not so much talk and endless ruminating. So much quiet, and aloneness, and being aware.

How did it come about, I wonder, you and I? How little we know of what life will be like later, when we are young. Is it a matter of chance? The odds (I haven't calculated them) must be impossible, a fool's game. There should be an age limit for players—say, thirty-five and over? (Were we ever in love, you and I? All we have is reconstructions, feelings, memories. They mean what they mean, or nothing.)

I would still live with you. I want to. But I don't know why. Does that seem silly? Am I so cynical that I don't believe it could ever be any different, with anyone? Yet I do believe it could be for you, if you could meet him (but where, who?). Why can I see him better than I can see someone for myself?

Will we be together in five years time? An exciting question, to wonder what your life would be like if the person you are with most is gone.

I do have passion. But not, apparently, the kind of which dream loves are made. I do feel something. I know it isn't' what you want. I don't know what it is. It's a feeling that I like to see you when you're not with me. It's a feeling that we somehow are together even though, maybe, we shouldn't be. A feeling of is. Why don't I love you, then, when we're together? It isn't clear what I feel. And I'm not proud of what we have. I wish it could be better. I want to love you. Nor will I until, possibly, it's too late for young joy. (Is that so bad? Might we not find something in the future, good friends, close friends, who need? But we are old then. We are old. And that is not now. What will happen to us? What lies ahead? Who might you meet, or me? We do live in hopes, and we know better.)

All right, then, I will live it out. But is it only curiosity? (That's a ghastly thought.) The end will come so hard if I think, then, I have missed something. It could be bitter. To be old and bitter. The young can smell the old when they sour. Let's hope we get better than that. I wish it for you. It never seemed to be much for me anyway.

MARION POTTS:

The mocking man laughed—I hated him. How could anyone not take me seriously when I wanted to be? There are indeed many frustrations which others heap upon us and which we justly deserve, being no less than human.

CRETE SEWELL:

When we tell others what we think is good and bad, what we feel is worthy and unworthy, we tell people what we would like to be taken as. Not necessarily what we are, but what kind of object we think is good and therefore if we were ourselves treated as an exemplification we would feel we were being treated as someone good.

DURAN SEEKER:

There is time to languish and muse and let one's depression set in. Relaxing in its posture, stimulating of one's meaningfulness. To find oneself empty is a great solace when one is looking for justification. We love to catch ourselves in agony.

LEWIS A. TELLURIAN, JR.:

An interesting feature about church as theatre is that it "works" even when the acting isn't particularly good. The "script" calls for shame, guilt, and the promise of redemption, all of which we find stimulating.

PHILLIP MARKINGS:

There is a niche for someone who suggests that the worlds of others wobble, although most people will soon tire of listening. In making assertions we push against something firm—we base ourselves in a context which has an absolute. To say the world (whatever world it is) wobbles is also based in a context with an absolute, although few have thought through matters that far to handle the question in this way. Generally he who holds that all worlds wobble (including his own) have a higher degree of tolerance for wobbly worlds. Hence people will find the discombobulation of confronting their own wobbly world matched by the, if not cheerfulness, then at least calm acceptance of the discombobulator.

And this gives the advocate of wobbly worlds an edge. People must not only see their own world as wobbly, but must do so within an unexamined (by them), paradoxically firm position.

HUGO POTTS:

In the arbor where vixens grow a child of nine sits musing. Floating above through a lilac bush terrestrial fantasies waft.

I'm alone on the inside—quite alone. I do not desire that anyone join me there but sometimes it would be nice to come out and play with others, those who, I can see, are alone too on the inside.

But I cannot budge—it takes too much strength, and my self, inside, is weak from languishing. Will I die, do you think, here?

Have you ever felt the feeling that we're in each other's way, that we're going somewhere (important one supposes), and it takes a long time (yes, it must be important), and we knock into one another because we're not sure exactly how to get there? I have.

The time is now (the time for what?) to do it (what was that?). If we let slip (what slip, pray tell?) it may not come again.

Yesterday I had it, didn't I? Or was I expecting it and what came wasn't what I hoped it would be, at least looking at it from today? Or did nothing come at all, I seem to forget? Funny, isn't it? Well, no matter, it may come today. At least it might. But I doubt it, don't you? Tomorrow, then, do you think?

No one would think of asking: why does someone ask a question about someone asking a question about the question Cervantes asked? But that may be where the answer lies. Shall we then?

I see again the portrait of a man whose eyes are almost closed. He knew, the artist knew, and now I know, again. We learn from the old after we are no longer young.

It's time now to say it. Yes, I'm quite sure, it's time. Ah . . . hm . . . yes . . . well . . . Perhaps not quite yet. But I'm close now. Yes, I'm getting close. I'll just work on it some more. It will come. You'll see. Soon.